Lordship to Patronage

Scotland 1603-1745

Lordship to Patronage

Scotland 1603-1745

Rosalind Mitchison

Edinburgh University Press

© Rosalind Mitchison 1983

First published 1983 in The New History of Scotland by
Edward Arnold (Publishers) Ltd
and reprinted 1990 by
Edinburgh University Press
22 George Square, Edinburgh

Printed and bound in Great Britain by
Billing and Sons Limited
Worcester

British Library Cataloguing in
    Publication Data
Mitchison, Rosalind
Lordship to patronage: Scotland, 1603–1745.—(The
New history of Scotland)
1. Scotland—History—17th century
2. Scotland—History—18th century
I. Title   II. Series
941.106   DA800

ISBN 0 7486 0233 X

To Kirsty Larner
with affection and admiration

Contents

Acknowledgements

I am conscious of having used specific pieces of information or pondered on ideas gained from conversation or correspondence with T.C. Smout, Maurice Lee, Jenny Wormald, Christina Larner, R.E. Tyson, Rab Houston, Eric Forbes, Christian Hesketh, Leah Leneman, Rosalie Stott and Richard B. Sher, and I am grateful to all of these. But this represents only the tip of the iceberg and I owe enormous debts to the wider academic community from whom I have received stimulus. Like many others, I have benefited from the increased interest and activity in research in early modern history which has taken place in the last 20 years. But my greatest sense of obligation is to my immediate colleagues, students, friends and family, for conversation, criticism and support.

Rosalind Mitchison

1

Government by the King's Pen

On 5 April 1603 James VI rode out of his Scottish capital Edinburgh for London, to take up government there as James I of England. It is worth, at the start of this study of Scotland between 1603 and 1745, considering what kind of country he was leaving and what his departure and the new link with England were to mean during the rest of his reign and after.

The two countries, England and Scotland, had been drawing together in dynastic entanglement and in a common and interacting Protestantism for much of the previous century. They had been at peace from the early years of the reign of James's mother, and during James's rule as an adult their relationship had progressed till the English queen had started granting the Scottish king a small annual subsidy in return for a degree of control over his foreign policy. The obvious development of bonds between the countries, culminating eventually in the Act of Union of 1707, has had a misleading effect on the study of Scottish history, forcing constantly the comparison of the institutions, economies and achievements of the two countries and discouraging the examination of the relative position of Scotland among countries more nearly her equal in development. England in 1603 was not yet the richest part of Europe, but she was certainly one of the richer and more powerful individual states, and was about to develop economically more rapidly than any other. Her government was not particularly sophisticated, but the amateurish nature of much of her administration suggests a high degree of cultural homogeneity and social stability. Though she was not at the centre of any major intellectual movement her art and literature showed remarkable and increasing vitality. By contrast Scotland was poor, only loosely held together in terms of government and, though responding to the main movements of the day in terms of law, institutions and religion, still peripheral to the life of Europe. Dynastic linkage alone had made her of significance in European diplomacy since the mid sixteenth century. It is more fruitful to look at her in the company of the less developed parts of northern and western Europe than to draw comparisons between her and England.

Scotland should be compared with the Scandinavian countries, Ireland, Poland, Portugal or Castile (the less advanced parts of Catholic Europe). She was less unified than all of these except Ireland. Her broken land mass and the linguistic divide between Gaelic- and English-speaking populations fragmented Scotland even though the linguistic gulf had not yet become as great a cultural rift as it was to be in the eighteenth century. She had a more complicated social structure than the Scandinavian countries, and does not seem to have been as overweighted with men classifying themselves as noble as were Poland and Castile. It is an interesting comment on differences in social flexibility that Scots provided many small traders in Scandinavia in the early seventeenth century, as well as government servants and mercenaries. The powers of central government in a more strictly stratified society such as Sweden or Spain were likely to be greater than in Scotland. Royal power in Scotland also was not backed up by the Church as it was elsewhere. In Scandinavia the Lutheran Church was almost a branch of government, and in Spain the king had, in practice, a close control over Catholicism. In Scotland Church and State were theoretically separate, and Protestant political thought had been stressing this separation for some time.

In Scotland the bonds of kin were still strong, though declining. It was common for men to hold land from the head of their surname and to follow 'the Name' in politics and religion. Surname groups had tended, in the sixteenth century, to rise or fall as a whole. But surnames had a local preponderance so these movements meant an enhancement or decline of the significance of a whole district. Aberdeenshire was dominated by the wayward and violent Gordons, and the marquis of Huntly, head of the Name, provided political leadership and also gave justice through his courts. In the Borders a prominent surname, the Kers, was split into the two feuding branches of Cessford and Ferniehurst, and in the Highlands the great clan of the Macdonalds had broken into northern and southern clans, and the southern was further fragmented and demoralized. The rising Highland power of the Campbells, though led by the house of Argyll, had also in the Campbells of

Glenorchy a potential rival and in the Campbells of Cawdor a powerful outlier. Generally in landowning society a man's kin, defined in terms of agnatic linkage only, that is through the male line, followed the head of the Name. Hereditary patterns of behaviour in politics and government could be more significant even than the influence of great but remotely linked kinsmen.

The continuing, yet declining, importance of kinship among the aristocracy, the people we necessarily know most about, is shown by various episodes of the early seventeenth century. The house of Argyll was suffering from the eccentricity of the seventh earl, who had reversed a long tradition of co-operation with the crown and was threatening to divide the succession to his lands between sons by different marriages. The whole, widespread clan of the Campbells was unsettled by his behaviour. His eldest son, Lord Lorne, learning by this, took the trouble later to place his heir for fosterage with the second most important Campbell house, that of the Campbells of Glenorchy. The special attachment that a foster link created would go far to re-establish solidarity within the clan. The heir's mother urged the Glenorchy family to give the boy opportunities to use the Gaelic he had learnt, which implies that both Campbell households normally used English. Yet clearly the bulk of the clan spoke only Gaelic. The 15-year-old earl of Montrose spent the several weeks of long vacation from university in 1628 visiting his kin, the various and not very numerous houses of Grahams, most of them already chosen as curators for his minority. Here kinship ties existed but needed to be strengthened by charm and personal acquaintance. The southern Macdonalds, under pressure from the crown and from the Campbells, were showing strain, and opposition and violence were apparent within the clan, even between father and son. Yet at the same time the branch that had settled in Ireland continued not only to nurse hopes of regaining old Macdonald lands, particularly Islay, but was prepared to ally with and support the Scottish holders of the surname.

We have as yet little accurate information on the role of kinship at lower levels of society, the peasantry and the urban work force. Here kin seems to have counted for less than among landowners, and here too kin links were not easily sustained. In the more economically sophisticated areas these links were weakening rapidly. In the Highlands, kin, real or fictitious, made the political unit of the clan. By contrast the mid-sixteenth-century baptismal register of Dunfermline shows that it was not particularly likely in this small burgh that a child would have members of the father's kin as witnesses to its baptism. But even at the end of the seventeenth century, as poll tax returns show, surnames were repeated several times over in the tenantry and work force of the joint farms of Aberdeenshire. The process of breaking up such farms into single tenancies, which had, even by 1600, gone some way in the Lothians, was probably among the economic forces reducing the significance of kin. Rural society was increasingly held together by the discipline and communal structure of the farm and the parish in place of that of kin.

Besides the kin network Scotland had another internal structure of lordship which might or might not follow the same lines as a surname. In early days royal policy had promoted feudalism. Feudal obligations were clear cut and the system had provided dispersed military protection and justice in a way that the rudimentary central government could not hope to do on its own. But although the crown did not formally attempt to reduce the rights and functions of feudal magnates, and indeed in the Highlands had been encouraging feudal overlordship as an alternative to clanship, there was a consistent drive in the sixteenth century to ensure that the greater magnates be kept within the framework, such as it was, of law and order, and answer, eventually, the monarch's demands. This change was similar to that taking place in other kingdoms. There was a trend to 'absolutism' in many parts of Europe which was limited more by the confusion, weaknesses and incoherence of the central governments themselves than by ancient rights of the feudatories. Scotland, again backward in government, was still more localized in authority than were most, but even so she shared in the trend to increased central power.

Some elements of lordship were feudal survivals. The formal land law used feudal terminology, and the system of franchises held by great men was feudal, though it also included the holding of some royal offices such as sheriffdoms by magnates, but the real strength of lordship lay in what it had to offer in terms of power and protection. Great men had brought under their domination, leadership and protection lesser men whose lands lay near to theirs. Many such relationships had been expressed in bonds of 'manrent', that is of loyalty and protection, some were simply implicit. There could be advantages for a family of minor nobility or baronage to be within the orbit of a magnate, and such a position was worth the surrender of independence.

Disputes could be settled by great men for their dependents, sometimes through the formality of franchise courts, sometimes by other pressures, and the interests of dependents could be sustained in other courts. It is an anachronism to regard the pressures which could be exercised both within and outwith the framework of formal justice as unjust exercises of power. Power was a fact which had to be accepted. Men who had power were expected to wish to use it, and justice was not expected to be impartial in the face of such realities. Men did not stand equal in the sight of the law in the late sixteenth century because men were seen not as individuals but as elements of group power, great men as personal manifestations of such power. Today an individual does not quarrel as an equal with an insurance company or a big trade union, whether in the courts or elsewhere. Nor did he, in James VI's reign, oppose a great man with impunity. Yet the modern concept of justice, as emanating from the crown, open to all and aimed at legal fairness, was being asserted, with some hesitation, by the organs of the central government, and in the long run was to become the dominant ideal.

Kinship structures and lordship provided much of the main social bonds, but also weakened the power of the government, as did the primitive and largely subsistence economy. But feudalism and kinship by their hierarchical nature imposed some sort of order on society. Scotland's great houses were not ancient in their establishment: they had come up often by aid from the crown, or by using the king's authority without his true consent. Kidnapping the king and ruling in his name had been a recognized means of gaining a short-lived advantage in the fifteenth and sixteenth centuries: probably the mysterious 'Gowrie conspiracy' of 1600 had been a late attempt at this device. The technique is a reminder that honours, status and lands ultimately came from the crown. Scottish society was extremely conscious of rank, for all that the formal privileges of nobility were not enshrined in law. The order in which nobles rode to Parliament, the place in which a landowner's family stood or sat in church, the numbers that followed the head of a Name to a funeral, the total presence at occasions such as funerals and baptisms, all these showed the significance of rank in a society where there was considerable opportunity for mobility. By the late sixteenth century educational opportunities provided by the Scottish universities, as well as by foreign ones, the chances of advancement at court, particularly with a king with a known fondness for handsome young men, increasing opportunities of employment in the king's service in diplomatic excursions or in legal duties at home and the existence of Church lands and teinds which could be distributed as rewards, all made particularly for the rise of new men and, eventually, of a new aristocracy. The inflation of the late sixteenth century had worked to the advantage of those lairds who held land by the fixed rents of feu farm, and the class of lairds, together with the baronage, provided candidates for royal advancement. Men on the make, hoping for greatness through royal advancement, were a means by which a shrewd and relatively long-lived king could promote his own authority. He could use such men as individuals, particularly if they came from lesser names, and so did not lead to promotion of a whole vast surname.

Another source of strength to the crown came from the acceptance, simply, of the concepts of kingdom and monarchy. In the Highlands where the crown could not expect to extract any revenue, recognition of notional sovereignty came easy to the chiefs, and might have been denied if it had demanded much in the way of obedience. Scotland's boundaries had been fixed for many centuries, and her royal line was accepted unquestioningly in the Stewarts. Since most of the nobility descended by one line or another from the disputed marriages of an early Stewart king, and since acceptance of a king as king did not in any way preclude opposition, even to the lengths of rebellion, to his policies, there was little desire to promote dynastic alternatives.

Fashions in ideas and institutions will spread from great nations to small ones, and Scotland had followed general European trends in the late sixteenth century. One of these was for government to become more bureaucratic: kings, ruled as holders of the pen rather than the sword. Literacy was increasingly a common attainment in middling and upper ranks in the Lowlands, and many of the clan chiefs had been educated by the book. Perhaps a product of this extending literacy was the trend to secularization of administration. Churchmen were no longer necessary in state office. There had been a shortage of trained ministry in the new Protestant Church which made it unwilling to see the state mop up its skilled labour, but even after the Reformation had become sufficiently established for churchmen to be about in abundance, and even after James VI had established an episcopacy and begun securing lands to support it, he did not use the clergy to any conspicuous extent in his civil government. A few bishops sat on the Privy Council, proving regular attenders, and they qualified as Justices of the Peace in the shires where their lands lay when this office was created, but this was all. There would have been advantages to the crown then as earlier in using these professional men, and the omission to do so must be taken as an indication that there was a sentiment of anticlericalism in landowning society.

In Scotland, as elsewhere in Europe, the role of the nobility was changing. The greater magnates were not much involved in the king's government, partly because that had developed into a heavy and regular burden which would require frequent attendance in Edinburgh. The power of the magnates depended on their local base and local leadership: such men could not make themselves available for the work of the central government without risk to their own power. The great franchises that they held, which made someone like an earl of Argyll or marquis of Huntly almost a king in his own area, meant that they like the king had a government to supervise. Nobles all over Europe were shedding their historic military function. Young men might be trained in some aspects of the arts of war, and many of the physical skills involved, such as archery, were ones by which social prestige was still won; some among them might study the subject of war academically, learning how to use new techniques of arithmetic to plan siege or battle, but it was no longer to be taken for granted that a nobleman could automatically command an army. On the other hand in the wilder parts of Scotland local feuding made it unwise for the magnates there to be inexperienced in the ordinary business of aggression. The houses of the upper class were still being built with castellations and turrets, but more as assertions of rank than necessary aids to defence. Continual pressure from the king's government towards law and order, to the ending of feuds, for compromises and settlements, compensation and redress, and occasional severity by the king in response to brutalities considered to have no redeeming features, did much to make life more peaceable, at least in southern Scotland. Occasionally members of the king's own Council were disciplined: in April 1611 incidents of abuse and violence in a long-standing quarrel led to the earl of Lothian being 'warded' in Edinburgh castle by the Council of which he was a member, to the king's approval and, eventually, to the earl's financial loss. Though great men still took it for granted that they should ride abroad with considerable retinues, these followings were being reduced in number and allowed less to do. In 1591 James had compromised on legislation on this issue and settled that for attendance on the king or at a

Justice court in Edinburgh, an earl might bring 24 men, a lord 16, a mere baron 10: the limitation was still worth making.

Nobility, shedding its military role, could and in much of Europe eventually did, turn for its occupation to patronage of the arts, splendid building and the cultivation of an expensive private life. This was not yet happening in Scotland, though great men had to live in style for the prestige of the kin. The surname had to present a front to the outside world.

James was not only disciplining the lay magnates. He was concerned to bring the ministers of the Church to greater seemliness in their language and less intransigence in their attitude to the monarchy and to the king's ministers. A king who could write 'Monarchy is the true pattern of Divinity' could not have enjoyed the scene when the ecclesiastic Andrew Melville plucked his sleeve and called him 'God's sillie vassal', even though his style of monarchy was informal. But personal slights were less serious than the systematic thwarting of his policy by the ministry. The ministers objected to his lenient handling of the still Catholic northern earls, were liable to inflame the populace of Edinburgh and, on a more general issue tried to force on the crown a crudely retributory approach to criminal cases. James held that this was unwise with the upper ranks of society. He wished to extend law and order and to settle feuds by bargaining and placating rather than by tough policies towards the miscreants. His was the safer policy for a weak government since it reduced the likelihood of backlash.

Neither Church nor State have, historically, been good at keeping off each other's territory. James had gradually devised methods of containing the extremism of the Church, by re-establishing bishops, by insisting on his right to choose the time and place of General Assemblies, by exiling a few firebrands and threatening the stipends of others. He was to go on to arrange better stipends for ministers and to aid, by subsidy, the representation of the less extreme individuals from the north at General Assemblies, but at the time of his accession to the English throne his policy of blending financial aid and containment was only beginning. As it progressed it was, as was his policy for law and order, to accentuate the differences between the north of Scotland and the south. The north was to remain under the control of the irresponsible great magnates, several of whom were Roman Catholic; it was to remain in kinship society longer than was the south, for only in a relatively tranquil world would the kin bond cease to be valuable as protection. The ministers of the north were not particularly attached to 'parity', the doctrine of equality in status and function of all ministers of religion which James called 'the mother of confusion'. James's exaggerated assertions of the rights and status of monarchy, which bore little relationship either to the actual situation in Scotland or to his own policy, probably resulted from his need to repel the self-appointed voices of an arrogant group of churchmen.

The claims of the Church to authority exerted pressure on society in other ways. Calvinism made demands for more than mere assent from the mass of Church members: it required active commitment, the realignment of priorities, total acceptance of its values. Tridentine Catholicism, when it could reach the surviving Roman Catholic enclaves in Scotland, which was not often, was also a faith with intrusive demands. Religion, particularly when, as in the Lowlands, it was partly politicized, could produce pressures which were additional to, and sometimes in opposition of, those of kin and overlord.

In some ways the Reformation led to increased personal freedom. One of these was marriage. The reformed Church set forth a narrower range of forbidden degrees and abolished the concept of spiritual affinity, changes which made it easier for a man and woman to seek each other in marriage. It held that marriage should be a mature and public-spirited decision, and that people should not marry against the advice of older kin. In the early days after the Reformation in various areas the Church had simply forbidden marriage to those it thought unsuitable candidates, but in the seventeenth century it came to accept that when people married against the wishes of kin or of kirk session, such a marriage was valid provided the consent of each party was freely given. Irregular marriage also had to be regarded as valid. Such breaches of convention or regulation were, in fact, rare in the seventeenth century. The Church also put penalties on couples who broke off an engagement after it had been proclaimed, and penalties placed on those who went ahead with sexual activity before marriage. There is some evidence that its pressure to confine sexual activity within marriage was becoming effective in many areas during the seventeenth century.

The freedom of decision making that reformed religion gave may have led to the strengthening of the forces of individualism in opposition to the social organization of kinship, but only to a small degree for some time. Society was, in any case, to be under close

Church control. In the disturbed decades in the middle of the seventeenth century the Church was to win when its claims clashed directly with those of lordship or kin. The fears produced by accusations of witchcraft could also lead to the overriding of kinship and marital bonds.

By 1603 James had embarked on another long-term policy, that of using the lands and teinds of the old monastic houses to reward his servants, and so to build up a new aristocracy of service. These men, the 'lords of erection', built up estates by series of separate personal grants. Such grants depended on the usefulness and obedience of the recipients. As a result by 1603 James could leave Scotland to be governed by his Privy Council, with the occasional aid of a direct order from himself. Councillors were, in many cases, also judges of the Court of Session. In both capacities their concepts of their role was high. James was gaining, in government, advantage from two characteristic features of the seventeenth century, the techniques of government by committee and the rising professional ethic. The same features were to be found in the Church, for the strength of the presbyterian system lay in its hierarchy of committees through which the clergy were held to a common policy, standard of behaviour and system of values.

James's new creations did not, at first, weigh much against the existing aristocracy. Forty-nine peerages existed when he took over political control; to these he had added another 14 before 1603, some of which were creations there is no reason to believe he viewed with personal enthusiasm, for instance Francis Stewart, whose mother was heiress to the Bothwell lands, was made Lord Bothwell in 1581. In the 22 years of his rule after 1603 James created a further 29 peerages, enough to change the basic character of the order, but not as drastically as it was being changed elsewhere in Europe. Some of these were affirmations, as had been the Bothwell one, of the facts of inheritance, others carried on the process of rewarding the regular servants of government and elevated men already serving on the Council in 1603, or working for the Court of Session. An example of this is Thomas Hamilton, Lord Advocate, Lord of Session since the 1590s, enobled in 1613. Others were of men administering a tough and probably one-sided 'law and order' policy in the unsettled areas of the nearer Highlands or the Border: a couple were friends who had engaged in the bloody fracas with the Ruthven brothers in 1600. The increase in peers reflects both a lowering of the standards of personal influence or wealth considered suitable for the nobility, a trend more conspicuous in England after 1618, and also the fact that since James could no longer exercise close control over the Scottish administration he had to tie his servants to him by benefits, by lands, revenues and titles. His new men, for the most part not of powerful kin, looked to him for support. Their enhanced status increased their authority, and hence their usefulness.

The new nobility of service, which most of these 43 creations were, had characteristics which marked it off from the older nobility and which promoted change. Many of the new peers were the younger sons of lairds or barons. They married among the social group from which they had been drawn, occasionally in the newer sections of the older nobility. Their children did the same, a fact which shows that this nobility was not yet accepted as the equal of the older. One or two new families built up extensive matrimonial networks, yet these do not seem to have made political blocs. The gifts and endowments which had come from the king had come in driblets, and did not make for territorially coherent estates. Even though the gifts might include jurisdictions, such men had not the powers or leadership within their estates of the older nobility. What they owned was rents and teinds, not lordship and leadership. The new nobility marked a step in the change from a society of kin and power to one of money. Also, by its dependence on the goodwill of the king, it accentuated the arbitrariness of this goodwill. The conspicuous example of this is the story of James Elphinstone, James's Secretary of State, made Lord Balmerinoch, who, in 1607, was sacrificed to the king's literary ambition. James was engaged in an arid ecclesiastical controversy with Cardinal Bellarmine and wished to retract some indiscreet statements he had made in a letter to the pope in 1599, so he pinned the blame on Balmerinoch, forced a bogus confession from him and then tried him for treason. It ended with Balmerinoch being sentenced to death, and though the sentence was not carried out and the estates which were forfeited were, in time, restored to him or to his heir, the episode stood as a reminder to the new nobility of how much they depended on the king's good will. It was also a lesson to the house of Balmerino, as it came to be called, that royalty was not to be trusted.

The inheritance by James of a larger, richer and politically more advanced kingdom was bound to have certain effects on Scotland. The English king Henry VII's judgement of a hundred years before that 'the greater will draw the lesser' would obviously be fulfilled.

Scotland could no longer have an independent foreign policy: in practice her external relations had been under English dominance sine 1560, so this was no great change except for the matter of relations with Ireland. Scottish kings had been in the habit of exiling troublesome Highland chiefs, who often had near relatives in Ireland. This meant that they might transfer their trouble-making across the sea and be a nuisance to the English government. This could no longer be encouraged. It was also obvious that the king would spend more time in England than in Scotland, because of the greater comfort to be had and because English affairs would be the more important. James foresaw this problem, and had promised to return to Scotland every three years, but in fact came back once only. His prolonged absence meant the disappearance of the Scottish court, and so the lack of the influence that a court, even an impecunious one, can have in patronage of literature and the arts. James, a writer himself, had encouraged literature, particularly drama, and earlier monarchs had gathered artists round them. Now this relatively unsophisticated cultural centre would cease to be available as a focus for the arts. Residence in England was bound to lead to some degree of anglicization, both of the king and of the Scots who accompanied him. His success in England would depend on some sort of accommodation of this kind. Exactly in what matters and to what degree this happened is, of course, the story of the second half of his reign. James could, and did, retain a detailed understanding of Scottish issues, but given the distance between London and Edinburgh, for which the post took more than a week and individual statesmen usually a month on the road, there was bound to be selection in what pieces of information came through to him. James, nervous of intrigues and disliking the pursuit by creditors, added to the inescapable difficulties of contact by ruling, in Parliament, that travel by Scots to his new court, even by his leading statesmen, required his permission.

Life in England necessarily strengthened James's position in Scotland because it meant the end of the long-established practice of factions of nobles gaining control of the administration by confiscating the person of the king. It is quite possible that no faction would have aimed at this after the bloody end to the Gowrie conspiracy of 1600. The technique would flourish only when royal policy would otherwise be in opposition to the wishes of an influential section of the nobility. James, though he complained of the continued existence of heritable jurisdictions and private feuds among the nobility, basically wished to live in harmony with his leading nobles and with their aid to put pressure on the lesser nobility and lairds to keep the law and abandon feuding. But from the safety of residence in England he was able to insist on a new level of severity in dealing with particularly outrageous disturbers of the peace. An example of this increased severity was his insistence on the execution in 1613 of Lord Maxwell, at last incarcerated for 'murder under trust' five years before of Sir James Johnstone with whom he had been at feud. The Privy Council had dragged its feet over the execution. James wrote sternly to say that 'in all tyme comeing in such materis' it should 'directlie proceed to the execution thairof'. Nevertheless severity had not been automatic. The attempts of the Maxwells to get the sentence reduced give a very interesting glimpse of the workings of law and the role of the Privy Council. The Maxwells were ready to arrange marriages between the houses, in particular for Lord Maxwell to marry the daughter of Sir James without a dowry. The king's demand for punishment was conditional on the Johnstones' refusal to compromise. Since they insisted on punishment, compromise was off. The Council's function was that of an administrative agent, a court and a place of compromise. None of these activities was yet separate. 'Murder under trust' had been named as particularly heinous by a statute of 1587, and the concept was an important sanction in efforts to get feuding parties to meet and discuss their disagreements in a society where men of all ranks carried arms as a matter of course and impetuous slayings were treated with considerable leniency. It remained a specially serious offence until the early eighteenth century. Ten years after the execution of Lord Maxwell, a considerable cooling-off period, the heads of the two houses vowed friendship in the presence of the Privy Council.

James, in 1603, had high expectations that the union of the crowns could be made to lead rapidly to a closer union of his two countries. In his own somewhat oversexed imagery he developed the theme of union: he was the husband and the whole island was his lawful wife. He wished specifically for unity in religion, law, parliament, manners and allegiance, so that the separate names of England and Scotland should disappear in Britain. It was one thing to create the title of Great Britain. It was another to persuade the two legislatures to merge trade, law and institutions.

We have a very intelligent discussion of what full union would mean, and how far apart the two countries then stood, in the work of

Sir Thomas Craig, *De Unione Regnorum Britanniae*. Craig considered that the two countries stood very close in religion, were almost identical in language and criminal law, close but with a widening gap in private law, and had economies at very different levels. He held that a real union would necessarily involve the opening of the offices of each country to citizens of the other. He saw that this issue would be more difficult for the English to accept than for the Scots, since the English offices were the more attractive prizes, but as a distinguished Scottish public servant, he did not make as much of this as might be expected.

James managed to persuade his two Parliaments to set up commissions to treat on a limited concept of union, but even this failed and all that he could secure towards this treasured end was a concept of dual citizenship for the future, and the repeal of laws specifically directed by one country against the trade of the other. The loss of the main scheme did not stop James still aiming at drawing the two countries together, but since from 1603 it was to English institutions that he was principally exposed, and since the capacity for resisting royal wishes was far more developed in the English Parliament than in the Scottish, it was inevitable that his policy should be one of the anglicization of Scotland. The king had grasped the fact that the union of the crowns was unlikely to be the climax of the relations between the two countries. Either the consciousness of separate nationalities would keep them apart, and the junction might eventually fail, or mutual interactions would create new links and bonds. James wished to hurry up the latter process. The failure of some of the European dynastic unions of the sixteenth century to last for more than a generation without a revolt by one or other partner indicates that his wishes were sensible, even if his time scale was too short.

The king was obliged to reduce the personal contact that he had had with individuals in Scotland, and in part to replace it with a strengthening of institutional links. He could no longer nobble ministers of religion before a General Assembly, but he could still keep a close eye on where it met and who attended. The Scottish Parliament was very much under his control because of the managing committee, the Lords of the Articles. The Articles provided the agenda and the drafts of legislation, and much of its work was to confirm the proposals of the Privy Council. The choice of this committee was largely in royal hands. James could also obtain legislation by calling a Convention of Estates, a body similar to a parliament which could be convened at shorter notice. Its limitation was that it was tied to the specific agenda for which it had been summoned. The Privy Council itself could issue 'Acts' of considerable authority. The legislation which inaugurated the Scottish parish school system came from an Act of the Privy Council in 1616, subsequently confirmed by a parliament.

The problem of Scottish government was not legislation but execution. The king's authority extended effectively to less than half of Scotland. The silence in the Privy Council's register about feuding in, for instance, Aberdeenshire, compared to the considerable amount of discussion of the same problem in Galloway or Fife, could not be taken to mean that all was peaceful in the north-east, merely that the Council had little power within the Gordon empire. The great franchises were still largely independent of royal intervention provided that there did not arise in them disputes that led to gross disorder, and provided that the holders of the franchises were prepared to appear obedient to specific orders from the Council. On various occasions both before and after 1603 a northern earl had been exiled or 'warded' in Edinburgh or Stirling castle. The king was occasionally strong enough to insist on this. But once back in his own area such an earl was not really under control.

In 1609 James borrowed from England the institution of Justice of the Peace as a device for improving the level of local order and law enforcement. The Justices eventually appointed, substantial resident landowners, were to deal with minor disturbances, control beggars, control weights and measures and wages, and carry on the general business of local government. It is often asserted that they never developed the authority of their English models, partly because there was no available slot for their jurisdiction in the network of franchises. There is some truth in this, but they added an element of authority and order at a level where it was needed and the class of lairds gained in status and cohesion through receiving these new powers, even if in the seventeenth century the powers were more apparent than real.

The Council was even able, in James's later days, to bring under some degree of control the Borders, the Highlands and the Northern Isles. In the case of the Borders, the policy was steady pressure and a ready use of the gallows. Elsewhere a more oblique approach had to be used, except for the notorious case of the McGregors, with whom its policy was a more ineffective edition of that used in the Borders. James had decreed the proscription of this weak and violent

Highland clan in 1603 because its internal dissensions had led its chief to attempt to maintain his power by slaughtering a royal servant and engaging in a battle on the fringe of the Lowlands. Behaviour of this kind could not be tolerated so near to areas of relative peace. The Council carried on James's policy by pressing other Highland chiefs to cease harbouring McGregors: at times 'Commissions of fire and sword' would be issued, that is licence to some magnate or chief to harry and loot, as a technique of control. As a political organization the McGregor clan was destroyed, but groups of McGregors hung out in many areas exercising protection rackets. Others made temporary changes in the surname and in allegiance. Some ended calling themselves Gregory and providing a distinguished element in the academic community in Aberdeen. The number actually slaughtered was far fewer than that of Borderers picked on in policing Border raids, but, perhaps because it was the society of a whole clan that was broken, not simply isolated bandits that were extinguished, sentiment has concentrated on this particular display of administrative ferocity. The broken McGregors made an unexpected contribution to Gaelic culture, for it was in their disordered society that new and freer forms of poetry were developed.

The Council had its doubts about the policy of Commissions of fire and sword. It was a mockery of law and order, and it tended to lead to the aggrandizement of one or other of two great houses difficult to control, Huntly or Argyll. An earlier policy of colonizing the Highland, with Lowlanders had given advantage to the McKenzies, and had not produced any real infusion of Lowland culture into the Highlands. In 1609 the Council devised a new, more peaceable if not particularly honourable form of pressure. Lord Ochiltree, one of the Council, captured several chiefs by fraud and he and the bishop of the Isles, Andrew Knox, worked out with them an agreement on regulations for the keeping of the peace. These became known as the Statutes of Iona. They reasserted the accepted technique of the General Band, by which men bound themselves to maintain order already established in Highland policy. The Statutes gave official recognition to clanship by placing responsibility for the behaviour of clansmen on their chief, but also, by prohibiting the support of bards and by requiring a Lowland education for the chief's heir, struck a blow at Highland culture. In the very long run it was the second policy that was to prevail. The dishonourable technique was understandable in the light of the chronic warface and brutal feuds produced in the southern High-lands by the break up of the great Macdonald clan, and the pressure of the powerful and unscrupulous clan Campbell. The policy at least contained the disputes and brought a little revenue to the crown. But the extension of royal concern was not adequately matched by the crown's ability to offer security.

Another bishop, James Law, enabled James to create an alternative administration in the Northern Isles, and so to bring down his cousin the earl of Orkney, who was imprisoned and eventually executed. Here again royal control involved an attack on the local culture. The separate laws of the Northern Isles were declared invalid and Scots law was to take over. This gave the opportunity for a Scottish landowning class to enter the Norse society. It is doubtful whether this meant any improvement in liberty or material living conditions for the islanders, but there is no doubt that James had increased, in three different areas, the range of his government's arm and the prospects of its revenue.

Bishops thus proved themselves useful administrators in lay matters, but to James their main function was the control of the wilder elements in the Church. The bishops were men of no great social standing in origin. Some were from the families of lairds, some married into this class. Enough was scraped together in Church lands to make their position respectable without preventing the improvement of the incomes of the clergy in general, but they could not expect to become great men in terms of wealth. One at least, Patrick Forbes who went to Aberdeen in 1618, was a scholar. In 1610 James emphasized their link with the pre-Reformation episcopate by insisting on consecration from bishops in England where the apostolic succession, through the laying on of hands, had not been broken. But this did not mark a break in the character of the Scottish Kirk. The existing clergy were not required to receive episcopal ordination, and though from then on bishops presided over ordinations they did so with the clergy of the presbytery, and the emphasis of such occasions was on the admission of a new minister to his parish rather than on the reception of a sacrament. The stress which the Scottish Reformers had placed on the congregation was maintained.

Partly through the presence of bishops and partly by other pressures James changed the role of the General Assembly and reduced its administrative function. Some part of this change would probably have happened without his intervention, since the inter-

mediate Church court, the synod, had become regular in its meetings, but synods also gained strength when James inserted bishops
as permanent moderators into them, and became a significant
element in the maintenance of the standards of education and
behaviour in the ministry. In 1610 James created courts of High
Commission in the two Church provinces to be the means of
discipline and conformity. In 1605–6, in the quarrel with the
outright presbyterians led by Andrew Melville, James had, at the
cost of exiling Melville and a few others, established that a General
Assembly met only when and where the king chose, but he still had
not the control of its deliberations that he had of Parliament's. He
therefore chose to call it rarely, and ceased to summon it altogether
after he had forced from it, at Perth, reluctant consent to the famous
Five Articles.

The problem raised for James by the Scottish Church was not
simply one of finance and administration, areas where on the whole
he was successful, but also of the nature of its ministrations and
services, where he was not. A Church needs a liturgy to preserve its
accepted doctrine from deviation, to maintain the links with other
Churches of similar belief and to ensure that the formal outward
signs of the sacraments are truly performed. A liturgy is also useful,
though not essential, as a means of religious education. It can direct
and stimulate the activity of a congregation. The Scottish Church
had adopted the *Book of Common Order* at the Reformation from
Geneva as a book of common prayer, but it was bound only loosely
in the observance of it, and in many matters the book itself was
permissive rather than directive. In some parishes ministers used
parts of the English *Book of Common Prayer*, in others they devised
services as they chose, but for most the *Book of Common Order*
provided the general pattern of worship. James had not concerned
himself with liturgical reform in the first half of his reign, being
more concerned with government than with procedure. In England
he accommodated to the English Prayer Book, and since he saw
church practice as an element in the unification of his realms, it was
understandable that he should wish to bring English usage to
Scotland. He may have added to a desire for unity an affection for
the English usage after many years of use. At any rate it was the
English liturgy which was used in his chapel when he visited
Scotland in 1617. The year before a General Assembly had
redrafted the Confession of Faith to make supralapsarianism
explicit and had brought out drafts for a new liturgy. In 1617 James

proposed to a General Assembly at St Andrews five regulations. These were refused on this occasion but passed by a later Assembly at Perth and forced through a largely unwilling Parliament in 1621 as the famous 'Five Articles of Perth'.

The substance of these Articles was to impose on Scotland observation of the principle traditional dates of the Christian year, to require communion to be taken kneeling, to require confirmation of the laity by a bishop, and to permit private communion and baptism in cases of infirmity. Already there had been an order that communion should take place at Pasch (Easter). None of these articles directly required a practice incompatible with the Reformed faith, but those on private sacraments went against the long-established Scottish emphasis on the role of the congregation, that on baptism suggested also that the sacrament was necessary for salvation, those on communion and the Christian year offended the growing puritan tenet that the only pure practices in a church were those for which precedents or instructions could be found in Scripture. These also demanded overt observance, so that performance or omission could not be ignored. Kneeling was normal for prayer at this time, but it could be argued that any action for which parallels could be found in the Mass was idolatrous. One of the bishops and several nobles had already refused to kneel for communion during James's visit, and resistance to this Article continued. The opposition to the Articles in the Perth Assembly, where they passed by two to one, when the king's strong wishes were known, is revealing. There was also a large opposition in the Parliament of 1621, and this included members of James's own aristocracy and most of the middling rank of burgh and shire representatives. The king had caused opposition in the groups which normally supported his policy.

In practice most of the Articles could be ignored, but that on kneeling at communion could not be. The Privy Council appears to have made little attempt to enforce the new practices. Ignored or grudgingly accepted, the Articles created a general suspicion of royal policy towards the Church, and in this atmosphere it was impossible for James to go on to obtain a reformed liturgy. They also led a few opponents to start holding their own religious meetings, the first 'conventicles'. These dissentients did not break totally with the Church: it was still a long time before there would be formal dissent in Scotland. They did not associate the Church with any doctrine deemed heretical, but they held that it followed practices some of which were impure. The Council made some, not very strong, efforts to stamp out these irregular meetings.

There are indications of other forms of stress than puritan in the 1620s. The colonization of Ulster, which had been going on from Scotland, and had led to a settlement said to involve some 8,000 adult males, seems to have come to a halt in this decade. But men were leaving Scotland to serve as mercenaries in the continental wars in large numbers. This export of manpower suggests that though the economy had expanded in the last 60 years, population growth had been faster than that of resources. In 1622–3 a sharp reversal of growth took place. A double harvest failure threw the country into famine. Belated attempts of the Council to get landowners in the counties to intervene and raise funds for the starving produced an answer either of refusal or of incapacity in the face of wide-spread starvation. The decade also saw a surge in the number of witchcraft accusations and trials. The number of these so far located rose from 74 in the years 1610–19 to 358 for 1620–9. We do not know enough about the sociology of witchcraft fear and accusations to assess the meaning of this. The proliferation may indicate a growing desire for more effective policing. Uncritical attitudes to causation, shared with most of Europe, certainly played a part. All that can be done at present is to note the growth of the trouble as a sign of some sort of dissatisfaction.

In spite of the elements of social stress James was entitled to feel in his last years that his reign had been a success. He had boasted in 1607 'I write and it is done, and by a clerk of the Council I govern Scotland now, which others could not do by the sword'. Royal authority was at a level never before safely achieved. This was largely because, except in his only half achieved Church policy, James's 'orders' did not clash directly with the claims, of entrenched and powerful groups. Also it is clear that some of the success of government came from decisions of the Council and not of the king. Some policies were suggested by the Council to the king and became his own, some involved a tacit refusal to follow James's line. James had known the country and its aristocracy well enough for most of his decisions to be implemented by the Council, but before his death in 1625 the situation between Council and king had become similar to that between a colonial administration and the mother country. The subsidiary government would at times go its own way, convinced that it knew best. A more serious weakness was that the heir to the throne did not know Scotland. He ruled a part of it, the lands given to him as prince of Wales and named the Principality, but he did not know the passions, priorities and prejudices of the aristocracy, nor had he acquired through watching it at work a respect for the professional expertise of the Privy Council. Yet for all that, James left a country more prosperous and more at peace than it had ever been before.

2

The Rule of Charles I

Scotland's real, but limited links, with general European culture are shown by the state of the arts in the early seventeenth century. Painting was as yet amateurish, though Scottish commissions managed to sustain the leading portrait painter George Jamesone in comfort. His work enables us to capture some of the personalities of the period. The partly fictitious portraits of the Stewart kings in Holyrood Palace show an artist unable to manage the human nose: the distinguished portrait of the young duke of Hamilton, now in the Tate gallery, was by a foreigner, and in Scotland, as in England, those of the aristocracy who wished to be portrayed in a style in keeping with their importance looked to the Netherlands for the artist. Scottish architecture was beginning to absorb Renaissance features from abroad. George Heriot's Hospital in Edinburgh, for which the symmetrical courtyard plan was made in the late 1620s, shows an appreciation of late-sixteenth-century Italian trends, even to a piazza on which to enjoy the rigorous blasts of an Edinburgh summer, and an elaborate entrance, but the detailing, especially as the storeys mount, has a northern flavour. And at the roof line the building buds into the corner turrets typical of a Scottish tower house. Castellation and gunports of an ornamental rather than a useful nature remained in the repertoire of Scottish masons because their past military relevance indicated the noble status of their owners. Heavy iron gates, on the other hand, stayed in for a natural desire to control entry in an age when almost every man was armed, and law and order not guaranteed. The tower house, in a enlarged L-shaped form, was at its peak of design in Aberdeenshire, and its defensive features were by no means only for social assertion, but in some more secure areas the houses of the upper classes had reduced their defences and been allowed to spread out. The supreme example of domestic architecture from this period is the Argyll

Lodging, Stirling, which adapted and enlarged for Charles I's favourite, the adventurer William Alexander, earl of Stirling, an earlier town house into a stately but irregular courtyard mansion with ornamented windows almost establishing a feeling of symmetry. Painted ceilings or elaborate plaster ones could be installed in the houses of the aristocracy to indicate refinement. The plaster ones relied on foreign workmen. There is a cheerfulness and joviality about much of this ornamentation, and in the case of the more modern houses, such as the Argyll Lodging, enough light came in from new-fangled windows for the occupants to appreciate the decoration fully. A further reassertion of nobility here, as in Old Castille, lay in the fondness for large and elaborate heraldic devices, and in both cases the explanation is the same, a nobility valuing inherited status rather than wealth.

In the designs of smaller items indicative of rank and status taste in Scotland more nearly kept up with that elsewhere. Scottish coins had long been of high aesthetic standard. The silver-ware of tankards, candlesticks and spoons shows enough technical mastery – it was not an area of technical change – and has beautiful restraint and judgement, though the surviving specimens to be seen today are blemished by the failure of silversmiths of this period to polish off the firescale which came from the copper needed to harden the silver. Hangings and cushions were luxuries for the few, and probably came from abroad.

In intellectual matters Scotland experienced, as did the rest of Europe, the impact of printing. This meant a widening and secularizing of written culture. The world of the book was open to all with a small amount of money to spare. It is clear from the efforts of the Privy Council to control and licence (printing of books had required royal licence since 1599) that there was a sizeable number of printers in Edinburgh, and testamentary evidence shows that booksellers also were numerous. Most of their stock was routine educational or religious material, but works written to be read for pleasure, such as Sir David Lyndsay's *Thrie Estaits* were available in quantity. The adaptation of Scotland's universities to the needs of reformed religion meant that academics were not encouraged to be scholars. The universities existed mainly to make lawyers and ministers out of the children who attended them: these were drawn from the middling ranks of society, merchants and lesser lairds, as is evidenced by the high protein diet provided in Glasgow by the university caterer. But St Andrews held to a higher social tone; it was there that the aristocracy went for a secondary education. The regenting system, by which the whole Arts course was taught to a year's entry by the same man, gave the student the type of personal care today regarded as appropriate only in a primary school. By forcing the regents to teach all subjects on a big curriculum it prevented specialization. In the 1590s under the dominance of Andrew Melville some of the Scottish universities had accepted Ramism, the philosophy of Theodore Ramus, a method by which topics were chopped up into small, memorizable segments, and arguments constructed on similarly minced elements. This was an obviously easy way of disciplining the thought and knowledge of adolescents, but had little creative to offer. It cannot be said that the quality of logic used by Scottish ministers in sermons of the early seventeenth century reflects well on it. In the English universities Ramism seems to have become associated with a dissenting puritanism, but in Scotland its short-lived dominance does not seem to have raised any challenge to authority. It merely reinforced the other influences which limited profound thinking. We know from the *Autobiography* of James Melville, nephew to Andrew, what books and languages formed the university curriculum, and we also know that he started as regent at 18. In Aberdeen alone scholarship seems to have survived the processes which turned the universities into drilling machines for the Church. The combination of remarkable men and the relative remoteness of the city from the political heart of Scotland enabled the 'Aberdeen Doctors', a group of true scholars, to survive and to cultivate a learning which embraced the works of the early fathers of the Church as well as of medieval philosophy.

The most interesting aspects of early-seventeenth-century intellectual life are on the lay side. Sir Thomas Craig's writings on the Union question show a detachment and an interest in comparative law and institutions which foreshadow the preoccupations of the late eighteenth century. James VI, trained as a classical scholar, was a penetrating literary critic, fancied himself in theological disputation and wrote with skill and vigour. It was a pity that his education had not run to any study of the economy. A man with his pungent wit did not like having fools around, and the surviving library from his crony Thomas Hamilton, earl of Melrose, and later of Haddington, shows that this minister of the crown had a civilized and cosmopolitan taste. Hamilton bought and used books in Latin, French and Italian, and would scribble marginalia in the French works in French. His interests were in political thought, particularly in the works of Macchiavelli, and in topics with direct political or practical significance. His lack of interest in theology and in Scottish history are both interesting lights on the fashions of his day.

Indisputably the most distinguished thinker of James's reign was John Napier of Merchiston. He aided the king in the fixing of the Scottish currency in relation to the English and wrote a significant pamphlet on the historical interpretation of the book of Revelation, but his fame rests mainly on his mathematical work, his construction of a primitive analog calculator and on the 'discovery' of logarithms. These logarithms were tables produced to aid trigonometric calculations, a fact which is an interesting comment on the sophistication of Scotland's material culture. They were not based on any deep mathematical insight: indeed until reorganized in the form we have today, by the contemporary English scholar Briggs working with Napier, they were needlessly cumbersome to use. Napier's logarithms were not, in fact, what are today called Napierian or natural logarithms. His formula was

$$\text{Napierian Log } y = 10^7 \log_e \frac{10^7}{y}$$

which gave a negative figure for numbers over 10 million. A similar discovery was made a few years later by a Swiss calculator, a reminder of how the technical needs of an age are common to large parts of its multifarious civilization and consequently met by multiple discovery. The discovery was, for two generations, an intellectual cul-de-sac. Napier did not understand the concepts he had stumbled upon, nor could anyone else until Newton and Leibniz produced calculus in the 1670s and Euler in the eighteenth century sorted out the exponential function.

Napier's career shows how an intellectual in Scotland could be part of the world of learning which still used Latin as an intellectual language. But when his career is contrasted with that of his coadjutor Briggs it is also clear how his achievement was held back by the smallness of his intellectual circle and by the unsophisticated level of Scottish technology. Briggs at Gresham's College not only had other mathematicians to talk to, he had the needs of the royal dockyard in measuring techniques and calculating skills to which to respond. Napier was on his own. He was also on his own when he wrote about Scotland's civil society, for he found it difficult to attach the generally accepted theory about the nature of a cultured society and its law to the backward state of Scotland.

In impact on the mass of the people the intellectual area that was of greatest significance was, of course, theology. Scotland had followed without serious question the intellectual developments within continental Calvinism. One of these was the defining of Calvin's predestination into a supralapsarian form. In its new precision the doctrine stated that before the creation of Adam, the fall of man, the redemption by Christ of the elect and the reprobation of the bulk of mankind had all been decided on by God for the manifestation of His glory. This was worked out by Calvin's successor Beza, and brought to its most explicit formulation in the Synod of 'Dort', or Dordrecht, of 1618. Dutch Calvinism was led to this sharpened form of Calvinism by the desire to repudiate the reaction from the increasing Calvinist emphasis on predestination and the construction of a concept of salvation open to all which is associated with the name of Arminius. Arminianism, formulated in the early seventeenth century, is often associated with free will. It is sounder to see it as stressing the various means by which grace is made available, and the recognition that grace is not irresistible. Such a doctrine reduced the extremism of Calvinism, and replaced predestination in its directive sense with divine foreknowledge. Scotland was not directly represented at the synod at Dordrecht, though King James had commissioned an observer, and the doctrines of Dordrecht were not formally declared the doctrine of the Scottish Kirk until 1645, when the Westminster Confession put forward that:

> by the decree of God, for the manifestation of his glory, some men and angels are predestinated unto everlasting life, and others foreordained to everlasting death.
>
> These angels and men, thus predestinated and foreordained are particularly and unchangeably designed; and their number is so certain and definite, that it cannot be either increased or diminished.

This delay did not mean that the doctrine did not prevail. It was expressly laid out in the legalistic theology of Samuel Rutherford, and there are occasional specific references to Dort which show that the synod was regarded as authoritative. But no serious exposition of arminianism had been made in Scotland. William Forbes, put into the new diocese of Edinburgh in 1634, is often stated to have been arminian but his writings more truly show him to have been an augustinian, that is a repudiator of free will who had not narrowed his concepts into the rigidity of full predestination. Like the other Aberdeen doctors he was deeply imbued with earlier theology and saw the Scottish Kirk as the inheritor of patristic and medieval Catholicism, so his writings draw heavily on the literature of the early Church. Forbes was one who hoped to see a reunion of the Churches, and therefore stressed their areas of agreement rather than those of difference. Other accusations of arminianism launched in this period usually mean that the man accused was not using the common stereotypes of theological language and imagery. The Scottish mind at this date was not particularly theological. Theology was a subject in which the young were drilled, not one explored by mature minds in search of refinements of truth.

The area of doctrine which received most comprehensive and detailed development was 'covenant theology'. This doctrine is to be found in an incipient form in Calvin's *Institutes*. Calvin saw God as having formulated a Covenant of Law with Moses, and a later Covenant of Grace through Christ. Subsequent writer called the first of these the Covenant of Works, and this was held to have been made with Adam; by it the moral law of the Old Testament was set out. This covenant, though broken by man, was none the less binding on him. From this addition to the text of Scripture had been built up an elaborate theological construct. It was already sufficiently established by 1596 for the General Assembly of the Kirk to have bound itself in an explicit 'new covenant' with God, and in the same year in a parish church in Fife the concept of such a covenant was expounded in a corporate catechism drawn up by the minister, which included the statement 'Christ is the Cautioner of the Covenant and Contract for us, and so principal debtor'. (It is one of the oddities of Calvinism, a belief that stressed the vastness of God's creativity and His omnipotence, that it should have come to credit Him with the values of a small-town notary pubic and to explain to Him what He could not do.)

Covenant theology prevented Calvinist thinking slipping into anti-nominianism, the tenet that faith supersedes the demands of the moral law, and consequently that anything is permitted to the justified. The elect would persevere in grace but the moral law was not abrogated by the assurance of salvation. It therefore filled an important ministering gap in theology. It also carried on the stress that Calvin had placed on the witness of the Old Testament and on the basic unity of Scripture. This meant that the primitive punitive concepts of early Israel could be put forward as moral standards. It provided its adherents with a clear, though limited, view of their place in time, an historic perspective rather like that possessed by today's Israelis, of an early Biblical world and the events of the last few decades made acceptable by a total ignorance of anything in between. To the limited historical consciousness of seventeenth-century Scotland this was attractive, and it was not countered by any acute sense of the antiquity of common law. Also attractive was the obvious parallel between the covenant between God and man and the 'General Band' in which Scots were in the habit of binding themselves to preserve the peace. The General Assembly's assertion of 1596 was seen as a general band in which God had been included as the principal participator. Such a band would enormously strengthen the clergy of 1596 in disagreement with the crown over Church policy. Banding and covenanting gradually merged into a practice which, by associating the civil precedures of the Scottish people with God, encouraged a belief in a peculiarly close relationship between the Scots and their God. Finally it presented theology in the crude legal language attractive to a society in which law was rapidly expanding its functions and with it the importance of the legal profession. Ideas of God could be put into terminology suitable for routine lectures to the young, requiring no grasp of difficult concepts such as eternity, omnipotence, etc. Abstruse refinements of covenant theology were drummed into students and congregations, and the drumming reinforced the self-esteem of the clergy. The clergy formed a professional group with good internal communications: regular meetings at presbytery level (weekly in summer) sustained orthodoxy and discouraged inclinations to original interpretations of Scripture. To such a body the idea that the monarch might be toying with a different theology would bring instant suspicion and hostility. There is no sign of any serious development of this kind in the reign of James VI: under his son it was a different matter.

The basis of government was still, all through the seventeenth century, one of personality rather than of institutions, so the succession of the amicable, intrusive and wily personality of James VI by his colder, more austere and more rigid son Charles was bound to lead to change. Since James's band of administrators, led by Thomas Hamilton, earl of Melrose, was by then a group of old men, set in their ways, the change was likely to be disrupting. The year of the new accession, 1625, was also one of war: Charles's foreign ventures led him to quarrel in rapid succession with Spain and then with France. Scotland was expected to contribute to the resulting wars in men and materials. There had been no foreign war for her since 1560, and it is clear that war placed a burden on the economy and revealed inadequacies in adminstration. Even countries in the habit of going to war found each time that the enhanced level of expenditure was a strain: it was much worse for a country completely out of practice. The king attempted to give office and powers to his favourites, in particular to the earl of Stirling, poet and adventurer, who had, as Master of Requests for Charles before his succession, mediated all contacts of Charles with the lands, usually called the Principality, which he held in Scotland. Stirling had been away from Scotland for most of his adult life, and though his 'try anything' approach led to some new ideas, the most long-lasting being an attempt to raise funds and promote colonization by selling baronetcies of Nova Scotia, he lacked administrative talent, application and the personal weight necessary to deal with the ageing bureaucrats of the Council. Two other of Charles's associates were out of Scotland because of trouble they had caused there: Robert Maxwell, earl of Nithsdale, brother to Lord Maxwell the murderer, was too deep in debt to enter the country, and Sir Alexander Strachan of Thornton was not only a thoroughly bad hat but one whose criminal activities had involved the Privy Council in action in the later days of James. With men of this stamp as the king's main advisers a gap in confidence between the king and his Scottish administration was inevitable.

The gap was made into a yawning gulf by Charles's mixture of poor communications, petty hostilities and a plan for the reconstruction of Scottish landed society, which was in part to put the clock back behind the revolutions of 1560 and 1567, when the aristocracy had annexed much of the wealth of the Church. Some such restructuring was overdue. Though the country had under James VI made great strides in peaceableness it still had serious weaknesses in government. The crown lacked an adequate financial base. The mixture of sources, royal property, burghal dues and customs duties venially collected from selected commodities gave a normal revenue of something over £16,000 sterling – less than the personal income put together by James's corrupt but effective favourite the duke of Buckingham in England. Taxation, levied by Parliament, had become increasingly frequent, so that its impact was almost yearly, but it was raised only from those who held directly of the crown. The miserly resources, inadequate even for the routine business of government, did not enable the king to reward his friends except by starving other functions of government. In practice most of the routine cost of government was being met from English resources because the royal court was in England.

Lack of money was paralleled by lack of law. Even though the level of peacekeeping had risen since James's early days, there was still obscurity about the content of various areas of law and the methods by which new law was made. There was also the exclusion of considerable areas from the king's courts in favour of those of a franchise holder. No map of the various franchises, the heritable jurisdictions, has ever been drawn, and franchise courts varied in the powers they exercised, but in general the existence of these feudal survivals meant that cases involving vassals based within a franchise would be handed over to the franchise court, 'repleged'. Also some royal offices such as sheriffdoms, were in private hands and, in the opinion of their holders, hereditary. Justice had a tendency to be mixed with expediency. The judicial bench of the Court of Session consisted of men who worked also in the Privy Council, and the function of the Council was a blend of justice and administration. There was also uncertainty about the distinction of the law-making powers of Privy Council, Parliament and Convention of Estates, though since the passing of an Act did not necessarily mean its enforcement this was not important in practice. A Convention of Estates was identical in membership to Parliament, could be called at shorter notice, but was restricted in debate to the agenda prepared by the Council in advance. Acts by either Parliament or Estates which might have been of major significance were sometimes not observed, as was the case with various poor law statutes, or observed only partially, as in the case of the recent requirement that there should be parochial schools.

Backwardness in the formulation and administration of law extended also to the profession of lawyer. There was no systematic education for these men, and many of the judges were administrators rather than lawyers. There was a conspicuous overlap between membership of the College of Justice and the Privy Council, and it was as Senators of the College that many admintrators received a salary. If the functions of the two bodies were to grow apart, this would become an anomaly.

Law's weaknesses were part of the general weakness of the central authority, Power over men lay in the hands of great magnates rather than in those of the crown. The renewal of the office of Justice of the Peace by James in 1609 had been an attempt to find support from a class of unpaid servants among lesser landowners, but these officers did not find it easy, even when they tried, to exercise effective jurisdiction, and seem to have lacked the sense of administrative responsibility acquired over the sixteenth century by the English Justices on whom their office was modelled. The traditional prestige of local office, so conspicuous in England, did not exist in the Scottish landholding class, nor did the social and politicial cohesion of the county. The central officers of state had little supporting staff, and the fact that under James his Lord Treasurer Dunbar had spent most of the year in England is a comment on the limited role of his office at home.

Perhaps a more serious weakness was that the country did not possess an institution for debate and consent to which its citizens would feel themselves bound. The king in Parliament was a figure of authority, but not the great symbol to which allegiance was paid that it was in England. Parliament was hardly a place of discussion since most of its business was done by the committee of the Lords of the Articles, and the method of choosing this committee made it easy and convenient for the crown to prevent dissent being adequately represented on it. Even so it had, particularly over the Five Articles of Perth, made the existence of opposition clear. The Council was more truly a debating body than was Parliament, but it too was not a place for opposition. The General Assembly still carried on real discussions, but the voices raised there were likely to be doctrinaire, and in any case it had not met since 1618, In most monarchies of early modern Europe such interchange of opinion in the formulation of policy took place within the social life of the royal court. Courts gave out information, misinformation and gossip to all who hung around near them, and in this way news and plans percolated through to provincial landed society. But with the headquarters of action 400 miles away from the administration in Edinburgh, this system did not work well, and in 1625, when Charles took over, it is clear that his government in Scotland, though ready to disagree in a spirit of encrusted conservatism with whatever the king would propose, simply did not know what was going on or why. Charles's attempt to put Stirling in charge of business merely resulted in James's old servant Melrose rescuing some level of efficiency from general disorder and carrying on without being officially in charge.

There were deeper problems pending, though, than the king's desire to provide comfortable jobs for his friends. His father had expressed dissatisfaction with the powers of the greater nobility but had contented himself with winning their confidence at first, and had passed on to discipline them only when he himself was safely away in England and only for unusually outrageous actions. Charles wished to alter the basis of aristocratic power, and weaken the sources of influence by which a magnate could build up an unwilling following and also to reduce the links between the aristocracy and the Court of Session. He further wished to secure a reliable income for the parish clergy out of teind and to enlarge the revenue of the crown. He may also have wished to create some system of check on the omnicompetence of the Privy Council.

For all these purposes he focussed his attention on particular features: the membership of the Court of Session and Privy Council, the grasp by landowners on Church lands and teinds, the feudal superiorities over lesser men. Initially he set up a commission of grievances which was to operate as a check on misgovernment, claimed the right to dismiss the judges of the past reign, and brought out in haste his famous Act of Revocation to exploit the generally accepted practice by which a monarch who had succeeded as a minor could, before he attained the age of 25, annul gifts made in his minority. Charles had succeeded in March 1625 and would be 25 in November. The Act annulled not only his own grants within the Principality but also the gifts of Church lands and teinds made by his father.

Most of these actions lay in a grey area of law, or were openly outwith his powers. It was doubtful whether judges could be dismissed for anything other than fault. In no way could the grants of James VI be considered as grants made by Charles himself as a minor, and in any case Charles had not succeeded as a minor. Even given the relative lack of experience in Scotland of the accession of an adult king, it was unlikely that men would fail to note that the law was being stretched or broken.

There was great uncertainty for some time about what the changes were to involve. Seventeenth-century governments were not in the habit of moving briskly and efficienty, yet haste was necessary to preserve the vestiges of legality. At first the Privy Council in Edinburgh thought that the Revocation extended only to the Principality, the Scottish lands settled on Charles when Prince of Wales. Later it was made clear that it covered the whole kingdom for grants made as far back as 1567, later still that it went back even to 1540. Even more slowly as the king pressed for formal surrenders of old Church property, were his ultimate intentions revealed. In 1633 the final settlements were made, and these showed that Charles's aims were those of a good administrator. Few lords of erection lost lands that they actively exploited: land not feued out mostly stayed in their own hands, but feued land had its feudal superiority compulsorily bought up by the crown. For teind, every heritor was to receive the teind of his own land, paying a fixed amount in grain as stipend to the parish ministry, and 6 per cent to the crown. Charles also gathered back various offices which had become hereditary possessions of magnates, and changed the forms of certain other tenures. The final result gave to Scotland the benefits of the considered plans of a man with a love of order. The ministers, already comfortably off by Protestant standards, became secure, and the means by which great men could trouble the lives of lesser men were restricted. But these powers, hitherto exercised, belonged to the central role of lordship in Scottish society. In 1625 the plan had appeared as a vast confiscation. Even when worked out and modified its administrative advantages were counterbalanced by the political stresses it created among the king's most powerful subjects. Members of the aristocracy lost influence and, sometimes, superiorities. These changes were to mean a significant reduction in aristocratic power, a change which even if formulated clearly and with full consultation would have needed the complete and trusting co-operation of all institutions of government for success, and particularly the support of the Privy Council.

Unfortunately for such a programme, Charles was handicapped by a minimal administration and had to move quickly if even the faint degree of legality which existed for the Revocation could be claimed. The Act was composed in May: it reached the Council only in July in a form by no means clear: it was formally issued in October before the Councils' doubts had been cleared up. At the same time the king was planning an agenda for his first Convention of Estates, a mixture of sound proposals for better government, requests for money and indications of considerable ignorance of the way of life in his northern capital. In November the king was restructuring his Privy Council in a manner which the existing Council regarded as offensive as well as unworkable. Early in the new year his leading officers of state managed to meet with the king and his London advisers. We have an account from the Treasurer, the earl of Mar, of these meetings which is doubtless biased in its recapitulation of the exchang of views but which faithfully reveals the astonishing fact that Charles had no idea of both how drastic and how illegal his programme had been.

The effect of this lack of communication and understanding has been summed up by a distinguished historian as the wrecking of the system of government of Scotland by the Privy Council. The king took into his own hands the making of decisions for which he had neither the knowledge nor the judgement. Eventually he had to build up new and lesser figures to do his work for him, and the confidence in the intentions of government which James had given to the aristocracy was destroyed. As the earl of Mar wrote 'no subject in Scotland in effect have any securities of his land'. Yet those who benefitted by the policy, the lairds and clergy, had their own grounds of suspicion of royal policy, for they soon came to mistrust Charles's apparent aim of religious assimilation of his two kingdoms. There was no support there to set against that which he had lost. It is worth noting that it was a similar royal disregard of law in part of a dual monarchy which was to lead to rebellion in another kingdom in the mid-seventeenth century, with the revolt of Catalonia against the crown of Spain.

The problem which must concern the historian over these events is whether if Charles had presented his plans with more understanding of his northern kingdom, he could have been successful. He aimed at undoing part of the change in power which had accompanied the Reformation, not in the covert way in which James had built up royal power, but openly. Such a policy, even if he had not attempted to cloak it with dubious legality, would have been against the personal interests of the Privy Council and the aristocracy who supplied both Parliament and Convention of Estates. If the king could have handled his administration with tact, and not been distracted by English politics and the English Parliament, war, marriage and impending further war, it would still have been difficult to have got the necessary changes legally established. In any case he wanted to be rid of the entrenched civil service of his father's Council, and could see no reason to treat these men with consideration.

Even at James's funeral Charles had shown insensitivity to the separate nature of the English and Scottish Churches by trying to bully Archbishop Spottiswoode into appearing in English vestments. The king's concern over ecclesiastical haberdashery was to be confirmed in the Parliament he held on his visit to Scotland in 1633 when he forced throught two Acts concerning the Church, making explicit the powers that James VI had assumed over the Church and extending these to the clothing of the clergy.

Charles had not wished to wait until 1633 before making his first visit to Scotland but, besides being delayed by the distractions created by his own policy, he had come to power just after a severe famine when the country was in no state to receive the swarm of locusts that made up an early modern court. One of the enactments of his first Convention of Estates had probably been stimulated by this disaster, an attempt to make the Poor Law into an effective instrument for supporting the destitute, but this had, like much other legislation, never got beyond intent. Before he could be received in Edinburgh the palace had to be repaired and transport for the furnishings of king and courtiers provided. Scots were supposed to be restricted from an over-competitive display in finery by a recent sumptuary law, but they still had to have and make available funds to improve the accommodation of the city. In the end, as Clarendon recalls, Charles was received with 'no less lustre' at Edenborough than at WhiteHall'. The rotting heads of malefactors had to be got off the city gates: supplies had to be ensured by putting the country on a Lenten diet for several months in advance, and special regulations had to be issued about the state of pewter and linen. Olfactory offence was always likely in a country where well-matured urine was the main cleansing agent. At least the king responded to the efforts of his native countrymen by being genial enough to allow Edinburgh to greet him with a level of festivity and display which he had not yet allowed to London.

By 1633 what the Revocation was to mean in confiscation was largely determined and known. How severe in the instance it would be depended on the varying levels in which payments were still made in kind. Whereas feu duties and rents had become defined in money the price changes of the late sixteenth century made teind, still calculated in real terms, particularly valuable. It was the upland and pastoral areas, where rents were mainly money ones, since the specialized products, wool, hides etc., all went to market instead of being locally consumed, which particularly resented the attack on teind, since it was the remaining area where wealth had not shifted from lord to feuar. Another source of resentment, that of taxation levels, hit both noblemen and townsmen, for it was becoming regular. Another unpopular element in royal policy was the use of bishops on the Council. Charles had made Archbishop Spottiswoode President of the Exchequer and given him precedence over lay councillors: in 1635 he was to become chancellor, illustrating the restoration of the medieval pattern of clerics as royal administrators. There were other bishops on the Council, men of relatively obscure families, and the aristocracy was, as always, excessively sensitive about status and precedence.

The administrative use of the episcopate was understandable, if dangerous, for it was the group of men most totally under the control of the crown. Even if he had wished Charles could not have used the windfall of Church lands as gifts by which to bind men to his service. This, James VI's method of securing allegiance, could only be done once. But he could have promoted the available talent among the offspring of his father's service nobility. The way in which he snubbed the young earl of Montrose when this young man came to court shows that he did not appreciate the use of this group.

Charles's policy produced a lack of commitment on the part of his Council, and this may explain the apparent deterioration in law and order in his reign. It became again necessary to issue special commissions to deal with trouble in the Borders. The south-west Highlands had been in turmoil for some time through the internal disputes of clan Ian Mor, the southern MacDonalds. In 1630 a gruesome episode, the burning of the tower of Frendraught with Gordon of Rothiemay and a younger son of Huntly inside, had set a feud going in the norht-east. Huntly refused to be reconciled to the Crichtons of Frendraught. No head of a great name would retain authority if he did not carry the feud for his own son. The Council lacked power to force Huntly or the detective skills capable of finding out whether foul play had been involved or not. Charles ordered it to spend a day a week on the case but all that came of this was the execution of an underling and the torture of a maid servant who had given confusing evidence.

Charles's visit in 1633 did not succeed in setting up the personal links and understanding which would have justified its cost. Most of the nobility were not sufficiently skilled in the relatively new science of elementary arithmetic accurately to calculate what the visit had cost them, but they were conscious of expenditure without any perceptible benefits to themselves or to their followings. The visit also made it difficult for the Council to continue to turn a blind eye to non-observance of the Five Articles of Perth. James's episcopate had accepted the articles as things indifferent. Charles brought out their general import by insisting on using the English form of service with Laud, future archbishop but now only dean of his chapel, officiating. Laud was known to adhere to the new religious deviation, arminianism. Nervousness of Charles's position in the Church perhaps explains why for once there was actual opposition to the method by which bishops were used to secure a body of Lords of the Articles agreeable to the king, as well as to Acts now passed about the Church. There was a protesting supplication, which complained of the Church Acts and the methods of royal supervision in their passage. This was not, in fact, presented, but a copy was later found to be possessed by Lord Balmerino, the son of James's scapegoat, and Balmerino was accused of the capital offence of 'leasing treason', that is verbal treason.

The Balmerino trial, 1635, though it did not focus a constitutional issue as did the trial of Hampden in England, brought the issue of royal policy and its unpopularity into the searchlight of publicity. Charles's immediate servants, including Sir Thomas Hope, the Lord Advocate, as prosecutor, and Sir John Stewart of Traquair, the Treasurer, as president of the court, supported his policy. Balmerino was convicted by a majority of one in the court: subsequently the sentence of death, as it had been for his father, was remitted. The trial was the epitome of the marginal legality within which Charles chose to operate, and, in its lack of political wisdom, set the scene for the later crisis. The nominal powers of the crown were great, but they had been allowed to remain so because kings had not been secure enough in their own persons to use them. The English connection, by removing the king to apparent safety, had drastically altered the facts of the Scottish constitution, and made these powers dangerous.

The treaonable 'supplication' had voiced a widespread unease over the crown's Church policy. The Church already included a small group of ministers and adherents in the habit of going their own way in the conduct of services, sometimes meeting in conventicles or private churches, and who, even when fully within the Church, were building up cells of people of their own persuasion. Such a cell appears to have been created in the south-west, and was led by Samuel Rutherford, minister of Anwoth; it included the family of Lord Kenmure, George Gillespie, Kenmure's chaplain,

David Dickson, minister at Irvine, and Robert Blair, temporarily based on Ayr after his ejection from a parish in Ireland. There was also a group of lay men and women in Edinburgh holding 'conventicles', or private services. Rutherford had written a catechism for his parish, and this form of indoctrination explains the concern of the bishops that his activities should be supervised. The bishop of Galloway, a new appointment, tried to bring the group in the south-west under control by exiling Rutherford to Aberdeen. It has been claimed that this action was the result of a large doctrinal work he had had published in Amsterdam, written in Latin, attacking arminianism. But it is unlikely that a Church court could have proceeded against a minister for publishing within what was the official doctrine of the Church, expressed in the 1616 confession, unless his statements were creating disorder, and little public disturbance was likely to be generated by a work in the international academic language of the day. Some Scottish clergy had acquired, from the English debate, a fear of arminianism, but there is no firm evidence of anyone in Scotland at this time holding to such opinions. Rutherford had already been in trouble for not observing the Five Articles, and the claim that he was being persecuted (if that is the right term for an enforced stay in Aberdeen) seems to be an attempt to build a dissident on Church practice into a martyr on Church doctrine. In Aberdeen persecution did not prevent him keeping the members of his cell inspired by exhortatory letters in language based on the more sexy parts of the Song of Solomon.

Early in 1636 Charles displayed his Church policy more overtly in a book of canons. This was a remarkable document for it bore no apparent relationship to the Church as it existed in Scottish law and practice. There was no reference to presbyteries and only a single oblique reference to a national synod which might be taken to be the General Assembly. Instead authority was taken to lie with bishops for the dioceses, as their units of operation were now called, and the book referred expressly to the 'Royal Supremacie in Causes Ecclesiasticall', language which had not been stomached in the Reformed Church in Scotland for over two generations. The book thus directly confronted the presbyterian system. It opposed one element of current practice in insisting that no minister preach in the parish of another without episcopal licence, for it was common during presbytery visitations for visiting ministers to preach. There were positive injunctions which sincere Calvinists might resent, for instance an express direction to preach the necessity of good works, and the canons took the Five Articles further in ordering all ministers to baptize on demand, though they modified the unpopular Article on kneeling at communion by the cautious phrase of 'bend the knee'. There were features bound to be unpopular with the more vociferous ministers though not contradictory to accepted doctrine: there was an order that sermons be short and not be made occasions for quarelling with other ministers. There was also prohibition of extempore prayer. Instead the new liturgy was to be used.

The new liturgy was not yet in print, so that opposition to any restriction had time to gather force. The book came out in 1637. Recent work has shown that it was not, as often asserted, the work of William Laud, but of some of the Scottish bishops working on traditional materials and restricted by the personal prejudices of the king. Its issue was the occasion for organized protest and riot.

It has been argued that this service book, if considered dispassionately, was not directly opposed to existing practice, though it contained instructions, particularly in the forms for baptism and communion, which would grate on Calvinist opinion. But it was not going to be considered dispassionately. The people at large deeply resented any change in forms of worship, and were not so totally determinist in their belief as not to think that methods of worship could not affect their prospect of salvation. To a very real fear for the hereafter they added a loathing of anything which they thought resembled the Mass, and they took the view of their clergy as to what the Mass was. A special source of annoyance was the inclusion of certain passages from the Apocrypha in the book, and the omission, to make room for these, of parts of the Old Testament. Protestant sanctification of the whole text of the Bible had gone a long way by the 1630s.

Much of the vociferous objections from ministers, as with the canons, focussed on aspects where the ministerial role was curtailed, or even where any form of discipline over ministerial activity was imposed. Particular hostility attached to the substitution of short, set prayers for long extempore ones, and to the participation of the congregation in responses. An anonymous protest, thought to be by George Gillespie, objected to any settled liturgy: 'might not able Ministers (at least) make a prescript forme to themselves which would fit them and their people best'. No set form of prayer would satisfy this 'do it yourself' school. Gillespie also argued that set prayer, replacing extempore prayer, curtailed the range of worship to which God was entitled, a comment which is an interesting forerunner of the idea of 'opportunity cost', but which also reveals little understanding of the psychology of prayer. But his protest ended on a note which contained the essence of valid opposition: if there was to be a new liturgy it should come from a General Assembly. The same was true of the canons.

In 1637 when the riots broke out over the new book, the situation in Scotland was one of a fragile administration in a country where royal policy had deeply annoyed three important sections of the nation. The Privy Council was by then a collection of not very able men with no particular attachment to the policy it was expected to implement. Royal intentions had not been conveyed to it in advance, advice sent by it to the king had systematically been ignored, and the only way in which it had made its views felt had been in general foot-dragging. The traditional institutions in which support for policy was gathered, Parliament and the General Assembly, had either been coerced or dispensed with. The nobility had had its strength curtailed by the legislation of 1633 and its pride affronted by Charles's exaltation of the bishops. A small but highly articulate group of ministers felt outraged and the ministry as a whole had been ordered to conduct worship in forms which were unfamiliar and against which serious doctrinal objections could be lodged. The great bulk of landed men and merchants were carrying a new level of taxation. To this was added an inflammable popular temper, and a well-advertised opportunity, the first reading of the service book, for displaying it. Men of power and men of words were both ready to influence and use the violence of the mob. Religion provided a useful tool for disturbance, which is not to say that it was not sincerely felt. The liturgy called on changes in personal practice with spiritual implications.

Behind this combination lay rumours of the spread of the new doctrine of arminianism. Fears of this and of practices which might support it had combined in 1629 with hostility to other elements of policy in England to produce a violent demonstration in the House of Commons. In 1637 in Scotland the elements which combined to oppose the king were even more powerful and more intemperate, and the king's remote power came to the country through men only half prepared to support it.

This state of government and opinion makes the outbreaks in the capital and elsewhere easy to understand. The leaders of protest rapidly spread their cause from the towns to the rural Lowlands. Recent study of revolutions in seventeenth-century England and elsewhere has attempted to relate them to a body of 'revolution theory'. It is doubtful if the theory, mainly designed to give a pattern for examples of revolution in the nineteenth and twentienth centuries, in states politically stronger and with more elaborate structures of representation, but socially more unstable than those of the seventeenth century, can be applied to this period. Those who decided to oppose royal policy did not at the same time envisage altering the system of degree and ranks into which society was divided. It was not just that, like many revolutionaries, they wished to appear conservative, but that essentially their aims were conservative except for the narrow area in which royal policy operated. In Spain the Catalan revolt was based on a refusal to share in the financial burdens that the crown had placed on Castile, and on a rigid adherence to legal custom, and it may have been hastened by the failure of the government to suppress banditry. France experienced the seventeenth-century revolts of the Fronde which appear to have been attempts of particular groups to preserve privileges against increased state power. Similarly in Scotland the mainspring of resistance to the policy of the crown was conservative – in the case of the nobility a desire for the more privileged position it had enjoyed under James VI, in the case of the populace an insistence for the patterns of religious observance as these had become established in the 70 years since the Reformation.

If there had been, in 1637, a king resident in Scotland, even one as obstinate as Charles I, the scale of the disorder and resentment would have been brought home to him. But communication came only through the missives of the Council. Was anyone, after the Balmerino trial, going to express in adequate terms the facts of the situation in Scotland, state the views of the forces of resistance, urge a reversal of policy? It is true that Charles had made a practice of keeping on his English and Scottish Councils men he knew to be opposed to his policies, but this was done to immobilize them, not to make them a source of independent opinion. The main body of councillors was not enough committed to the king's policy to attempt to forestall the moves by the protesters or to try to put pressure on the king to give way. It made no effective answer when the clergy complained of the need for a General Assembly to consider the service book. It did not prevent the nobility and barons holding a meeting in Edinburgh in September 1637 to organize a petition. Already the Council had been inundated with petitions against the liturgy. These may have been spontaneous, or they may have been organized by a small group. Organized or not they represented widespread indignation in the country. By October when the Council, in response to direct orders from the king, issued a proclamation ordering the nobility to leave Edinburgh, the various ranks and elements of resistance were already organizing a system of representation which was a counter government. This was the 'Tables', comprised of representatives of the burghs, the parish ministry and the nobles. The leading figures of the nobility, by whom this structure was probably inspired, were the earls of Rothes and Loudoun, to whom soon after the young Montrose attached himself. By holding firmly to the service book as the immediate cause of disturbance and claiming that it, the canons and the court of High Commission endangered estates and liberties, the nobility was able to keep within the popular movement against the crown. In February of 1638 a fanatically religious layman, the lawyer Archibald Johnston of Wariston, perhaps in collaboration with other lawyers, compiled the document which crystallized this movement, united it with legal norms and current theology and called the work the Covenant.

The Covenant began by repeating the 1581 Confession of Faith, listed after it, at tedious length, Acts which confirmed and enlarged the Protestant Church settlement, and then asserted the promise of all its subscribers to maintain the Kirk, sovereign, laws and liberties of the kingdom and to be bound together in this enterprise. It was both an enlargement of the traditional band and a revolutionary conservative programme. It was revolutionary in that it stemmed from the mass of the nation rather than the crown. It carried the theme of the Balmerino supplication a step further. It was a protest apparently mainly over religious policy which contained a constitutional demand for the rule of law. The revolutionary nature of the Covenant was also shown in the way it was pressed home and received in the various parts of Scotland. It was signed by many of the nobility, lairds and ministers in Edinburgh, and copies were sent to all towns and parishes for signing. Those who could not sign were expected to affirm their support in public. Though we must not assume that all adherence was willing, clearly the Covenant appealed to a vast body of outraged opinion, much wider in scope than that usually concerned with politics. With the only effective power in the country that which stood behind the covenanters, the military might of the great magnates and a population which was used to having arms at hand, subscription to the Covenant was a threat to the crown's authority. The Covenant bound the Scots together on a revolutionary enterprise, and in so doing destroyed the frail apparatus of royal control.

3

The Great Rebellion and Interregnum

The Covenant created a revolutionary situation, for it was seen at once to mean more than it actually stated. Because of this attempts at verbal compromise which sounded innocuous were repudiated with vehemence by the covenanters. In spite of its claim to be a voluntary band, the Covenant was to be forced on all. Montrose, with support of churchmen and a cavalry escort, took ·it to Aberdeen, and secured a degree of assent to a modified form. It was already apparent that an attack on the bishops and resistance to the crown were implicit in the document, and Aberdeen wished for neither. Sermons preached with covenanting approval assaulted the bishops: covenanters armed and drilled: the reinforcement of royal castles was prevented by force. Charles sent forth the court magnate with the most effective foothold in Scotland, the marquis of Hamilton, to negotiate or browbeat. Neither policy was successful and the king, while issuing his own edition of the 1581 confession on which the Covenant was based, had to promise a General Assembly, a meeting of Parliament and to renounce the canons and liturgy. The Assembly met in November, but the process of packing it had begun even before it was announced. The alliance of nobility and ministers was effectively dominated by the nobility, and they proceeded to change the nature of presbyterian church government by the creation of a new office, that of 'ruling elder'. This meant that elders as well as ministers were to sit in the higher courts of the Church. But such elders, even if theoretically as elders they were not laymen, were clearly representative of landed power. Many of them were magnates, and where there were disputed elections to such positions the dispute was not between lay and ecclesiastical interests but between local noble power groups. In one such dispute, for the representation of the presbytery of Peebles, the Treasurer Traquair won the eldership, a fact that suggests that if the members of the Council had so wished they could have put up some sort of a show for royal policy. All in all the new eldership marked a sell-out by the Church to lay power, which would never be reversed. The new Assembly was still predominantly of ministers, in the ratio of three ministers to two elders. It is worth noting that the sell-out was made possible by the extremely limited historical sense of the ministry: medieval struggles to reduce lay influence within the Church were ignored except in so far as they involved the power of the crown.

The Assembly was packed, and surrounded by armed men when it met. It was no place for those who opposed the Covenant. It refused to be bound by the remit set forward by Hamilton as king's commissioner, and when he tried to close it, went on illegally. The bishops were accused of a mixed bag of offences combining crime and heresy, their office abolished and abjured, but not explicitly stated as contrary to God's word (that was to come later). The Five Articles, canons, liturgy and High Commission court were also annulled. Implicit in such actions was a claim of supremacy of Assembly over Parliament, for it was by Parliament, however unwillingly, that much of the structure of royal control of the Church had been created. With the bishops also disappeared the mechanism by which the king controlled the membership of the committee of the Articles and so the work of Parliaments. The prospect of a meeting of Parliament was suspended and the country moved to war.

Revolutions of the seventeenth century do not fit well into modern theory on the immediate and remote causation of revolutions, but the Scottish story belongs in the sequence of events to a pattern better known as it was later shown in the French and Russian revolutions. There is an initial and easy seizure of power from the nerveless hand of the established government by a group with widespread support, followed by further revolutions and coups during which the support base is drastically narrowed. Internal campaigns are instituted to compel the adherence of dissenting groups. The dominant segment holds tightly to a justifying theme: the Will of God or the dictatorship of the proletariat are both issues which do not admit of argument. The narrowness of the power base of the new dictatorship is disguised by a special vocabulary or by special meanings given to words of general currency. Those who break away from following the dictatorship, in particular those who expose this double talk, are attacked fiercely and, where possible, exterminated. 'Cruelty and hypocrisy' have been attached as labels to the successful Bolsheviks, but they apply equally well to the Mountain and to the regimes set up in Scotland in the 1640s.

It is of particular interest that the revolutionary development in Scotland should be an early example of this type, since the ensuing rebellion in England, made possible by events in Scotland, was not. The English revolutionaries never in the struggle for power lost their preoccupation with the need to make a sound legal base, consonant with existing concepts of law, for their regime. This ostentatious legalism in England may be the explanation for the less bloodthirsty though no less serious attack on royal power there. The Scottish revolutionaries were pushed towards extremism by the basic fact which Charles had exploited at the start of his reign, that there was no single explicit source of law which could be made binding on the crown.

The first revolution was the seizure of effective power by the Tables in 1637–8, made easy by the lack of commitment of Charles's councillors to his policy. This lack of commitment in Hope of Craighall, the Lord Advocate, went as far as treachery, for he pronounced the Covenant legal. The General Assembly at Glasgow was ostensibly a religious revolution, but marked a further secular event, the take-over of the Church by the nobility. At this point various other members of the Privy Council, most notably the young earl of Argyll, defected to the covenanters. Internal war was shown in the campaign by Montrose in the north which produced at least acquiescence and a façade of unity, and by two successive campaigns against the English forces that Charles managed to bring against the Scots, the first Bishops' War, an almost bloodless series of manoeuvres in the summer of 1639, and a similar but more drastic invasion of northern England, the second Bishops' War, in the summer of 1640.

The army raised in Scotland for these campaigns, by various methods of coercion, profited by the return to Scotland of many professional soldiers who had been making their living in the wars on the continent. Each regiment was equipped with a senior officer who had seen service abroad, and most had both a major and a colonel in this category. The cost of the army was originally met by syphoning off the customs duties through the adherence to the Covenant of the collector general, William Dick, who also advanced a loan from his merchant resources. Subsequently a heavy fee was landed on the English for the privilege of having a Scottish army of occupation in the northern counties. The Scots had learned from the Swedes how to make other countries pay for being invaded. The king's need to extract supply from England led first to the abortive 'Short' Parliament of 1640 and then to the Long Parliament, and it was the Long Parliament which eventually in the summer of 1642 found itself at war with the king.

With the calling of the Long Parliament the king's attention was necessarily deflected from Scotland to England. The negotiations over the recent wars had led the Scots to reflect on problems created by the regal union. Some of the ideas had become incorporated in an apparent constitutional settlement in 1641. The core of the new situation was that effectively the king had lost any choice of ministers in Scotland. His choice had to be confirmed by the Scottish Parliament, now free itself from royal control, and recalcitrance by Parliament soon shifted the real choice into its hands. Its standing body, the Committee of Estates, was a governing cabinet in the intervals between Parliaments. In 1640 the Scots had put to the king the 'eighth demand', an attempt to settle his dual position as king of Scotland and also of England. There should be freedom of trade between the two countries. The king and his heir should have spells of living in Scotland, and when in England the king should keep more Scots about him. These men should be more representative of the reality of power in Scotland than had been his previous courtiers. Neither nation should go to war without the approval of both Parliaments. The aim in all this was an interlocking system; two nations ruled by king and Parliament co-operating. The real problem was how to create the institutions which would sustain and operate this. Another problem, shown when the Scots tried to encourage the demise of episcopacy in England – a reasonable enough aim since both countries regarded religious truth as indivisible and the Scots for their part had proclaimed in 1640 that episcopacy was against God's law – was that the countries were still separate nations, with differing societies, priorities and consitutions, resentful of interference by the other. In the storm that this unwise action by Scots produced the longer term proposals were sunk.

Revolution had been achieved in Scotland: it was still, late in 1641, possible that it would be staved off in England, though the king's visit to Scotland to help win support there by concessions, which in any case he could no longer refuse, made the situation in England more critical. In the end it was rebellion in Ireland which lost him credibility among enough of his English subjects to bring on the Civil War. So all three kingdoms came to be in a revolutionary or rebellious state. Other parts of Europe were to be sufficiently disturbed in the next two decades for some historians to have speculated on 'the general crisis' of the seventeenth century. It is worth considering whether there were general reasons for governments to be unable to keep control, though in each country the immediate triggers of revolt are idiosyncratic. For nearly a century in most states the actual power, still more the claims to power, of the central government had been on the increase. Costs of government had therefore, even in peace, gone up, and new military equipment meant that they had gone up even more for war. States faced higher levels of taxation, or new forms of it. Old privileges in law and finance were destroyed or ignored in the new intensity of government. The long period of inflation from the mid sixteenth century had ended before 1640, but it had left permanent changes in economic strength and security. Everywhere it had weakened the resources of the crown: often it had reduced the incomes of magnates and exalted those of the middling ranks. In some cases it had pressed heavily on labour. The spread of new elements of culture, of Protestantism, of advances in science, and new methods of communication, particularly the spread of printed matter, all meant that the issues of politics and the participants in political issues were changing. Some of these forces had a particularly close bearing on Scotland.

There is no doubt that after the union of crowns the monarchy had a new immunity to established methods of pressure in Scotland. It was also aiming at new types of control, and wished for greater resources. Charles's reign had taken further the innovations of taxation that his father had devised, for instance the taxing of 'annual rents' or interest, and taxation had, since the 1580s, been almost regular. In 1625 there had been a tax of a twentieth on lands and on interest, repeated for four years, in 1630 another for as long, in 1633 a sixteenth for six years. The country had found itself involved in a foreign war for the first time in 60 years. The crown had forced an unpopular religious policy on Church and Parliament, and had continued to carry it through without the aid of either.

The issue of the price revolution certainly affected Scotland. It has been asserted that the price rise largely passed the country by. A better informed verdict is the assertion that the price rise was more marked in Scotland than elsewhere, but even this needs qualification. The general price rise arrived later in those parts of Europe which can be considered commercially as outliers, and there also it was less marked in terms of the change in value between precious metals and commodities. Scotland, peripheral and economically undeveloped, but still in touch with the continent, had in this aspect experienced what one would expect, a limited and late change in values. It did not begin until the 1540s and was over by 1600. In terms of the silver content of the coinage the price of grain had doubled between these two dates, whereas in most other countries it had gone up between three and five times. But there had been a much greater change in the nominal coinage and the price of food. This was a period when many hand-to-mouth governments debased their coinage, and the financial incompetence and irresponsibility which led them to do so were well marked in Scotland too. The result was that in currency terms the price rise had been eight fold. This figure is high in European terms, but not the highest. The small proportion of people in Scotland who lived by wages experienced a drop in real income, but not on the scale suggested by either real or monetary values. This drop suggests that behind the inflation there was real pressure of growing population.

But the Scottish economy was still, in many areas, one of payment in kind rather than in money and this fact had cushioned many from inflation. In the late sixteenth and early seventeenth century there was devised a system of accepted annual 'fiars prices', to ease translation of obligations from grain to money, but most regular obligations, most notably teinds, were still paid in grain. It was in the higher stretches of annual dues, most notably in feu duties, that the inflation and debasement had transformed obligations. Lairds who held of great magnates by feu ferm benefited by the fall in real value of these fixed dues. The shift in prices meant that teind became a more important source of revenue to great landowners, and feu duties and rents where these were paid in money less important. Understandably the prospect of a sharp drop in their share of teind was a real threat to these men. By contrast the class of lairds would continue to benefit by monetary changes and by greater security of teind, but these men were not strong enough politically to compensate the king in support for the hostility of the aristocracy. The main burden of price change had fallen on the great owners, but apart from this new threat to teind, most of the difficulties of adjustment were over a generation before the Great

Rebellion. By 1638 we must assume that the aristocracy had learnt to compensate for loss of income by the exercise of new powers or the acquisition of new lands. Charles's magnates faced a threat, but they had already overcome economic stress. The issue behind the Revolution stays with political confidence.

The bloodthirsty rebellion in Ireland in October 1641 brought English and Scots again into negotiations. Both countries had settlers in Ireland who were at risk, since the rebellion aimed at Irish resumption of plantation lands. The number of Scots in the Ulster settlement is uncertain, and not clarified by wild assertions of the English lord-lieutenant, Wentworth, who did not like them. He alleged, on different occasions, that there 50,000 and 100,000 of them. It is clear that the number fluctuated: the plantations were treated by both English and Scottish adventurers rather as were railway shares in the 1840s, temporary investments which could easily be got rid of. It was easy for supplies and men to cross the channel to and from Galloway. By 1641 the number of Scots in the plantations may have been over 10,000 and there were others not on plantations, for instance the Macdonnell refugees from the fracture of the great southern Macdonald hegemony who had left Scotland to settle the glens of Antrim. These refugees were Gaelic in culture, Roman Catholic in religion, and looked for leadership to the wayward earl of Antrim. The earl looked to Scotland for gain because he hoped to regain Kintyre from the Campbells. The Irish rebellion created or enhanced suspicions of the king's goodwill, since the confederate rebels, many of whom had been in the army raised by Wentworth in Ireland to deal with the rebellious Scots, claimed understandably but without authority, to be acting on the king's behalf, and Charles's denials carried little weight. Refugees flooded back to both England and Scotland adding wrath to suspicions. Ireland raised not only colonial concern but religious fear, since the Catholic confederates rapidly established links with the papacy: indeed it was papal pressure that allowed their most successful general to leave Spanish service and start to organize an Irish army.

The joint interests of England and Scotland in the affair led rapidly to an agreement that the Scots should send an army of 10,000 men to Ireland which would be largely paid for by the English Parliament, and which should take orders from the English government in Dublin. The terms are easily comprehensible. Events of the last few years had given both the English and the Scots an exaggerated idea of the ease with which the Scots could raise men and the English be prepared to raise money. The Scottish army for Ulster was to be an ally of the English, not a mercenary army in England's pay, yet the ambiguities of its position were to be more important than the obvious convenience. Within a year the English were shown not to have fulfilled their financial obligations and the Scots to have ignored instructions from Dublin.

The Irish war completed the breach between Charles I and his English Parliament, bringing forward first the demand for ministers in whom Parliament had confidence, and later for parliamentary control of the army. In this way it created a royalist party in England, and military aims for its opponents. These two developments made the Civil War possible and in the summer of 1642 England slid into the war.

In this development the Scots remained passive. It has been a common diplomatic error to look on revolutions and civil wars in neighbouring countries with complacency in the mistaken assumption that the victor is bound to end up with a state weakened by the disorders. In practice, as the Scots were to find, revolutions enhance the central role of the state and provide it with new aims, resources and machinery. War, however, certainly provided business opportunities for neighbours, and some Edinburgh merchants were soon selling reinforced doublets to the royalist defenders of Newcastle. By the end of 1642 the Scots themselves were divided. In the year before the ambitions of Montrose and Argyll had proved unreconcilable, both in public aims and in personal interests. The young earl of Argyll, who had already played a significant part in the Glasgow General Assembly, was a competent politician in charge of the most powerful and tightly organized of the Highland clans. Montrose was of lesser status, from a family of no great wealth but of a tradition of royal service. He had played a leading part in the early days of the Covenant, but by the end of the second bishops' war had come to be suspicious of the way royal powers had been annexed by the covenanters, and hostile maltreatment of his supporters by followers of Argyll. He had formed a party of the disaffected in the Band of Cumbernauld, and when news of this Band had leaked out the Banders had been in trouble for breaking the unity of the covenanters. At this stage the revolution had not yet developed the full ferocity of which it was to be capable and the policy was only to execute minor figures who strayed from the path, so Montrose had merely been imprisoned for some time, to prevent contact with the king. There was also, in 1642, a further breach with the Hamilton faction, a central block of nobles, ill at ease in relation with the radicals. Early in 1643 there was a confrontation between the Privy Council and the General Assembly over the statement that was to be made about the English struggle, an issue which the Assembly won by forcing its text on all parish ministers for publication. The Scots accepted the invitation to send representatives to the English Assembly at Westminster which was set up to reform religion in England. Convinced that the divine will had been revealed to them alone they could hardly refuse, even though they were to discover that the the distinguished ecclesiastics they sent were to be treated as observers, not as leaders, of the Assembly. These Church negotiations and the somewhat fractious dealings over the army in Ireland kept the two sets of opponents to the king in touch with each other, and it was therefore relatively simple, after the inconclusive campaigns of the summer of 1643, for the English Parliamentary leader Pym to insist on opening negotiations with the Scots for support in the English war. But it is somewhat surprising that the new agreement should involve terms similar to those which both parties had disregarded in Ireland.

The new alliance was the Solemn League and Covenant: 'League' meant a treaty and 'Covenant' meant to the Scots another band with God. In return for a Scottish army which the English would pay, reformed religion of the Scottish type was to be imposed on England and Ireland. The English negotiator, Sir Harry Vane, of Independent rather than Presbyterian affiliation, slid a small qualifying clause into the religious part of the treaty: the reformation of religion was to be 'according to the Word of God'. As the treaty expressly approved the Scottish Church settlement, this did not appear to the Scots to pose any difficulty. The League also spoke of the preservation of the 'Priviledges of Parliaments', 'the King's Person and Authority' and 'Peace between the two kingdoms'. There is no reason to believe that except on the question of the king's authority the document was disingenuous.

'The English were for a civil League, we for a religious Covenant' wrote an observer, the Reverend Robert Baillie. The reasons for the Scottish insistence are worth examination. One element was unconscious nationalism: the Scottish revolt had been based on a repudiation of religious observances accepted in England: now the Scots were pushing their own religious pattern on the English. They were showing that they stood by the view that episcopacy was contrary to divine law. In Scotland Parliament might legislate but was not necessarily supreme. Laws passed by it could be ignored and become accepted as invalid. One Parliament might reverse the decision of another, and the decisions of a Parliament could be manipulated by committees, perhaps by a resurrected Articles. The line between the competency of a Convention of Estates and a Parliament was not precise, and this made room for further manoeuvre. In some way, though, it was accepted that decisions competent to religion were more final than those on lay matters. What a General Assembly said was the law of God was likely to remain such. The actions of the Glasgow Assembly had been based on the discovery and reaffirmation of the early intransigent Assemblies of the immediate post-Reformation period, and this could be seen as evidence that decisions by Assemblies held firm. Schism had not yet forced the Scots to the more sophisticated concept of deciding which General Assemblies were to be treated as valid. Since it was religion which had given the occasion for the recent wars between the two kingdoms, religious unity, however imposed, would be a step towards confirming peace. Peace with the English Parliament would ensure a crown too weak to reverse the political settlement of 1641. Furthermore the Scots not only saw the General Assembly as having a more effective sovereignty in its own sphere than had the Scottish Parliament, but as having the right to intrude into political matters, as it was already doing. State and Church were separate but only because the state was a mere civil instrument, carrying out the decisions of the Church: all important issues of policy contained religious issues, and so lay within the Church's competence. This scheme of things is more comprehensible when we remember that Scottish Calvinism, as shown in the sermons and diaries of the day, saw God as constantly intervening in the affairs of his elect, and the Scottish nation as in some way a chosen instrument of God. If there came up a divergence in opinion on religion or Church government, it was not for the elect to compromise, since any who differed from them belonged to the eternally reprobate. What the chosen people, the Scots, had settled on as the most pure and reformed system of Church government, even if it was one open to lay manipulation through the device of the ruling elder, must be the structure which the English would have to accept.

The unrecognized difficulty here is that the very word 'presbyterian' meant two different things in the two countries. In the

Scottish sense of the word there were no real presbyterians in the English Parliament, there were only puritans who might, or might not, accept some of the features of the Scottish system, but who would ultimately insist that the English Church settlement had to be made by an English parliament which would limit any attempt by Church courts at any level to coerce the gentry. By contrast in Scotland Parliament had been used merely to confirm the revolution initiated in the laicized Church. The concepts were incompatible.

The attitude of the Scots meant that initially when they joined in the English struggle they took the more militant side within the English Parliament, the 'war' party who wished to see the defeat of the king in the field, and not the 'peace' party who wanted a negotiated settlement. The view of the peace party was voiced by the half-hearted English general Manchester, 'if we beat the King ninety nine times he is King still, but if the King beat us once we shall all be hanged and our posterity made slaves'. The Scots helped the war party to set up as executive the Committee of Both Kingdoms. Yet as the war went on their alliance shifted to the peace party, and the word presbyterian came to be attached to this party because of their adherence, not for its views on Church government. The English parliamentarians came to suspect that the Scots would sell out without seeing a permanent constitutional settlement for England, provided the king would accept their presbyterian system. The Scots themselves came to suspect that Parliament in England would sell out on presbyterianism for a constitutional settlement. Both were proved to be right.

It is also worth pondering why the English were prepared to bind themselves by the Solemn League and Covenant. Their negotiators had included Vane, who was opposed to presbytery. The English approach seems to have been a normal wartime hand-to-mouth decision. Long-term difficulties were ignored because of the current emergency. They needed what they thought the Scottish army could give, a professional and effective fighting unit. But the army was not necessarily the disciplined and holy force that the Scottish General Assembly envisaged. There was an understandable tendency for parishes, required to send in a number of recruits, to take them from the local undesirables. Still, the unsettled nature of Scottish life meant that most men were accustomed to weapons.

The army, some 20,000 men, entered England early in 1644 and was set to the siege of Newcastle. The siege was already going badly, and continued to do so, and the usefulness of this necessary holding operation was not obviously apparent to the south of England. Meanwhile, Pym, the architect of the Parliamentary war effort, died. His death weakened the realism of the English Parliament. The campaigns of 1644, however, brought about the creation of the New Model Army, and this showed that the English could be at least as effective in arms as the Scots. This army drew its strength and experience from the eastern counties of England, where the religious emphasis was for Independency, and so it became the military arm of the Independents. Meanwhile Montrose launched a royalist campaign in central Scotland in September 1644, and this forced the Scottish army to send back contingents for home defence. It also revealed that the Scots were not as united as they pretended. In 1645 the English Parliament passed some formal presbyterian regulations, but it was becoming clear that there was a fundamental difference between the two countries, not only on what presbyterianism meant but on basic political aims. The English saw their struggle as one for parliamentary rights, from which religious reformation would follow: the Scots looked to religious assertions, based on their view of God's will, to protect their new revolutionary constitution. So, though both were concerned for religion, their priorities differed. The Scottish belief that a religious settlement would be more powerful than a simple political one was not simplistic but was based on the lack of protective rigidity in their political institutions. Their Church was a state more powerful than the state. They failed completely to appreciate the central position that Parliament as an institution occupied in English thought and loyalty.

Montrose's one year of campaign was brilliant but divisive. He had linked up, as the representative of royalism, with a dual army of Highlanders and Irish Catholics brought over by Alasdair MacColla, a leader of a dispossessed Macdonald line, whose main aim was to regain lands from the Campbells. The cultural divide between Highland and Lowland, though it could be spanned by someone like Montrose whose lands lay near to the Highland fault, was already so marked that this army, flexible and hardy as it was, made it almost impossible for him to gain Lowland support until he had conquered central Scotland. The conquest, achieved in August 1645 at the battle of Kilsyth, was momentary, but deeply disturbing to the covenanters who chose to interpret any success by an opponent as a sign of divine intervention. The Irish and the

Highlanders went off after Kilsyth to conduct campaigns on their own priorities, and eventually to be slaughtered. Montrose's small core of supporters was scattered in the grey dawn of a September morning outside Selkirk by David Leslie with the Scottish cavalry withdrawn from campaigning in the English midlands. The camp followers were wiped out and those of Montrose's group who were captured were executed. The king had already lost the English war at Naseby.

Montrose was not the only evidence of Scottish disunity. The Church acted, both in the General Assembly and in its executive Commission, set up in 1642, in apparent unity, but it contained diverse aims. In many cases the nobility continued to exercise the position of ruling elder, but in some districts, notably Glasgow, the lay power was inactive and the lesser folk dominated. Ministers whose aims had appeared similar in 1638 were now moving apart. By the mid 1640s there was a small group of really radical men ensconced in the Commission. Radicalism would prove itself willing to act without support from the nobility. It would also tend to prefer the action of a small revolutionary cell to the majority decision of the presbyterian structure. As the defeat of the king produced new political problems, this minority group came to wield disproportionate power.

Defeat of the king brought to a head the strain on the alliance with the English Parliament. Even before this the Scots in the Westminster Assembly had been dismayed by the unwillingness of the English Parliament to stamp on the wilder sects. The military successes of Cromwell and his army and the army's indoctrination with Independency frightened the Scots further, and led to the shift of Scottish support to the peace party. They would negotiate with the king for a presbyterian church structure in England, but these negotiations failed on the intransigence of the king. The political shift of the Scots, and their domestic embarassment over Montrose meant that their army in England was sent on minor matters during the concluding campaigns. Its ineffectiveness encouraged the English in their failure to pay its expenses, and shortages of supply which resulted from this reduced its military potential, and also, because of plunder, increased local English resentment.

The hopes of the Scots that England would set up a discipline and structure for their Church similar to their own also met frustration. The Scots accepted the doctrine as laid down by the Westminster Assembly, but were dismayed when Parliament intervened to prevent the English Church achieving an effective discipline. The Westminster Assembly had to acquiesce in lay control over discipline, not at the kirk session level as was familiar to the Scots but at the top, which they called 'erastian'. Erastianism, which had little to do with the actual opinions of Erastus, was the term of abuse for state supremacy over the Church. In fact both church systems were erastian, the Scottish one more subtly than the English. Melvillian thought might regard the Scottish ruling elders as an order of the ministry, but in reality they acted and thought as members of the estate of nobles. It was the unwillingness of most of them to take time for the detailed business which gradually liberated the Church from their control.

Charles may have preferred to negotiate with the Scots rather than with the English because in Church affairs Scotland still accepted the leadership of the relatively moderate Alexander Henderson, and also because it was likely that a surrender on Scottish matters would be more easily reversed afterwards than on English. Anyway, it was to the Scottish army at Newark that he gave himself up, to prove a burden as well as a prize. The Scots did not wish to take him back to Scotland in case he provided a focus for anti-covenant elements (the English were later to feel the same about having him in London). On the other hand Newark was dangerously far into England. The army cautiously moved north to Newcastle, where negotiations were initiated and where eventually they failed. The Scots wanted the king to take the Covenant, but since 1643 this meant the Solemn League and Covenant, and acceptance of it would bind him to setting up presbyterianism in all three kingdoms. They proposed also that the English Parliament should control the army and nominate ministers for 20 years. The king proved adamant, and the Scottish army was in difficulties from the failure of supply. Eventually agreement was reached with the English, and at the end of January 1647 the Scots accepted a large payment, which still did not amount to what had been promised, and assent to the idea that the English would consult with them in any further negotiations. With these assets they left the king and walked home. The promise of consultation would be of value only if negotiations stayed in the hands of the English parliament, but by then this body represented only a part of English opinion, and had no military force. Both English and Scots treated the monetary transaction and the abandonment of the king as entirely separate matters, a pedantry not convincing to those who had some residual regard for his safety. More seriously, while the Scots had had possession of the monarch, an apparently advantageous bargaining position, the basic decisions of the future political and religious settlements had not been made, and they were unlikely to be made now in a way the Scots liked.

Scottish negotiations with Charles continued, in the hands of a group of nobles, Lauderdale, Hamilton, Lanark and Loudon, all ambivalent about the promotion of presbyterianism in England but all possessed of some concern for Charles's safety. Stewart kings in Scotland had exercised a personal type of kingship with close contact with, and sometimes affection for the nobility, to most of whom they were related, and in life style were members of the natural club of magnates. Though they themselves had destroyed the monarch's political power in Scotland the Scots expected the English to be able to find a compromise with him on his position in England. Meanwhile those who took the more radical stand in Scotland, led by Argyll, gained control of the reconstructed Scottish army. It was a setting ripe for disagreement: the action which precipitated this was a bargain made by the peers involved in negotiation with the king, beyond what they were empowered for, of Scottish military support for him in return for a promise of a presbyterian system of an emasculated kind for three years in England and the suppression of Independency. This was known as the Engagement. The *quid pro quo* to the Scots was to be an enhanced presence in court to the amount of a third of the royal entourage, and on the English Privy Council. At intervals the king or his eldest son was to reside in Scotland. An aim of the Scots since 1640 had thus been met, but to the personal advantage only of the nobility and at the expense of the wishes of the Kirk and the interests of the English army.

War with the English army was an inevitable consequence of the Engagement, but it was possible that English force would be distracted by internal differences and even a royalist rising. In Cromwell's eyes the Engagement threatened to 'vassalize England' to a 'foreign nation'. English nationalism was often a force which the Scots failed to recognize. The great bulk of the Scottish parliament gave assent to the Engagement, which can be seen as rebellion of the aristocracy and lairds against clerical dominance. The alliance of the two groups, which had made the Covenant and Glasgow Assembly was over. A majority of the Assembly also accepted the deal, and the army chose to be neutral. It was the radical clergy, and some of the less radical, who repudiated it.

This division, over the Engagement, was to be the source of long-term conflict. The opposition set up conventicles, meetings which were as much political as religious, and through these a force was developed which was suppressed only by the army at Mauchline Moor. The conventicles showed an alliance between lesser gentry, clergy and the more articulate of the common people against the aristocracy, though some of the nobles, notably Loudon, had changed sides and abandoned the Engagement. A body within the Kirk refusing to accept a majority decision of a General Assembly on a matter basically political, was now set up and to remain. Meanwhile the Engagers found their capacity to raise troops for the coming war impaired by the resistance and protest of ministers. They went south on an incompetent invasion of England in the wet summer of 1648, to be defeated by Cromwell at Preston.

The battle was largely determined by Cromwell's possession of nerve and Hamilton's loss of it. It left a vacuum of power in Scotland, because the greater part of the traditional governing class in Scotland had been defeated. Into this vacuum moved the radicals, with the 'Whiggamore raid', as it was scurrilously named: an invasion of central Scotland by the anti-Engagement forces of the south-west. 'Whiggam' was said to be the order given to urge on horses by the men of this area when they made their long annual journey to exchange their pastoral surplus for grain: the word defined not only the geographic base of this body but its social level.

This party did not get to complete power at once, nor even eventually by its own effort. It had to make a treaty at Stirling after some fighting with an Engager remnant, and its dominance came from the intrusion into Scotland of Cromwell and his army. The Whiggamore leaders usurped the title of the Committee of Estates, crammed it with lesser men and negotiated with the English power. Soon it had a local structure and a central body of its supporters in the south-west and Argyll called the Western Association. It was indubitably minority rule. The belief of the early struggle for the Covenant, that the nation was the instrument of God, had to be drastically modified to allow for the narrow base of power. The middle of the road line which Hamilton had followed all along, and which had adherence by 1648 of most of the aristocracy, had been based on the idea that it would in some way be possible to reach a compromise between the king and the Covenant to which a powerful enough segment of English force would adhere to guarantee the success of the Scottish revolution. The policy had foundered on

military incompetence, in itself an indication that the role of the
aristocracy was due for change, but, even before failure, the king's
intransigence had made this middle route seem unlikely to achieve
success. Hamilton was to pay for failure by execution by the
English. There was to be little active sign of a desire for a renewed
inclusive and moderate party in Scotland for the next two years, and
during that time the hopes of English support for the Covenant
disappeared.

England also was held by an extremist minority group, but this
minority comprised the army and so could force its will on the whole
country. Cromwell went south to force on the English parliament a
denunciation of the negotiations with the king. In Scotland the
Whig parliament fulfilled with excess zeal the promise to him that
those who had supported the Engagement, would be kept out of
power. In the Act of Classes it banned from office for life all who had
fought for it or promoted it, and also all who had supported
Montrose. Shorter periods of disability were attached to all who
could by action or passivity be labelled 'malignants'. The disabili-
ties were to remain until the Kirk was satisfied of repentance.

The policy of this Act was to make the minority nature of the
dominant group into a matter of principle, and to destroy the
professionalism of the officer corps which had given Scotland her
military reputation. In both ways it weakened the power base of the
Scottish government, a point which was not likely to worry
Cromwell, since his aim was to end the intervention by Scotland
into English affairs. But the Whiggamore government was in any
case insecure, for there were royalist armies operating in the
southern Highlands and the north-east.

Both countries had lost their appreciation of the need to find some
acceptable way in which they could collaborate. Cromwell made
this overt by forcing through the trial of Charles I, and his execution
in January 1649. The Scottish Parliament protested, though it
refused to base this protest on the sanctity of kingship, and went on
to show that it had no intention of keeping out of English affairs by
proclaiming the eldest prince Charles II of both kingdoms, though it
also stated that he would not reign until he had shown satisfactory
adherence to the Covenant.

This acceptance of monarchy brought the Whig ascendancy a
little nearer to general Scottish feeling, but broke the alliance with
England. For over a year nothing happened in practice. Charles
was hesitant about the Covenant. Meanwhile the Scottish Parlia-

ment carried through legislation appropriate to its social composition and its dependence on the Church party, some of which suggests a positive social policy. We know relatively little about the exact location of power within the dominant alliance of this period. Parliament still contained a few nobles, notably the marquis of Argyll. It met the wishes of the ministry by abolishing lay patronage: in future ministers were to gain appointment by a complicated division of activity between presbytery and kirk session, with some small role left to the congregation. The Act reduced an accepted right of the upper class, and would not have been passed by a Parliament with the normal aristocratic dominance, a point which made future dispute likely. Yet it was also carrying out a demand the Kirk had voiced in the First Book of Discipline. A purely secular enactment gave vassals of Kirk lands the right to buy up their feu duties, a step in the direction of lairdly independence. Justices of the peace were re-established. A new Act about the poor was passed, giving responsibility for their support to the kirk session, and in response to this some parishes, for the first time, were able to force their landowners to accept responsibility for those poor who were tenants on their lands. A crusade against witchcraft was also launched.

In 1650 the Whig ascendancy confirmed its position by bringing the apparently covenanted Charles II to Scotland, a step which made war with England certain, since Charles had no intention of surrendering his hereditary claim to the English throne. Certain that they had divine support, the Scots reduced their military strength by a drastic purge from the army of all of doubtful godliness. The result was slaughter at the hands of Cromwell's troops in the dawn battle outside Dunbar. Not content with this political shipwreck the extremists went on to ensure division within both Church and State by the issue of a document, the Western Remonstrance, a declaration against compromise with anyone, the king, the 'malignants' or royalists, and the English Independents.

Country and Kirk were now irrevocably divided. The radicals in the Church had adhered to the main body only so long as they could dominate it: now they formed their own presbytery and the tendency towards schism, which had existed since the 1630s, was fulfilled. Perhaps, though, it was a sign of the general unwillingness of both parties to force this breach that the dissentient minority had had a political organization and an army for many months before it achieved a separate Church.

There were by now four armies in Scotland. One was that of the disorganized remnant of the united Kirk party, now the group promoting Charles II as covenanted king; then there was that which the diarist Nicoll called the 'Holie airmy, that of the Remonstrants'; there was the 'malignant' army in the north, unreservedly royalist; and a fourth army 'that ran throw the Kingdom without opposition, under the charge and command of General Oliver Cromwell', and which was successful because of the bitter divisions between the others. Cromwell was able to knock off the Scottish armies in turn, starting with the 'holy' army, defeated at Hamilton after a life of only a few months. In an effort to promote unity the Kirk passed a resolution in December 1650 allowing Parliament to draw military strength from other than the holy, a reversal of the policy before Dunbar which accepted that the secular side could control its own sphere of action. Rapprochement between Church and nobility thus became possible at the same time as the split between the majority and minority parties within the Church was made lasting. The radicals protested at this decision, and from these two public statements came the future names of the two parties within the ministry, Resolutioner and Protester.

As the Protesters saw, compromise with the nobility, most of them Engagers, led rapidly to a shift of power to the laity and away from the ministry. In March 1651 parliament allowed 'malignants' a share in the control of the army; soon after this it repealed the Act of Classes, and the experiment of godly rule was over, though the Kirk party still hoped to regain political power. The main issue had become one of national survival, since Cromwell already occupied the eastern shires. At the end of August his lieutenant Monck captured the Committee of Estates, while Cromwell was involved in chasing the Scottish army on its invasion of England. He caught up with it and defeated it at Worcester in September. A few places in Scotland held out against the English through the winter but for the first time since the early fourteenth century Scotland had been conquered and occupied by her neighbour nation.

Conquest had not been easy or gentle. The various armies had requisitioned local supplies and had tried by confiscation of food to force each other out. Scotland had not considered she could support the armies she had sent into Ireland or England in the 1640s, so the supporting of the successive forces raised in 1650 and 1651 must have meant crushing burdens. There was widespread complaint of destruction of crops and loss of goods, more complaint about the

English policy of religious toleration, and even deeper bitterness between the different Scottish parties. 'Kirk and Cavalier cannot endure one another' wrote an English officer, and even deeper lay the feud within the Kirk. Conquest at least gave participants time to reflect on the past. Argyll was later to write 'I did not look upon our intended Reformation as any way taxable, since it had the whole stream of universal consent of the whole Nation'. But he misrepresented: unity had not been complete even in 1638. Samuel Rutherford went further and recognized that his party had been too obsessed with taking over the control of the state. But it was the essence of the Remonstrant position that there could be no compromise with any backsliders in the cause which this minority had decided was God's, so no steps could be made by this party towards ecclesiastical or political unity.

Cromwell had conquered Scotland to protect his own position, and for the same reason he would continue to occupy it. None of the varieties of royalism in Scotland could be expected, if given control there, to leave England alone. There was also a risk of Presbyterian imperialism. The Protesters still claimed that the Covenant of 1643 represented God's will, though it was unlikely that they would ever be strong enough to put it into effect militarily. A pamphlet of 1653 attributed to the Protester James Guthrie asserted that the reason for the military failure had been the inadequacy of the purging of the army before Dunbar: such an attitude shows that there was no connection in Protester thinking between military force and the prospect of success. It was no use to overawe such people. Peace would depend on occupation, and for this reason English rule in Scotland would have to be direct, not indirect.

Scotland was to be incorporated with England. Union was imposed, and the nominal consent given to it by commissioners from the shires and royal burghs was based on the absence of alternative. Scotland was given a small representation in the Westminster Parliament, but most of her political nation were disfranchised for having been involved in the recent war, and a considerable part even of the small number of representatives who went to Westminster, all nominated by the occupying power, were English brought in to rule.

The benefits of this incorporation were held back for a while by a serious royalist rising in the Highlands in 1653-4 under the earl of Glencairn. There were always clan groups ready to resist any attempt at control by a government, and to these was added a resurgence of royalism. This simpe type of sentiment, a desire to see the king enjoy his own again, had been gaining strength since Dunbar, and had supplied much of the support which had made possible the Worcester campaign. To this was added the chronic suspicion of the house of Argyll, for the marquis of Argyll, though trying to keep his lands independent of the new conquest, had begun to negotiate with the English. Argyll needed recognition of his position by some acceptable Scottish government so that he could pass on to this government a share of the vast debts which he had incurred by military action. The same burden of debt prevented many magnates from joining Glencairn, so the material resources of the rising came from coercing localities into paying their taxation to it rather than to the English regime.

Glencairn's rising was defeated by the usual policy for dealing with Highland military threats, the sealing of it off from support in the Lowlands and then a campaign in the Highlands to force a major action. It was carried out by General Monck. With the rising defeated Scotland gained a relatively beneficent and advanced government. Lord Broghill was installed as President of the Council, giving the country an intelligent and creative ruler and the appearance of civilian rule. Since he came from Ireland he was unlikely to anglicize aggressively. His position did not disguise that power rested on military strength, and that strength had to be paid for by the Scots. The English army, which numbered 18,000 during the Glencairn rising, was reduced to 10,000, but it was still far more expensive than anything the country had had before. A fort was built at Inverlochy, and Inverness, Perth, Leith and Stirling were garrisoned. The financial devices created by the covenanters were taken over by the intruded regime, and the customs were remodelled on English lines. An outward sign of change was that householders in Edinburgh were made to light the streets. More significantly, Scots were forbidden to carry arms. Eventually this ruling was modified for favoured groups in and near the Highlands and the Borders who could claim that they might need to defend themselves. All principal judicatories and feudal courts were abolished, and a replacement system of central courts was set up. Later baron courts and Justices of the Peace were given criminal cases, and the Justices had also wide administrative powers. The relatively unified system of justice was a great advance over the heterogeneity which had existed before, and a minor additional benefit was that it was one in which it was relatively difficult to prosecute witches. From being undergoverned, Scotland had passed to being held in a vice. A Highland chronicler was later to claim that the English army 'civilized us'. It is unlikely that many felt the same, but certainly life was safer in this disarmed world, and justice more even-handed.

But Scotland was being held in this way and governed because of English interests, and this showed in economic matters. Scotland was included within the existing English system and the trades encouraged were those that suited England. English industry could benefit by Scottish wool and skins, so these were not to be sent overseas nor were French wines, an unnecessary luxury, to be imported. Scotland could receive, so long as she could afford them, the rich variety of English manufactures. Many of these were goods previously imported from the Netherlands, the sort of wares which made for domestic comfort. The system of internal free trade within Britain meant that anyone wishing to set up an industry would receive no protection, but since most of these commodities were ones not made in Scotland, it was no hardship to get them from a new source.

One judgement on the regime comes from Cromwell himself. 'I do truly think', he said of the Scots in 1658, 'they are a very ruined nation. Yet . . . it hath pleased God to give that plentiful encouragement to the meaner sort in Scotland. The meaner sort live as well and are likely to come into as thriving a condition . . . as when they were under their great lords, who made them work for their living no better than the peasants of France.' This can be set against the description given by the Resolutioner Robert Baillie in 1656: 'Our Nobles lying up in prisons, and under forfaultries, or debts, private or publick, are for the most part either broken or breaking. . . . Money was never so scarce here, and groweth dailie scarcer. . . . What England may bear, to whom the Protectour remitted the halfe of their monethlie maintenance of one hundred and twenty thousand pound sterling, I know not, but Scotland, whose burden has been triple, besides the fynes, forfaulters, debts and other miseries, seems unable to bear what lyes on already'. Neither of these statements was, of course, based on a thorough survey of incomes. It is clear that the cost of good government was high, perhaps too high. But what disturbed men like Baillie more was that the Cromwellian regime made it impossible for the Church to heal its own rift. It was an English interest that the Protesters, who were opposed to royalism, should be encouraged and promoted. There was even an attempt to put them in control of the universities and so of the education of future ministers. By the forcible dispersal of the Resolutioner General Assembly in July 1653 and also of the rival Protester meeting, any possible move to unity had been frustrated. The rift was more truly political than simply religious, since it was based on the issue of compromise with royalism, and its existence gave space for the English policy of toleration of the sects, disapproved of by both Scottish parties.

After this there were to be no Assemblies, and so no formal expression of the views of either party. The English system favoured the minority party. Broghill had no intention of allowing either faction to establish control over the other, but his support of the Protesters allowed the even more extremist element in this extremist group to claim the right to be recognized as the whole Church of Scotland. By 1656 all the leading figures in a Church which had once proudly if mistakenly claimed to be free of 'erastianism' were negotiating with the English power for patronage in appointments and for the rights to stipends.

The suppression of the system of Church courts prevented the issue between the two parties being aired in the right place, a real General Assembly, in which also the relative strengths of the two might have been revealed. But otherwise the religious policy of the Protectorate was without much effect. No amount of toleration was likely to turn the Scots to Independency, and the only non-presbyterian minority which became established at this time was a small group of that radical and assertive body the Quakers.

The period of conquest was too short for major political development to be achieved. Scotland suffered even more than did England from the impatience of the regime with any legislative body which attempted to show any signs of independence. Parliaments were experimented with and dismissed. The long-term effects of the period came out from positive enactments but from the continued exclusion of the nobility from power. Left to herself it is difficult not to think that Scotland would have seen it recover from the political collapse after the Engagement, and regain political power, though the debt burden would have handicapped individuals. Conquest kept the nobility out and also removed from it the private jurisdictions. The vacuum of power left by this change was there for such lesser men whom the regime approved to occupy. Not very many took advantage of it, for royalism, even if passive, was still strong. But many men acted in minor capacities and gained in prestige. Encouragement of the lesser landowners who made up the commission meant surrender to one of their strongly held ideas of good order. The initial cessation of witchcraft trials, achieved by using the English definition of malicious activity for the offence rather than the concept of intrinsic criminality in the status of a witch, was reversed in 1656 and a sizeable witchcraft scare occurred in East Lothian. The two strands of landowner, 'barons' or tenants in chief, and lairds, holders of feu charters from tenants in chief, combined in the new definition of heritors, proprietors of land on whom was placed the burden and privilege of maintaining the ministry and the church. This change waa not only the promotion of a class but the bringing forward of the concept of property as against feudal superiority. The power of this class was not to be laid at the door of God's will, but of the fact that they were present and acted during this Interregnum. In their new status it was clear that property had become the basis of power.

4

Restoration Government and Society

Cromwell's regime in Scotland as in England rested on his personal qualities and the army. With his death in September 1658 went the first of these controlling influences, and the second soon disintegrated among disputing generals. In the ensuing uncertainties it became clear to most men of weight in England that military force, unwisely used, was no longer acceptable, and in response to this reaction General Monck left Scotland with his army on a leisurely march to London where he allowed the old Long Parliament to reassemble, and to call back the monarchy in the person of Charles II. The Scots had little part in these changes, except that by keeping their peace in the absence of the army they made them possible. They had to accept the Restoration as it was negotiated by England.

The Scots who had been in touch with Charles II in exile were successively disheartened. It seemed at first likely to the Resolutioners that Charles, who had taken the Covenant, and the old Long Parliament which had negotiated the Solemn League and Covenant, would together be bound to set up a presbyterian system in England and Scotland, and in the latter case confirm the Resolutioner party as true to the principles of both monarchy and presbytery. The Protester party which had broken with these would be excluded. The Resolutioners were represented by James Sharp, minister of Crail, but once Charles came to England he was in close touch with the earl of Lauderdale, an old supporter and crony, and the earl of Middleton who represented the royalist sentiment shown in the Glencairn rebellion. Lauderdale was in favour of presbyterianism and the Resolutioner interest, but also aware that Charles had little liking for either. He eventually decided to follow political rather than religious inclinations and acquiesce in Charles's decisions, in particular in the abandonment of the idea that presbytery should be set up in England. What neither Sharp nor any of the religious parties in Scotland expected was that the decisions about the future of the Scottish Church would be made on purely political grounds and by laymen. The nobility, who crowded to London once the king was back, saw that this was the opportunity for an aristocratic re-establishment, and their pressure on the king was effective.

So in May 1660 the king came back expecting to fulfil the ancient functions of monarchy. This meant that the courts, and the high court of Parliament, came back into being. So did the king's executive committee, the Privy Council. The first Parliament, that of 1661, took the country briskly back to the old days by annulling, in the Act Rescissory, all legislation since 1633. This meant that, at least ostensibly, the legislative decisions to which Charles I had unwillingly agreed, in particular the need for parliamentary approval of appointments and the abolition of episcopacy, were rescinded. So were all Acts of Parliaments held in defiance of royal wishes, and this included the abolition of lay patronage in the Church. To put this particular clock back the occupants of parishes were, in 1662, ordered to get presentation from the restored patron and collation by the bishop, actions which would oblige them explicitly to recognize the return to the 1630s. Though bishops were put back in Church office, and given their old function in Parliament as the key element in the royal control of the active committee of Parliament, the Lords of the Articles, the mistake made by Charles I of installing them in high offices of state was not repeated. Sharp became archbishop of St Andrews and thereby completed his divorce from the interests of the Resolutioners whom he was supposed to have been supporting.

Scotland was thus ostensibly re-established as a separate kingdom within which authority lay in the old instruments of government. The active Privy Council was a mixture in its social background and of factions of the past. The king thus tempered his desire to reward outstanding royalists or engagers with a recognition that a large part of the concerned nation had opposed the various royalist causes. There were some, but not many, vindictive executions. The most significant victim was the marquis of Argyll.

We cannot tell whether Scottish society as a whole wished to see this restoration of the aristocracy to power, even if in a lesser capacity than of old. The diaries and memoirs of the age show a well-learnt caution. But if the power of the magnates had been felt as oppressive in the first third of the century, rather than, as it seems, taken for granted as part of the social and political weather, then it is clear that this oppression was bound to be less after 1660 because it was exercised by men who had learnt that their power was not inexpugnable. But once people have found a system oppressive they may not take the trouble to measure its relative strength.

There was not, in Scotland, the strong wish for a government ostentatiously legal in its base that there was in England, if only because the system of law in Scotland was not strong enough to be the basis of such a sentiment. But there was in many people a sentiment for royalty, though one which did not necessarily mean assent to the policy of a monarch. There was also approval for a political structure which had regard for ancient differences of status and rights, for the end of English control, and of English support for religious variegation and English-based handicaps in the prosecution of witches. But since the power of the aristocracy was also an affirmation of the marked localism of Scottish politics and opinion, its restoration met certain needs. Of course clocks can never be put back. There had been a transference of power away from the aristocracy which had permanently lessened its prestige in much the same way as the defeat of European powers in the Second World War permanently injured their colonial authority. The central government too, in both Scotland and England, had developed new strength and tools, though these were different, and would have to be differently exercised, in the two kingdoms. Neither within Scotland, nor in her relations with England, would things be as they had been in the 1630s.

In both countries the financial resources of government had been enhanced. Men might object, as usual, to paying taxes, but the objections started at a higher base level than under Charles I. Scotland had not managed to pay the full monthly contribution of £10,000 from the county assessment, demanded by the Cromwellian regime, but she had paid about £35,000 in excise a year as well as supporting a more efficient customs service. The formal grant that Parliament made to Charles II of £40,000 a year, about three times the normal revenue of the 1620s and almost twice the civilian component of the Cromwellian resources, was a sum within the scope of the country. Yet even so the administration found it could not manage within it. Peacetime government had become expensive in ways unheard of before, and war costs were still beyond the system's capacity.

On the English side a similar expansion of resources marked a change in the relationship between king and Parliament. Raising supply and granting it to the crown was now totally the function of the House of Commons. This was to alter the relations between the countries. However much the Scots might hope, irrationally, that a trading Union could be retained, this was unlikely. The protectionist temper of the English Commons was shown in the rapid reassertion of the Navigation Act. The efforts of the king to prevent the English excluding or heavily taxing Scottish commodities were ineffective under the new distribution of financial power. At a slower pace the Scots were pursuing similar routes. It is clear from the different dates at which Acts were issued by Parliament that the whole Parliament convened at other times than its opening and closing sessions. There was some real political discussion over measures, and some of this was critical of the crown. It had ceased to be a foregone conclusion that a Parliament would produce the Acts the king wanted. Parliament had to be managed, and the manager to be fully acquainted with the royal wishes. The king's chief servant thus became the Secretary, who would stay by his side and be part of the caucus which came to be called the cabinet. When a Parliament met he would represent the king in it as commissioner. Lauderdale was the first man to hold (and for many years) this dual position. He was part of the 'cabal', an early cabinet in Whitehall, but the king took care to keep Scottish affairs out of the discussions of the English Parliament.

So to a limited degree the Scots achieved some part of the closer link with England and with royal policy which had been demanded in successive negotiations since 1640, but in a way which minimized the impact of Scottish needs and opinion on England. The new type of central government also enlarged the administrative resources. The monthly maintenance tax on land became the 'cess', and it had to be raised by special officials. These men, the Commissioners of Supply, gave the country the nucleus of a county government. That their qualification was the ownership of land, irrespective of feudal relationship, at the fairly low level of £100 a year also marked a continuation of the major change of the last 30 years, the advance of the class of lairds. A central criminal court, the Court of Justiciary, founded in lasting form in 1672, may have owed something to nostalgia for Cromwell's centralized judicial system.

In Church matters the return to 1633 was deceptive. As before the government of the Church combined bishops and presbytery, but the apex of the system of Church courts, the General Assembly, remained suppressed. It was accepted that any attempt to order services through a new liturgy was not on. Except in the north and north-east, the concept of ecclesiastical rule was unpalatable, and altogether the aristocracy of Scotland was strongly anti-clerical. The gulf between the two sectors and royal policy was the main point of agreement between the two presbyterian factions, Resolutioner and Protester (or Remonstrant). In England, on the other hand, there was considerable nostalgia for the Book of Common Prayer, and acquiescence, at least, in episcopacy. The two kingdoms were further apart here than on anything else. Once episcopacy came back in England the combined actions of a cavalier Parliament and the bishops made presbyterianism illegal. The relative ease of this change is a comment on how little support there had ever been for anything that the Scots could recognize as presbyterianism in England. The other sects were harder to suppress, but had no pull on Scottish sympathy. In both countries the Church settlement was made by the mechanism of Parliament.

At the local level the Church settlement worked much as before the revolutionary period. The kirk session carried on with the discipline of sexual, social and Sabbath offences. It is clear that in some areas, notably in and near the Highlands, it was not very effective, but there was nothing new in this. The records of the Inverness and Dingwall presbyteries show that failure of material provision – that is the refusal of heritors to build manses – meant that the ministry often could not be truly resident. This was the situation at Daviot in the 1670s. At Lochalsh the presbytery had reported in 1649 that there was 'nothing found in this kirk but the bare walls', not even glass in the windows. In Moy the minister 'kept no sort of register'. In lowland Scotland the local Church machinery carried on, and in many parishes it had provided a parish school; in some it was beginning to take the support of the poor seriously.

The continuity is the more impressive because of the massive expulsion of ministers which followed the Restoration. The issue was not episcopacy but patronage. A brisk order that this should be made effective on those already in the ministry led about 30 per cent of the total to leave their parishes. Already the Remonstrant clergy who had refused to acknowledge Charles II as their covenanted king had been expelled, and also some of the leading resolutioners had resigned. The vacancies were easily filled with young graduates, trained for the ministry but as yet without a vacancy. These if technically qualified were probably still unskilled preachers, and perhaps clumsy in their other duties. The open exercise of state power and the actual change of local figures of significance, a more drastic change even than that at the Reformation, was a blow to the spiritual standing of the Church. Moreover 262 'outed' ministers, a number which included the great majority of those who had served in the synods of Galloway and Glasgow and Ayr, made a focus for opposition or disobedience. North of the Tay there was little of this pushing out of men, but then the north of Scotland had not been able positively to influence ecclesiastical politics since the Reformation. If the northern ministers are disregarded, nearly half the ministry of the rest of Scotland had resigned or been ejected.

A large number of the 'outed' ministers were old resolutioners, who had accepted Charles II. They included Robert Douglas who had preached his coronation sermon. Yet the effective leadership of the group shifted towards a refusal to recognize the restored monarchy, and so to remonstrant sympathizers, though the actual leaders of this renewed covenant movement were not among those who had produced the original Remonstrance of 1650. The witness of these men was not on doctrine or liturgy, for hard-line neo-Calvinism and impromptu prayer prevailed both within and outwith the established Church.

The problem for the government of Scotland was not the individual ministers themselves, but the fact that in certain districts, notably Galloway, the home of the original Western Remonstrance, they were followed out by whole congregations. The nearness of the wild hills in Galloway made it peculiarly difficult to deal with disorder there. There were also dissident gentry who had incurred fines for too ready a support of the Interregnum government or who now refused to take the new oath of allegiance to the king. The prayer meetings of dissident congregations gradually changed into open, large-scale meetings of armed bands, the sermons into denunciations of the government. It was not a recipe for peace.

The nervousness with which the government, in spite of its enhanced resources, regarded these developments was partly justified by half-hearted rebellion, in the march on Edinburgh in 1666 of nearly a thousand men. This was defeated at Rullion Green in the Pentlands, but it has long-term significance because it was a movement of a new type. No magnate figured in it, not even a substantial landowner. It was therefore not susceptible to the usual political bargains made at court. It caused the supersession of the crown's immediate choice of ministers and the dominance of Lauderdale, who brought forward a Church policy of concession to the dissenting groups, but it was too late to win back many of those pushed out in 1662. 'Indulgences', special concessions, were made for ministers who agreed to conform in behaviour, and refrain from conducting services outside their own parishes. The main effect of this policy was outrage among those who fully accepted the Restoration Church settlement. The archbishop of Glasgow voiced this protest and was deposed, a gesture which might have been calculated to show the Church that it was 'erastian'. This position was made explicit by an 'Act of Supremacie' in 1669 which announced that the king had 'Supream Authoritie and Supremacie over all persons and in all causes ecclesiastical'. Still, in all some 80 parishes were given ministers prepared to compromise. Their actions did not stop the spread of armed conventicles, for all that it showed that there was a substantial group of ministers anxious not to step into schism. In fact it may have promoted the organization of those in opposition, for they had been brought together in meetings for the negotiations which had preceded the Indulgence. It also left opposition to the less moderate, and under their leadership the conventicles were to justify the fears of the government by making the expected step from opposition to a Church settlement imposed by the king to deny the political authority of the king. Violent language in large meetings of armed men did not have to go very far to result in actual bloodshed, and bloodshed by those in opposition inevitably led to extra-legal activities by the government; a policy of repression.

There is considerable difficulty in writing about the later covenanting movement because of the deliberately distorted yet scholarly historical work of Robert Wodrow in the early eighteenth century, which set out to show the covenanters as simple religious adherents of the true Church, made martyrs for their beliefs. In the nineteenth century a further layer of myth was put out, that they stood for liberty. Liberty of opinion was certainly anathema to them. Towards the end of the nineteenth century there came also a recognition that the government of this period was committed to the promotion of a particular Church establishment, chosen not even mainly for its Scottish context. Of course, the Solemn League and Covenant had put forward a religious policy for more than Scotland. The historiography of the nineteenth century appears, unacknowledged, to have attached nationalist feeling to its interpretation.

Those of us who have had the benefit of seeing various types of political extremism and patterns of underground revolutionary activity in the later twentieth century should be better equipped than our predecessors of the nineteenth century to recognize the genesis of such movements in frustration, and to understand the difficulties they provide for governments. In our lifetime such movements have been based on marxism, nationalism or fascism. They have usually been developed under a strong sense of disappointment by the extrusion from a larger party of a small group refusing to submit to majority decisions. Such groups are already equipped with a specialized vocabulary, a calendar of anniversaries and saints, and a complicated political theory which combine to mask to the perpetrators the actual effects of their actions on those for whom they claim to be working. They do not need a carefully worked out positive propaganda: it is sufficient to have a clear statement of what is opposed. The State, their opponent, often holds by a real but unacknowledged commitment to a particular policy and is unwilling to have the foundations of this submitted to dispassionate examination. Most important, for such movements, is the existence of a large, predominantly passive, body of the discontented, of people who for some reason of policy or mechanism of control are excluded from policy making and do not like what prevails. Such a body, usually a minority in the state as a whole, in sympathy with one or another element in extremist rhetoric, is prepared to give active or passive aid to the radicals. This makes it impossible for the established government to suppress its opponents without adopting heavy-handed measures, and this not only confirms the unity of its opponents but alienates some of the more conscientious of its own supporters. The opponents of the government either genuinely or for purposes of propaganda appear to expect higher standards of legalism from the government than from the radical group.

In seventeenth-century Scotland the usual Calvinist approach to decision making was to question whether a policy was expressly licensed by Scripture, without questioning whether opposition to it was so licensed. This produced a negative view of the functions of Church or State. There was, too, a tendency of the more extreme to private conventicling. In the 1640s the General Assembly had acquiesced in the manifestations of this to avoid open schism. The choice put by the Scottish Privy Council to ministers in 1662 led the extremist group which already tended to schism to combine with the bulk of conscientious presbyterians who supported the 1649 abolition of patronage. Lauderdale's attempt to separate the two parties failed, partly through its overt erastianism, still more from the impossibility of accepting the existence of large, armed demonstrations at conventicles, and these demonstrations pushed the dissenting body towards open rebellion. Lauderdale's fundamental weakness was that the episcopal Church in Scotland rested on a political decision, not on an accepted Church policy. So also had presbyterianism in the 1640s, for it had been based on the packing by the aristocracy of the General Assembly. But over time presbyterianism had gained legitimacy in the eyes of many, and may, in any case, have had greater support than episcopacy.

The government took great care not to make martyrs of covenanting ministers, but was apt to treat the laity with considerable roughness. Covenanters were imprisoned, not always in civilized conditions, or fined for not attending their parish church and, as feeling mounted, steps were taken in 1678 which were the equivalent of martial rule. Lauderdale brought in troops from Newcastle and Belfast and also from some of the Highland clans. This mixed bunch of regular soldiers and semi-alien freebooters was quartered on those who would not subscribe to a promise to keep away from conventicles. In case there should be another rising, as in 1666, the arms and horses of the aristocracy were impounded. Few events could more sharply mark the decline that had taken place in the power of the magnates than that a duke of Hamilton, leader of the parliamentary opposition to Lauderdale, should have to appeal to the king for the use of his own carriage horses. Hamilton, the third duke, had become the leader of those in the aristocracy who were concerned primarily with the restoration of their own position. They adhered ostentatiously to legalism as Lauderdale's attempts to deal with extremism came more and more to divert from it.

The quartering of Highlanders, as well as of a Lowland militia, on the south-west, was a device calculated to force many landowners to accept bonds promising to keep their tenantry in order, and weakened those who refused, since such quartered troops would loot and damage the goods of the tenantry and so prevent the paying of rents. But quartering, for all the distaste it raised, was not illegal. It was a regular mechanism used in extracting overdue tax from recalcitrant payers. The presence of Highland clansmen, the numbers of which have been greatly exaggerated, made it much more of a threat to the local power and influence of landowners than a simple financial device.

The Highland Host, as it was called, was in occupation for only five weeks. But it marked the end of the moderate policy which Lauderdale had set out to use. Opposition to it remained silent, for fear of the accusation of 'leasing making' or verbal treason, and Hamilton himself had a convenient attack of sciatica which prevented him showing open opposition. There were, however, anonymous but well-informed pamphlets published against Lauderdale. The crown's attention was in any case focused on England where the rising crisis in Charles II's reign was being staged, the Exclusion issue in which the Whig opposition party was attempting to get the Roman Catholic heir to the throne, James duke of York, cut out of the succession, and thereby to assert parliamentary control over the monarchy. When the English Whigs attacked Lauderdale's actions in Scotland the king was very angry, for it was an essential feature of his policy to keep the parliamentary concerns of the two countries apart. Junction of the two kingdoms was to be in the king and his policy, not in the legislatures. But if Lauderdale's technique of Indulgence was not winning many in Scotland, and the methods of control used over disorder were enhancing clamour in the English Parliament, there was little to be said for it.

In 1679 the outbreak of disorder in Scotland, long awaited, happened, with the murder of Archbishop Sharp in May, an armed rising in the west and the defeat of government forces under John Graham of Claverhouse at Drumclog. This led to larger military action under the duke of Monmouth, Charles's acknowledged bastard, at Bothwell Bridge. Victory left the government with a large number of covenanting prisoners and brought many who had hitherto supported the unrest to doubt whether armed resistance to the government was in truth the will of God. But Lauderdale's policy of attempted comprehension of the moderates and repression of the rest, was shown to have failed. The residual covenanters now made explicit what had long been implied in their position, the rejection of rule by presbytery and majority vote, in favour of domination by the self-appointed godly. In a paper proclaimed by Richard Cameron at Sanquhar, they declared war on Charles II as an enemy to God.

Bothwell Brig thus resulted in the fall of Lauderdale and polarization of the issue. The convenanters had become 'Cameronians', adherents of the *Sanquhar Declaration*, and the large body of Presbyterian adherents were alienated from them but not necessarily prepared to attach themselves to the episcopal Church, particularly since, for its part, the government was now making the erastian basis of that Church conspicuous. It was embodied in a Test Act, which demanded of all office holders acceptance of the Confession of 1560 and the recognition of the king as supreme in spiritual as well as temporal matters. It could well be argued, and was, that these two items were mutually contradictory. So while covenanters were returning to the church, a further body who could not accept the Act left it. Various of the nobility evaded the issued, but one important figure, the earl of Argyll, was brought to book. Argyll had been a chief beneficiary of Lauderdale's rule, and probably because of this was pursued when he took the Act with the qualification of 'as far as it was consistent with itself'. He was tried for leasing making, convicted, but allowed to escape abroad. Meanwhile the government sent Graham of Claverhouse, a professional soldier, to the south-west to force landowners to take the band, and fine those who attended conventicles.

The policy of the government became increasingly savage as, in the autumn of 1683, there came the repercussions of the Rye House plot in England. There were arrests and investigations in Scotland. The government had got the dissident minority on the run, and it can be considered as a sign of desperation that from this minority came an open declaration of war on all who supported the government in a document with the misleadingly humble title the *Apologetical Declaration*. Repression now took the form of shooting out of hand all who refused to renounce this statement. It was an understandable ferocity, for attacks and murders had been perpetrated by the Cameronians, and as a method of selection of the hard core of resistance it was probably sounder than the brusque investigation of contacts and arbitrary fines which had preceded it. These earlier methods were more likely to hit the passive supporters of presbytery than the resisters of monarchy. It is the ensuing period of summary execution which was given the name of 'the killing time' by Wodrow. Such a name is in itself a comment on the enhanced position of the law in restoration Scotland, but was the source of much historical misrepresentation. Perhaps as many as 100 were executed in all, mostly in the field, a small number compared to that involved in the slaughter of royalists after

Philiphaugh or the siege of Dunaverty, but remembered ardently by a society benefiting by an increased level of law and order, and commemorated in a distorted historical tradition.

One feature stands out in this period, which is that apart from the case of the earl of Argyll, the victims of government were lesser folk, lairds and tenantry, directly, but it was also the case that it was these lesser folk who had been holding conventicles, fighting at Drumclog and less effectively at Bothwell Brig, and it was from small landholders that the murderers of Sharp had recruited themselves. In ways troubling to the government an important social and political change was manifesting itself, the rise of the class of lairds.

The so-called lairds of this period were a fusion of two earlier groups, the baronage of Scotland, that is the non-noble tenants in chief of the crown, who might be under the sway of a magnate but were not within anyone's feudal superiority, and the vassals who had at one time or another received feus, either directly from a magnate or in the process of the disendowment of the Church, from an ecclesiastical estate which had later become part of a lay lordship. Feu-ferm tenure had carried with it, though not always explicitly, certain feudal obligations and restrictions. Marriage and the alienation of land required the consent of the superior, and a man would be expected to support his lord politically and militarily, but the main burden on the feu-holder was a money rent. In the drastic readjustment of money values in the late sixteenth century many of these rents became only light encumbrances, but the right of the feudal superior to extract teind could still involve a heavy burden of dependency. This right had been limited and regulated by the legislation of Charles I. This let vassals become independent, and they and tenants in chief were becoming fused into the category of 'heritors'. The stipends of ministers were defined in terms of grain, and so inflation proof. The cess had placed further burdens on property, but the whole long-term development of definition worked to the advantage of the moderate landowner. Local power also came to him, again without reference to his tenurial status, through the expansion of the role of the Justice of the Peace, which had occurred under the Cromwellian occupation and was only partly reversed in the Restoration, and still more from the new position of Commissioner of Supply. For both these offices the basic qualification was property, and not a great deal of it, rather than feudal status. The other practical qualification was residence, which kept out the nobility. Increasingly in the Restoration period the government cast together the two sections of the class of lairds as heritors, in its appeals and commands over Church policy. Only in representation in Parliament was the baronage distinguished from the rest of the class. And in Parliament there begins the series of improvingg statutes, Acts which increased the rights of landowners in the reorganization of their estates. These had started in 1647 with an Act making feasible some divisions of commonty, but more significant legislation took place later, in the 1660s with power to realign roads and adjust boundaries after enclosure. As land-owners, many benefited from the definitions of lawyers which inter-preted statute law to impose serfdom on miners and saltworkers. Heritors were liable to the drawn into a share of control in Church matters either as ruling elders, once the aristocracy had pulled out from its position of 1638, or as ordinary elders functioning at parish level only. The properties of landowners, whether tenants in chief or not, would usually form one or more baronies, and within the barony the baron court gave the landowner further authority.

The total body of landowners may have numbered close on 10,000, but four fifths of this number were very small beer indeed, the men to whom Walter Scott was to give the title of bonnet lairds, owners of perhaps a single farm which they worked themselves, more akin to the English yeoman than to landowners who lived on rents. But there were still over 1,500 more substantial landowners, whose resources ranged from a couple of farms to a great estate. Some of this class played an important part in central government. They provided the judges, and set a pattern by which it was common for the eldest son of a landowner, if of sufficient ability, to enter the profession of advocate, and supplement his rents withfees, or as he became more senior a judicial salary. They also provided what there was of a civil service. Various families were moving towards enhanced status through several generations of office holding: an example of this is the house of Primrose, to be ennobled in the early eighteenth century as earls of Rosebery. The Hopes held a network of estates and baronies, and one of them was sufficiently near to the duke of York to be drowned in the sinking of the *Gloucester* in 1682, but the behaviour of Charles I's Lord Advocate, Hope of Craighall, in effectively sabotaging the king's policy over the Cove-nant, may have led the crown to keep them out of office for the next 100 years or so. The presence of two Sir George Mackenzies in the government of the Restoration period showed that Highland families were, in some cases, following the same mandarin route as

Lowlanders. There were also openings for landowners in military careers, and it was in this way that Claverhouse advanced himself.

Baronies, with their baron courts, were basic units of rural society. They were single entities, originally created by royal grant, bonding together the law and practice of a particular area though not always geographically continuous. A baron court had criminal powers, though these did not extend to the pleas of the crown, i.e. major offences. In practice in the seventeenth century they confined themselves to minor matters, which, considering their lack of specialized legal skill, was just as well. But this is not to say that they were unimportant: most of the need of people to adjust the claims of others are shown in minor affairs. Petty thefts, encroachments and minor acts of aggression, and of course encroachments on the rights of the baron, formed most of the regular business of such a court, and the fact that some of these were criminal matters and others civil did not alter the need for decisions or the types of penalty available, which were mostly fines, but sometimes forfeiture. Justice had a profitable side to it to the owner of the court, but this does not mean that it was not also of advantage to the tenantry. Baron courts met at the instance of the baron, when business had accumulated, and the baron might or might not choose to preside in person. There were also the 'birlaymen' who might be chosen by the baron or elected by the court. In either case they would be men of considerable local knowledge, whose duties were to settle local issues and divide local burdens. Possibly these men were the surviving features of a system of justice by which the local community had made and enforced its own rules. Baron courts spent much of their time on local policing, cases of 'sclander' which meant verbal abuse, or 'ryot' which seems to mean any minor affray in which blood was shed, or 'straiks', blows. They also set penalties on activities which, though advantageous to the tenantry, damaged the laird's property: steeping flax in rivers, burning the moors to the destruction of nesting birds, or cutting green timber. The court might be used to enforce the payment of specific rents, in kind or services, and would supervise the joint performance of the onerous duties involved in keeping the mill in working order; repairing the mill lade, for instance, or bringing in a new millstone. It might also lay down fees, and see that they were paid, for routine smith work or milling, and would extract teind. There was constant business over damage caused by straying animals.

Our vision of the life of our ancestors is largely formed by the records in which we seek for information, and some of these can be distorting. In a purely criminal court men appear as solitary individuals because it is in their individual capacity that they have offended. Baron courts records show us that men were also part of a group with complicated and interwoven rights and duties. Both aspects are true, but selective. Where the farms were joint the domestic economy of each tenant household rested on communal effort, even though the draught animals put to the plough were individually owned. Cottars were also participators in the joint farming, as hired labour, as occupiers of small portions of land and as sharers in common pasture. There might on an individual farm also be grassmen with rights only in the grazing. Even where a system of single tenant farms predominated, as it did already in the seventeenth-century Lothians, and farmers made their basic decisions as individuals, there may well have been sub-tenancies which meant that the effect of such decisions was communal. Working through the cottar system as extra labour was not the same as using labour hired by the day, since the cottar had his own land to work. It looks, from eighteenth-century evidence, that it was normal for the children of cottars and tenants to leave home, probably before puberty, to work as 'servants', that is employees, for other farmers or in handcraft industry.

In a joint farm, the link between man and land was communal. When a tenant came to a new farm – and there is considerable evidence for seeing the tenantry as highly mobile – he would take on a third or a quarter, or some other fraction, intermixed with the holding of others, and this segment would have no territorial meaning until he sowed his first crop. The system might still be fluid, with redistribution occurring every few years, which would further weaken the bond between man and land. It was as a group that the tenantry would have to work the land, and all were also bound to use the same mill, and in practice also the same wright and smith. There would probably be joint work in bringing in the firing for the laird, or in statute labour on the roads. All possible labour was under orders not to withdraw and work elsewhere at harvest time. Farmers who held single tenancies might be richer than their neighbours in joint farms, even rich enough to conduct their ploughing without using the beasts of sub-tenants, but all were involved in the same sorts of arduous labour at various seasons. The social gulf was probably sharper between cottar and tenant than between prosperous and poor farmer.

The small amount of goods that can be seen in some surviving testamentary inventories for the farming population, and the low level of wages, beyond the allowances in grain, paid to even skilled men as servants or hinds, both show the narrowness of the margins by which families survived. Any unforeseen disaster, a crop failure, the drowning of oxen in river or snow, a fire in barn or house, would throw people into destitution. The Church had organized charitable support to some of those thus afflicted, and after 1649 had managed to get it accepted in many area that in general emergencies more than just charity was required. Landowners were to be 'stented', that is assessed, to support those on their estates. In practice this was done by requiring them to take responsibility for a list of those poor on their lands, not by direct assessment and the distribution of revenue by the kirk session. In financial matters the barony was still a stronger unit than the parish. Within the barony the court might order a further spreading of the burden. In 1650 it was reported to the kirk session of Yester that 'the barony of Yester has sett down upon ilk pleugh a stent besides my lord's proportion', and the published records of the baron court of Urie show the baron and his bailie laying down in 1698 which tenants were to support specific destitute individuals. These instances suggest that the proclamations of the Privy Council during the famine of the 1690s, subsequently ratified by Parliament, which formally laid down that half the burden of assessment should lie on the tenantry, merely made law out of existing practice. It also shows that some rulings, made in hard times by baron courts, such as that of Stitchill in 1698, that no alms be given to wandering beggars, had a positive social purpose. The resources of the barony would be needed for its own. Parishioners could be surprisingly generous in response to special needs. An appeal for aid to the town of Kelso, burnt down for the third time of the century in 1684 with what seems to have been unusual carelessness, produced in Yester parish 285 pounds Scots, and though most of this came from the principal landowner, nearly 60 pounds came from the various farms and settlements of ordinary people.

The kirk session might give way to the barony on finance, but on other matters it had powerful sanctions, which could, in the last resort, be backed up by imprisonment by the sheriff. It could control settlement, for it could insist on 'testificates' of good conduct and church attendance for those who wished to enter the parish. It imposed, apparently with success, conformity to sexual standards.

Illegitimacy appears to have been at a very low level in the late seventeenth century in the Lowlands, under 5 per cent of births often under 3 per cent, except in the north-east, and sinners of both sexes submitted to the discipline of the Church without protest or prevarication. In the years after 1649 Church discipline was effective even over landowners. The sessions promoted schooling, and raised money for the school fees of the children of poor families, even though in many cases most elders were still illiterate. There is a touching revelation in the comments of the session of the poor parish of Kingarth, in Bute, when in 1649 it had set up a school and the schoolmaster reported that only five or six children were attending. The session urged that all should send their children to it, but added that 'the most pairt of these that has children for the schole is illiterat and knowes not the good of learning'. Literacy was important to the Church, at least at the level of reading skill, for it was the route to use of the Bible, and though the theology instilled did not in practice depend on Scripture but on the dogma of the Westminster Confession, yet this Confession used Scriptural texts as reinforcements to its statements. Literacy was not, though, of much practical use to the peasantry, who might well grudge paying for its acquisition by children once they were old enough to be set to even a limited amount of work at home. The sessions recognized the economic needs of their people, and did not call failure to educate children an ecclesiastical offence, though they regularly paid for the schooling of pauper orphans. By the later seventeenth century many Lowland parishes had their schools, and children might attend merely to learn to read, with only a minority staying on to learn to write, or even, in exceptional cases, to be promoted to the study of Latin, mathematics or navigation. It would take some decades for a parish school to produce a population capable of reading, and only a minority, till well on in the eighteenth century, would have and retain the ability to write. The need to withdraw children once they could read, and the tendency to see no reason why girls should have even as much schooling as this, was obviously prevalent. This makes particularly interesting the overlap of governing function shown in 1688 when the baron of Stitchill, through his baron court, insisted on imposing fines on any tenant who should fail to send his children to school, or place his daughter at a sewing school before she had been two years 'reading'.

Kirk session and baron court often used the same men, those of wealth and prestige, as leading figures, and landowners might dominate the session as they did the baron court. Sir John Clerk of Penicuik in the 1690s used his baron court to pass rulings on Sunday observance, and also as principal landowner made it carry out an investigation when some teenage boys were alleged to have been for a walk on Sunday. He personally interrogated them in the court to find out what further heinous offences they had committed.

In the eyes of the Kirk men and women were individuals, each to be held within accepted morality, as evidence that the parish was a Christian congregation. The terms of religious control over the sexes were not strictly equal. Both would be reproved and censured for sinful behaviour, and this behaviour might include not just specific offences but simply being a bad neighbour. Over the years the preference of the kirk session for a specific offence on which to proceed tended to translate this into unseemly language for women and 'blooding' or 'straiking' for men. In sexual matters, though both sexes were reproved, it was often harder to bring home discipline on the men than on the women. If a woman named a man as her partner, and she was under very heavy pressure to name someone, he might deny it, 'unless the child was born at the appropriate time', whereas the woman could not deny visible pregnancy. A strong-minded session would threaten an accusation of adultery, rather than the milder sin of fornication, against a woman who did not produce a name. The man might have left the area, and not be available. If he was present and denied the case would be passed to the presbytery which could put him on oath. If he was willing to undertake perjury the Church had no further weapon. Women, without having offended, might be compelled not to live alone, for fear of 'scandal', and probably, also, risk of rape. But a peasant who had seduced a female servant would be allowed to continue to employ her if he said he needed her services. His economic needs overrode the risk of further sinful activities.

The Scottish peasantry did not have long-term rights in the land it worked. It held by a lease or as tenants at will. A man might move to another farm, and the sudden rise in numbers of those doing so after a bad harvest suggests either inability to continue farming through loss of stock, or eviction through failure to pay the rent. Sometimes eviction might be for the purpose of reorganizing the farm structure. All these pressures which might result in movement seem to have prevented individuals having a strong feeling for a particular piece of ground. Rights were those defined in contracts, not growing out of status. But peasants were conscious of their status as farmers and tenacious of authority over children and servants, and in this aspect both Kirk and government supported this view. Covenants and bands were taken by tenants on behalf of their wives, children and servants. What then was the status of women? They were part of the labour force, and often worked away from their parental home as farm servants. Part of their work was the basis of the expanding output of textiles in the country. They spun, set up the warps for weaver husbands, did the milking, soled their own shoes and took part in all the major tasks of the farm, in particular acting as shearers in harvest, by which labour often their husbands' rents were paid. The system of reaping known as the bandwin was mainly 'manned' by women. There is evidence of independent economic activity by widows, and, less clearly, by single women. These single or widowed women might keep a school, brew ale, engage in retail trade, and at the bottom of the scale of remuneration can be found wandering around collecting rags for the new paper mills. A Fala midwife was accused of witchcraft in 1678, a Glasgow woman schoolteacher was acquitted of the same in 1700. In 1662 the barony of Stitchill was ordered to pay the debts incurred towards an ale-wife in terms which suggest an extensive business. In 1641 the surgeons of Edinburgh complained to Parliament that women had been carrying on their craft. But the frequent presence of fairly young widows with children on poor rolls suggests that it was difficult for such to earn an adequate family income. In the Highlands we are told that women supplied most of the agricultural labour force, since men felt this work to be beneath their gentility. In both Highlands and Lowlands they retained their surnames or patronymics after marriage, as a sign that they had never become fully members of their husbands' kin group. They were treated as independent moral individuals by the Church: to a much lesser degree by the courts. Traditionally they had had no share in criminal cases. The courts had refused to regard them either as independent criminals, or as witnesses, so that responsibility over their actions had been assumed to lie with their husbands or kin, though in the 1640s there were special commissions set up to try women for child murder. The General Assembly pressed Parliament on the subject of the murder of bastards by their mothers, and in 1690 an Act of Parliament placed a presumption of the guilt of murder on a woman who concealed her pregnancy and whose child was subsequently found dead. At this point at least in the area of the end result of sexual activity, women had become fully criminalized. But till well into the eighteenth century they might be disqualified as witnesses in court except in matters where only women could give information, such as whether a child had been born alive or not. A statute of 1591 had allowed their evidence in witchcraft cases, presumably on similar grounds, but in the 1670s it was still occasionally successfully argued that it should be excluded.

In landed society women held a mixed position. In one aspect they were mere chattels to be given in marriage for political or economic reasons. The law of the Church, which made the law of the land in marriage, did not permit of forceable marriage, and allowed the legality of a marriage conducted in defiance of the woman's kin, but cases of this kind were rare. Abduction was a serious affair, it seems, because it was the forcible removal of some man's property, and the cases which came to the notice of the Privy Council were all those of women who, whether unmarried or widows, had links with property. In 1663 in Aberdeenshire the schoolmaster Alexander Brodie noted in his diary that a man had carried off a girl, with the aid of an escort of 24. The ballad of Eppie Murray had a foothold in real life. What happened when force was used on women without possessions or a powerful kin is not clear.

Yet also women might act with considerable independence. It is clear from the evidence in witchcraft cases and kirk session business that they might express themselves with vigour and animosity. When the government was trying to control the covenanting movement in the 1670s many of the gentry complained that they could not keep their wives from conventicles. Certain women had a conspicuous influence over the religious life of those they came in contact with. One such was the countess of Cassilis, who was patron and friend of the young Gilbert Burnet. Anne, duchess of Hamilton was no cipher in the running of her estate or household, and was well aware that the title was vested in her personally, not in her husband or son. Women might travel considerable distances. We have statements during the Commonwealth period of them going by road to London, in a coach, which contrasts with the death-bed scene recorded by Samuel Rutherford for Lord Kenmuir in which it is taken for granted that after the noble's death his wife will not have the use of the coach. For those in the upper and middling ranks, improvements in amenity and travel opportunities would give more personal independence.

It does not seem to be a complete accident that it is in the early post-Reformation period that we see the criminalization of women, a new interest of the law in sexual behaviour and the beginnings of the witchcraft craze. All meant a new look at the role of women. Of those accused of witchcraft in seventeenth-century Scotland, some four out of five were women, and though one would expect the figure to be slightly slanted towards women, from the tendency of the figures to be also slanted towards the poor, this preponderance is more than should be expected from simple social or economic standing. The Reformation made a transformation in the relationship of individuals of their Church: more than just belief was to be demanded from society by Calvinism, a sense of total commitment to God's plan, and activity which marked out the congregation as chosen of God. The godly life of a society was not valued as a means to God's grace but as a sign of the possession of it, and women had their part in the achievement of this sign. At the same time reformed theology carried on the mediaeval tradition in which the sexuality and availability of women was seen as a threat to the souls of men. Such a view is entirely comprehensible from the fact that all who wrote about religion and morals were men, and concerned with the temptations which they themselves had experienced. Protestant thought, though, seems to have had an enhanced distaste for women, as can be seen in the comments made in the Confession of Faith of 1560 about the Catholic practice of accepting baptism by women as valid. If sinfulness of women, which might in many cases also entrap men in sin, was a demonstration that they were independent moral personalities, it would seem anomalous to have their criminal activities regarded as someone else's responsibility. When withchraft became recognized as illegal, and the status of witch incurred drastic penalties (for it was the status, not any particular acts, which were criminal in the European tradition that came to Scotland under James VI), it was inevitable that no one would be prepared to take on the personal responsibility of such an offender.

Recent work on the witchcraft craze has not answered directly the simple question of its causation, but has offered instead the concept of 'associated circumstances' under which such a craze becomes likely. These include a high sense of the need for personal commitment to religion, a belief in the possibility of witches among the peasantry at large, and even more important in the class which controls the local institutions of Church and state, and the concept of criminal justice as implying not simply compensation for wrongs done, but specific penalties for specific offences. In such a setting the idea that someone had renounced their baptism – an idea which it is difficult to place in a Calvinist theology, since whatever grace had been conferred by baptism could not be removed by mere human action – had become the servant of the devil and often his concubine – an idea disgusting to a society which legitimated sexual activity only within marriage – produced a mixture of terror, intellectual muddle and deep antagonism. Accusations of witchcraft would arise only from long hostility, during which suspicion and fear fed on all misfortunes. Since the total executed during the main century of the craze, from the 1580s till the 1670s, was probably about ten times those executed in the 'killing times' to which much literature has been devoted, it is a topic worthy of consideration.

The pattern of witchcraft trials in time and location does not indicate any simple relationship to varieties of religious or political opinion, except that though people in the Highlands believed in a wide spectrum of magic, these did not usually lead to the execution of witches, nor does it indicate the degree of stress in a society. There was a natural tendency for places in which one generation had seen an outbreak of accusations to have another some 30 years later. There was a major outbreak of trials in 1629–30, perhaps a reflection of a high level in continental Europe, so that in all some 350 cases were heard in a little over two years. This outbreak may have exhausted the supply of local animosities, so in the 1630s the level of cases was low, for all that the events of the later years of the decade do not suggest a tranquil society. There were other years of high levels in 1643, 1649 and 1661–2, for all of which the political setting might be seen as an explanation, but since these general high levels are merely accumulations of local issues which varied greatly in type, a national political explanation is not convincing.

In the decline of convictions and executions however, national aspects played a crucial part. The Privy Council had, since 1597, issued commissions as the normal mechanism for starting a trial, but did not have full control for trials could take place also in the Court of Justiciary. In the Cromwellian period, with the Privy Council no longer in existence, the English judges were hostile to the use of torture for suspects and somewhat sceptical of the evidence produced by it. But as power became decentralized in the later years there was a recrudescence of cases, and a backlog waiting to be discharged in 1661. This backlog alarmed the Privy Council, which changed the rules to an insistence that its commission was necessary for arrest, and also banned torture. This made prosecution harder, and in the late 1670s the judges, particularly Sir George Mackenzie, the Lord Advocate, the 'Bluidy Mackenzie' of covenanting myth, did much to make prosecution ineffective. He and his fellow judges did not denounce the concept of witchcraft, but systematically picked holes in the evidence submitted, in a way which suggests that they were genuinely sceptical of the whole process. The local kirk sessions and landowners who made accusations were in no way sceptical, for the belief system held at the lower level, but there soon became little point in arduous and expensive procedure against local sources of trouble if this was bound to fail.

What is surprising is that in a century in which over 1,000 met death on this count, local records should indicate an unwillingness to proceed against people engaged in the deliberate use of super-natural techniques. For instance in 1671 a man in Yester parish admitted having gone to the Canongate to get a local wizard there to advise him where certain stolen goods were to be found. The kirk session soon found that public denunciation of this practice produced new examples, as local people of both sexes popped up to town to use the facility. The later cases were, therefore, merely reproved privately.

If charming or magic were in occasional use in the Lowlands, they were basic features of life in the Highlands and Islands. The Dingwall presbytery records show fascinated horror at the information gathered about magic practices in Applecross and Loch Carron in the 1650s, for instance the sacrifice of bulls to an early Celtic saint, the use of magic wells, etc. These customs seem to have been even commoner in the islands according to Martin Martin's account of his island tour in the 1690s. He described rituals with fire, the taking of auguries, visions, ghosts, special rituals to bring good luck in fishing and the influence for good or ill of particular animals. Post-Reformation Christianity, both Catholic and Protestant variants, with its austerity, zeal and puritanism had largely missed the Highland area, kept out by the difficulty of maintaining a regular ministry through clan warfare and by the lack of Gaelic speakers for preaching purposes (though Dingwall presbytery recognized this latter factor and was making special arrangements to find youthful talent). Ancient practices were not easily abolished even when they were exposed to the full rigour of

Calvinism, for the Gaelic songs later collected from many areas reveal a society with religious imagery and charming rituals entering into every aspect of daily life.

This continuation of the petty cults which had enabled Christianity to make itself acceptable in the early days of the Church was only one aspect in which Highland culture was marked off from Lowland. Highland culture was still aural, based on music and song, and as Martin Martin remarked in more than one island, the poets might be of either sex. The names and works of four women survive from the late seventeenth century among the poets of distinction. Poetic status was based on natural talent at manipulating complicated prosody, though it was enhanced by nurture in myth and symbolism and needed little in formal education. But it was becoming more common for the people of distinction in the Highlands, in terms of power, the chiefs and tacksmen, in terms of culture, poets and bards, to be lettered. Even at the time of the Statutes of Iona leading chiefs could sign their name to a document in English: by the late seventeenth century the state of relative peace was making it possible for the sons of chiefs to study in the south, and this promoted both literacy and the use of English. In fact such men might be literate only in English. Clans were ceasing to value the system of hereditary bards, though the MacMhuirichs were to stay with the Macdonalds of Clanranald to the fourteenth generation. The role of the bard had been the retention in memory and production when required of genealogy and verses about battles, and the lyric developments of the late seventeenth century were a very different matter.

A major puzzle about the society of the Highlands in the late seventeenth century is how far had it followed a separate line of development from that of the Lowlands? Certain features which are often regarded as characteristic of the kinship and clanship pattern of Highland society can be seen at earlier date in the Lowlands, particularly in the Borders which had had surname groups very similar in power and function to clans as late as the early seventeenth century. The system of justice by compensation worked out between two kin groups, was finally destroyed only in 1649 in the Lowlands, but traces of it can still be found in the eighteenth-century Highlands. Clanship gained much of its authority from the effective absence of any higher power, but added to this negative aspect the cult of loyalty to the person of the clan chief which does not seem to have obtained in the Lowlands. In the Borders obedience to the head of a surname, in the Highlands to a chief, was necessary for survival, but the literary emphasis of Gaelic culture transformed this practical necessity to an ideal. By the late seventeenth century the great surnames of Lowland Scotland had been tamed, and much of the authority of a magnate over 'his' men was being replaced by a lesser authority, that of laird, and this was manifested not so much by browbeating as by the occupancy of specific legal offices in Church and state and tenurial rights. Yet one of the hostile critics of Scotland in this period, Thomas Kirke, stated after a visit almost exclusively to Lowland Scotland in 1677, 'The Nobility and Gentry Lord it over their poor Tennants, and use them worse than Gally-Slaves; they are all bound to serve them, Men, Women and Children; the first Fruits is always the Landlord's due, he is the Man that must first board all the young Married Women within his Lairdship, and their Sons are all his Slaves, so that any mean Laird will have Six or Ten, or more Followers; besides those of his own Name, that are Inferior to him, must all Attend him (as he himself must do his Superior, of the same Name), and all of them attend the Chief. . . . Every Laird (of note) hath a Gibet near his House, and his Power to Condemn and Hang any of his Vassals'. We can ignore the traditional myths of the right of first night, and the private gibbets: otherwise this is much of what was said, in less disgusted terms, by the lawyers of the early eighteenth century about the Highlands: it is certainly overstressed, but may not have been total fiction as a picture of Lowland society. There are many instances of viewers from economically advanced societies registering surprise at the number of followers and inefficient servants attendant on great men in less primitive systems (Bishop Liutprand of Cremona sent to Byzantium in the tenth century saw the same thing the other way round and was surprised that the Emperor had to do odd jobs for himself). It seems likely that not only had the pressure of more effective central government reduced the domination of great men in the Lowlands but the growth of power in the middling ranks, as yet not so marked as in the society from which Thomas Kirke came, of merchants, ministers and lairds, had eaten into this domination from below.

5

The Economy in the Later Seventeenth Century

It might be expected that the landed aristocracy, after its mid-century loss of political power and its subordination successively to the Church and the central power of the state, would have turned to the economic promotion of its landed resources in much the same way as failed politicians in the eighteenth century tended to become agricultural improvers. Indeed instances of pressure on factors to increase production do exist. A notable example of a well-run noble estate in which the successive owners pressed steadily for enhanced grain yield was that of the earl of Panmure, but the Maules of Panmure were in no way typical of the nobility, having attained a peerage only in 1646 through court service, after a career in trade. A more typical response to change was that of the young earl of Kinghorne inheriting an estate heavily burdened from his father's military support of the Covenant, as well as fining by Cromwell, so that when he first came to his ruined castle he 'was not worth a four footed beast'. His response was to sell off some parts of the estate to free the rest, to rebuild his castles, and to make sure that his creditors were people favourable to him. Most of his rents continued to come in in kind. As he wrote the end of his life:

> Men who's fortun's are burdened with debt may when their children are young doe somewhat to less'ne ther debt by making annuall payments of some on debt or other, especially if corns, of which our estats must consist give any good pryce. But that has been the misfortune of my tyme that for the most part the price of corns one grain with another has not exceeded ane hundreth merks per chalder and oft'ne under that.

Landowners such as young Kinghorne had a strong sense of responsibility towards the future of the estate, an approach which contrasts with the total irresponsibility sometimes shown by an earlier generation, for instance by Sir Thomas Urquhart of Cromarty who when faced with disorder and debt in his affairs had gone on an expensive tour abroad hoping, mistakenly, that someone else would sort out his affairs. We have as yet no studies published of the way in which the greater magnates met their burdens, but it is clear that they eventually managed to restore their estates. The remarks of Kinghorne give a strong hint why agricultural improvement was not the general policy: grain prices were too low.

Prices were, in fact, markedly lower than they had been. The surviving runs of 'fiars prices', that is the annual levels asserted as normal for a particular crop, for Perthshire and for East Lothian show that between the 1650s and the 1660s these stepped down to range round a level some 28 per cent in the former case and 25 per cent in the latter below that of earlier year. This change implies an easier relationship between food supply and population, achieved either by more grain being available on the market, or there being fewer people to purchase and eat it. There is no reason to see the late 1650s or 60s as a particularly high period of population loss, so the former alternative seems the more likely. Scotland appears to share in the surplus grain which can be seen elsewhere in Europe at this time. Confirmation of this view comes from the remarks of an intelligent contemporary observer, Sir Robert Sibbald, on the increase of land under plough: 'a vast deal of ground now tilled and laboured that before was pasture', he wrote. The non-agricultural sector in Scotland was very small, though increasing, and grain export was becoming a regular feature of Scotland's trade, so altogether it seems likely that the reduction in price came from increased production.

The new price level may have discouraged such agricultural developments as were within the techniques then available. The obvious route to improvement was what the English called 'up and down husbandry', and which today we would call long leys. This means subjecting the land to long periods under grass and short spells of grain crops. It would mean the withdrawal of some land from the infield-outfield system then prevalent. Infield was land continuously cropped, manured in winter by the quartering on it of livestock. Outfield was land used for most of the time for pasture but part of which at any one time was broken up for the plough and used to produce grain until the yield made it unprofitable, whereupon grass and weeds were allowed to re-establish themselves. The repeated cropping, perpetually on the infield, and for up to four consecutive years on the outfield, was not as damaging, at least for barley, as was claimed by eighteenth-century improvers trying to get rid of the system. Studies of continuous cropping made at the research institute of Rothamstead show that yields go down sharply in the first three years of the process, but then stabilize: the creation in the soil of an uninterrupted structure of parasites on the parasites using the grain crop partly compensates for the loss of nutrients. The change from this system to ley farming required 'enclosure', that is the creation of moderate-sized fields, fenced or hedged, and this was capital expenditure not profitable unless there was enough stock to manure the land and build up fertility. It is also the case that by following the English principle of a legal maximum rate of interest, and taking the English level, which meant bringing down what was allowed from 8 to 6 per cent in 1661, a rate unsuited to an undeveloped economy, the Scots made it improbable that there would be much capital available for borrowing. The creation of a system of entail in 1685 also made it difficult to burden estates with debts, and thereby raise capital for development. The fact that this law was passed by the aristocratic Parliament when that institution was in general being used to give the landowning classes what they wanted, suggests that not many landowners were yet considering improvement except in the form of trying to push up rents. Bar a few men of unusual enterprise, the move to improved agriculture was to wait the rise in grain prices of the mid eighteenth century.

From 1660 till the mid 1690s the country appears to have had enough food, but the winter of 1674 led to great loss of stock in the southern uplands and consequent grain shortage from lack of animals as draught power or for trade in the following year. Otherwise Lowland Scotland appears to have been more able than in the past to feed itself, and the trend of county fiars prices on the east to move parallel to one another suggests improved communications.

The fall in grain prices seems to have benefited particularly the upland and pastoral areas of Scotland which needed to trade livestock products for grain. There may have also been a rise in the price of cattle, but this we shall not know for sure until systematic work is done on cattle prices. Study of Cumbria in the seventeenth century has led a demographer, A.B. Appleby, to assert that that district benefited from a favourable movement in the terms of trade, and such a movement might mean a rise in pastoral product prices as well as a fall in those of grain. Certainly the price of sheep appears to have risen in the seventeenth century. A change of this sort in

Cumbria would probably extend to Scotland too. Scottish graziers also benefited by the ban put by the English Parliament on the import of Irish cattle after 1664. We have glimpses of the large numbers of animals that might on any one occasion cross the border into England. In 1663 over 18,000 cattle went south through Carlisle alone: in 1664 altogether nearly 48,000 as well as over 11,000 sheep went across the border to England. In the late 1680s when more regular figures are available, the peak year of animal exports to England was 1683 with 27,000 cattle and nearly 32,000 sheep. The sheep mostly originated in the Borders, where large flocks were becoming common. For cattle we do not know the origin, and in any case we have to allow for the development of temporary halts in Galloway, and fattening there. Commercially oriented pasturing in Galloway was already big business which by the 1680s made necessary clearly demarcated drove roads. How many of these beasts originated in the Highlands is unclear. The exchange of Highland pastoral produce for the arable surplus of the Lowlands is shown by remarks of visitors to Scotland in the late seventeenth century, and Dunblane was a conspicuous cattle market. Martin Martin, writing of the islands at the end of the century, showed that cattle were being swum across the Kyle Rhea tied nose to tail in groups of five, and the Harris estate of the McLeods was aware that the price of cattle determined the ability to pay rents.

In the later seventeenth century the Border areas of Scotland were geared to growing sheep for marketing both wool and meat, and usually in England. This meant that the farmers were tied to market forces, even though weaknesses in transport and market system meant also that much of the lower ground went to cereal crops for subsistence, rather than on fodder for winter. Only in the early eighteenth century did these farms turn over to purely market-oriented farming, cutting down on their labour and so creating rural depopulation. In the Restoration period there was still enough sporadic disorder for manpower to have advantages other than as labour.

It was particularly in arable areas that the limited level to which the economy was monetized was displayed. Rents were paid largely in grain and in specific services, for instance in harvest work or 'carriages', that is fetching goods, particularly cutting and bringing in peats. The odd wether or goose, and, invariably, hens would figure. Wages too, for those in regular employment, were met with grain, cloth or grazing rights. Payments in kind divorced farmers from use of local markets; indeed it prevented there being such markets in many areas. And this meant that seed corn was not an object of purchase. If there were new varieties occurring by mutation they did not spread. Payment in kind spread over other activities. On the estate of Clerk of Penicuik the miners paid rents in coal and the smith and slater in repair work. Clerk's payments to his servants reveal mixed duties and payment largely in kind: 'Feid George Cowie to be grieve, serve at table, oversea my horses, ryde with myselfe for 51 lib. 12 shillings, yearly and a stone of woole, or 4 lib., a firlot of bear and 6 loads of coals', went one entry in his notebook, and another said, 'Christian Tomson, agreed with her to guard ye kie and barn, to look to the housse, keep ye kies thereof turn the beds and open the windows in fine weather and to put on a fyre against my coming . . . for 2 ½ bolls of oats and 1 pair of shoes. I am to furnish her 6 or 12 hens and she to gether their eggs for my use.' Similarly the earl of Wemyss paid his salters in a mixture of meal and money. Even where a payment was nominally to be made in money notes in a rental may show that what had been received was a bullock, some swine, butter, wool, flour, even strawberries. Such a pattern of payment made for strong social links and constant communication between the different layers of society, even if it was not the fastest route to the development of specialized skills.

Yet much of the farming was not simply for subsistence. There was a substantial grain trade, sending food not only to the capital, Edinburgh, but also to the Highlands and northern Isles. A reminder of this is the fact that the Gaelic poet Iain Lom referred disparagingly to Leith meal as a normal commodity. Whenever the Privy Council felt that domestic supplies were secure there was an export of grain. Galloway wool went for sale to principal towns on both the east and west coasts. Elsewhere the spread of domestic textile manufacture meant that many apparently subsistence farming areas were getting spending power by this activity. But there were farming practices of low productivity which it was not yet worth while eradicating if this involved cost. The Lothians grew large quantities of peas and beans and there and elsewhere landowners often insisted on these crops at the end of a lease. In the 1680s this policy was sustained by an Act of Parliament. They were, however, little used in Galloway, though the expected yield was high, because they would have had to be sown at a time when the land was normally kept open for sheep pasturage.

The main instruments which were eventually to help landowners to promote agricultural change were already established. Many farms were let on fairly long leases, and in numerous parts of the country, particularly conspicuous in the Lothians, the older system of joint tenancy had given way to single tenancies. This might not mean, however, that a single man directed the farming. There might be subtenancies within the farm, though only one man was responsible for the rent. Certainly eighteenth-century cases can be found of tenants abandoning farms having collected the rents of subtenants and not having paid the rent for the whole: it is only in such cases that estate records reveal the subtenancy structure. Enclosure, encouraged by Parliament, made possible increased cattle stocks and also the establishment of woodland. It was generally a means of better and more varied farming.

Strengthening and widening the market sector would eventually lower the risk of local famine, for it would necessarily improve transport facilities. It would also monetize the interests of all classes. It would increase the practice of purchasing seed corn, and this was the most certain route to higher yields. It would emphasize the role of towns and villages, and probably lead to the founding of new ones. Most of this still lay in the future. For the present, though, landowners were concerned to get as good a price as possible for their 'victual' rents and livestock. In upland areas where disorder was of recent experience, estates might still regard themselves as representing and defending kinship groups rather than encouraging commercial relationships. Farms might be reserved for members of the Name. The Buccleuch estate in the 1680s was using Scotts only to assess the stock losses of bad winters: the Ogilvy estate had a strong tendency to use kinsmen as factors: the Argyll power in Tiree still gave preference in tacks to Campbells.

Given the unrewarding climate of grain prices it is understandable that those landowners concerned to enhance revenue would choose to do so by promoting their industrial or commercial resources, which were more readily elastic than was the revenue from farming. The linen industry, already expanding, could use spare labour and made it easier to shift from subsistence farming to a more commercial mode without reduction of the local population. Coal, salt and salmon fisheries were all the subject of particular concern. In particular, efforts were made either to confine trade to burghs over which the landowner had domination, or to set up new markets in villages and burghs. The young earl of Kinghorne obtained the right to hold two fairs a year in Longforgen and one in Glamis, where there was also to be a weekly market. The Acts of the Parliaments of the 1670s and 1680s contain substantial wedges of grants of this kind which show a readiness of landowner to expand local trading, and to get a share of it for themselves.

On the foreign aspect this was paralleled by the celebrated Act of the 1672 Parliament which opened foreign trade, hitherto restricted to the 66 Royal Burghs, to burghs of regality and barony, reserving for the Royal Burghs their privilege only in particular commodities such as wines, wax, dyes, silks and spices. The terms of the Act give a very accurate survey of Scotland's overseas links. It lists the exports of coal, corn, cattle and other stock, salt, wool, skins and hides, and the import of timber, iron, tar, soap, lint and linseed, hemp, onions 'and uther necessars for tillage or building or for . . . manufactors'. The significance of this picture is that the country exchanged its primary products from agriculture and mining for the basic goods that kept her industries going, the timber needed in all building, the iron for every occupation, the tar for shipping, the soap and lint for textile manufacture.

A common theme of many seventeenth-century visitors to Scotland was the smallness of the burghs. Thomas Tucker reporting to Cromwell in 1656 referred to many of them as 'pittifull small' and no better than villages. In terms of population this is true. Except for Edinburgh and her subsidiary burghs, Canongate and Leith, and the concentration of burghs on the Clyde, the urban population was small and dispersed. Dunfermline, a Royal Burgh with long standing links with the monarchy, has been estimated at holding about 1,600 people, a figure based on the description of the effects of a fire which destroyed most of it, 220 houses containing 287 families. For comparison, Carlisle was not very much bigger, 309 houses and 447 families, and Penrith in the 1680s had 270 households. These comparisons show that the frontier of commercial backwardness was not the international boundary between Scotland and northern England, but the geological change which marks off the hill country of northern England from the plains.

The small burghs of Scotland were not cut off from agriculture: they used their common grazing, took peats from the hill where possible, and had arable land to which their regulations restricted their own labour force in harvest time. But still, in architecture, way of life and links with the more distant outside world the little burghs were urban. A frequent form of building structure, the long main street of tall buildings with vennels, wynds or alleys off it, still surviving today as a traffic hazard in many places, is in no way rural. The formal demarcation of group within burghs set out separate rights for each. In rural Scotland a man's status depended on a tenurial agreement; in a burgh it depended on whether or not he was 'free', had been admitted as a burgess, and before he could achieve that status he had been through a formal apprenticeship to a merchant or a craftsman. The power in the self-governing area of town life lay in the hands of the merchant burgesses, with a share, but never a dominant one, in the hands of the crafts. Burghs existed for and by sustaining privilege. They claimed sole rights to hold markets, or to conduct specific manufactures over considerable areas, and within the burgh the separate groups guarded their own privileges. The easiest way to this privileged position was by inheritance or marriage, but occasional disasters, such as the plague which, when it struck Edinburgh in the 1640s, reduced the population of the city and its satellite burghs by probably over 10,000, would lead to surges of incomers, far beyond the normal trickle of those migrating to town life. Edinburgh in fact picked up her population again promptly, and other towns, such as Glasgow, with perhaps 12,000–14,000 inhabitants and Aberdeen with 9,000, managed to sustain these levels by immigration at a time when towns of this size lost more people by death each year than they gained by birth. Town life was evidently attractive, even though it involved these as yet unrecognized risks. Towns were at risk from food shortage as was the country but, since most of them were ports, might receive cargoes from abroad to prevent starvation. They were more at risk than the countryside from human-based disasters such as fire, war or plague.

The attraction may have lain partly in material conditions. Samples of urban housing which still survive, for instance the parts of the Edinburgh Royal Mile which lie under the present City Chambers, were more solidly built than rural, and might even be more spacious. Goods could be bought without long journeys or long waits for a pedlar bringing ribbons, laces, minor iron ware, drugs and copies of the new testament. Diet was more varied wilt cheap French wine and fresh fish available, and sometimes dried fruit or sugar could be afforded. More of the attraction probably lay in the different way of daily life. The community was bigger, more assertive, and laid on a consciously designed programme of events. Craft work involved the pleasure of developing and using a specialized skill. It also often meant working indoors. Schooling also was more available than in the countryside, and to a higher level.

Though the small towns in Scotland matched those in the north of England her major cities matched the regional centres of the south. The population of Edinburgh and her satellites may have numbered 40,000 whereas Norwich, the second city of England, stood at only 30,000; similarly Glasgow, at up to 14,000 and growing fast, was not out of scale with Bristol at 20,000 and Newcastle at 16,000. The Irish scene was also similar to that of Scotland, with one big city, Dublin, and then, much smaller, a set of regional centres, which is perhaps surprising since Ireland in the late seventeenth century appears to have had a market-conscious economy. What appears a relative lack in the Scottish scale is the moderate-sized regional centre, the town of some 3,000 or 4,000 inhabitants, acting as more than a supply centre for local agricultural needs, providing skilled workmanship and luxuries for a fairly large upper-class market, though these did exist: Elgin, Ayr, Dumfries, Falkirk and Paisley all filled this function even if some of them were probably under 2,000 in population.

This weak area in the scale probably relates to the fact that the thriving activities of the late seventeenth century, soal and salt, linen and the cattle trade, may have used the towns to supply special needs but did not need them as places where produce was processed. The larger cities gained their support from international trade, and also made specialized goods for the aristocracy and for their own richer burgesses. Gold- and silver-smithing had been a significant activity in Edinburgh and the Canongate for a long time. By the late seventeenth century there were craftsmen there making wigs and coaches, even if not many of the latter, and a powerful incorporation of surgeons and apothecaries was available to deal with the results of upper-class dietary excess by purging, blistering and bleeding. Craftsmen were also necessary to keep in repair luxury equipment, furniture or armaments, bought abroad. The spending habits of the aristocracy bred skills. By the end of the century the Scottish landed class was investing in a big way in sumptuous country houses, and these, even if they used some foreign workers, relied mainly on local labour.

The activities of the towns emphasizes the dual nature of the Scottish economy, a characteristic often found in the undeveloped parts of the modern world. There was a basic agricultural sector, weak in its market aspects but nevertheless producing a surplus which sustained a landowning class, which bought in essential tools, farm and house utensils, pottery, ironwork and leather, and there was also a sophisticated sector supplying a small minority with the luxuries expected by the wealthier parts of Europe, fine textiles, wines, pictures, books, silver and jewellery, arms and furniture. Much of the materials sold in this sector were imported but some, and probably a growing share, were home made. In particular the Restoration period saw attempts to widen the manufacturing base of luxury goods. Monopolies and patents were granted for glass and leather work, soap, sugar, alum and paper, lead and woollen cloth, though mostly with no great commercial success.

Most of Scotland's Royal Burghs and a considerable number also of lesser burghs, were ports. The harbours were often barely improved river mouths, and the ships of necessity small, usually of under 40 tons. Some of the leading towns with larger docking space had bigger ships; Dundee for instance in 1665 had two of 120 tons. But many of the ports lay on great firths and vessels could ride at anchor before they faced the difficult task of getting in to harbour. Leith, which could accommodate large ships, carried on the most significant trade of eastern Scotland, and on the as yet undredged Clyde Glasgow had developed, in Port Glasgow, a satellite capable of taking big ships. Forth and Clyde were the great trading areas, though Montrose and other northern ports were expanding a trade in agricultural surplus. The growing unfree port of Bo'ness, described in 1656 by Thomas Tucker as second only to Leith, reflected both the burgeoning coal exports of the upper Forth and the needs of the west of Scotland for commodities which were small enough to be carried over the narrow Forth–Clyde gap.

The burghs gave specialized services to their hinterlands, markets and consumer goods that everyone needed, though not necessarily at a high level of craftmanship. Some of them had very specialized offerings. Canongate's wizard for theft divination was one such. It has also been asserted that in two years in the 1680s 16 foundlings were abandoned there. In most parishes a single foundling only might crop up in 30 or 40 years, so this suggests that here again it was providing a regional service. By the 1670s the main exports of Scotland were already escaping the grip of urban monopoly in trade. The Act of 1672 was as much a recognition that the narrow funnel of the legal outlets was an anachronism as it was a concession to the vested interests of the superiors of the lesser burghs.

The leading exports owed little to any high level of craftmanship. Coal mines had begun to need surveying skills, but the working was crude. Exports went to Ireland from the Ayrshire field and in much larger quantities from the Forth to the continent, particularly to the United Netherlands but also to Ostend, France and even to London. In 1670 the export was valued at 100,000 pounds Scots. The small coal, called chews, was used to boil away sea water in great pans, for a somewhat tainted salt, which though it could be used for cooking was not pure enough to be a preservative. It was an industry allowed to flout the Sabbath. The export coming to the fore in the late seventeenth century was linen, both cloth and yarn. Between one and two million yards of cloth went out each year, mostly to find the bottom of the English market. There was also a considerable export of skins, both of cattle and of wild animals such as foxes, though the increase in the trade of live cattle to England was reducing it. Woollen cloth went both to the Netherlands and to Scandinavia.

There still survived in the Restoration era a feature of the old, regularized and privileged system of commerce, the staple port of Veere in the Netherlands. All commodities for the Netherlands in woollens, salmon and cattle produce were supposed to be marketed through it. The system was in decline: it did not suit the forceful way in which trade was making its own tracks. Veere lay in Zeeland, and the expanding cities of the Netherlands were mostly in southern Holland. Royal patronage had also landed the Scots with an inactive factor in Veere, but even if the man had been a forceful figure, a system of trade which concentrated on a failing sector of exports and sent them to a waning town was not going to have much impact on the economy.

The spread of markets within Scotland in the 1670s occurred when there were increasing problems on the export side. The Dutch were learning to coke their coals and make them go further, and also turning to Newcastle for supply, for Scottish coal did not coke well. They, and the Norwegians, were giving up using Scottish salt, and the English had clapped a differential duty on this, thereby encouraging the import of the superior sun-evaporated salt of the Bay of Biscay. They were also penalizing Scottish shipping services by the renewed Navigation Act of 1660. The Act was aimed primarily at the Dutch carrying trade, but it also took a swipe, in extra duty, at all non-English shipping, and banned it totally for the import of colonial goods. The Scots had no colonies, but were in the habit of acting as general carriers: their own similar restrictive Navigation Act of 1661, doubling duties on foreign shipping but not daring to insist that Scottish shipping meant ships built in Scotland since there was almost no shipbuilding going on, did little except annoy the French. Scotland's traditional customers, France, England and Sweden, were in one way or another pursuing policies of self-sufficiency and protection which handicapped her trade, and against which retaliation, unwisely tried, was ineffective. The economic thinking of the day was shown in Colbert's policy for France, self-sufficiency, and Scotland was not important enough to justify concessions. But her big and prosperous neighbour England could use certain agricultural imports from Scotland to release energies and resources for more profitable products. Hence Scotland could still send cattle and linen to complement England's specialization on sheep and woollen cloth.

English members of Parliament might, and did, put inconvenient impediments in the way of trade in other commodities, but a full-scale trade prohibition was unlikely so long as the two countries shared a king with a parliamentary veto. But the quarrelsome developments of the century, in particular the fact that France and England were coming to represent the chief rivalries in Europe, was disruptive of Scottish links with France. In the period when Mary queen of Scots had also been queen consort of France the two countries had made a treaty of free trade and joint nationality, but that was at a time when restrictions on trade had often been not national but local, and in any case it was a long time ago. By 1670 all special privileges had disappeared in the face of rising protectionism. The three Dutch wars of the seventeenth century had probably less effect on Scottish trade than had changes in Dutch methods of manufacture. Dutch and English manufactured goods remained vital purchases for many Scottish consumers. It had long been Dutch practice to trade with the enemy, but Scottish privateering in the second Dutch war had taken advantage of the fact that Dutch naval efforts were concentrated on the English. The effects of this had been to provide Scotland with some really large ships as prizes, which still stand out in the survey of shipping taken in 1692. Unfortunately these were too large for most Scottish harbours, and at 500 tons, too large for most of her trade. Scotland had little of the long-distance or general carrying trades which could find such a size an advantage.

The most obvious response to restrictions in established markets would seem to be the development of new export areas, but in this the Scots were sluggish. Trade was most easily carried on through members of a partnership, often kinsmen, with one of the partners located in a foreign port who could act as factor for cargoes dispatched and give advice on what could be marketed where. Cromwellian military defeat had involved the sending of some Scots to Barbados, but most of these were not in a position to be commercially useful. The Scots had not shared in the seventeenth-century expansion of trade in the Levant and of Italy. But they had many links with Scandinavia, some with I reland, and a few individual members in the English West Indian or American mainland colonies. This last group represented the innovating trend of the period. Direct trade with these colonies was forbidden by the Navigation Act, but it was made possible on a small scale by the complexity of the American waterways and the smallness of the controlling forces. The most important features of this expansion were the imports of sugar and tobacco to the ports of the Clyde and Solway. The English colonies had constant need of a wide range of minor industrial goods of all qualities, so the trade could be mutually advantageous.

New trade need not simply mean new routes, it can mean new commodities. On the whole, though, it did not. A certain amount of English tinplate came into Scottish domestic use, but most change was in scale rather than in items. The new 'colonial' luxuries, tea, coffee, and chocolate with attendant use of sugar, had become available at a staggeringly high price for a minority. Coffee was the most significant of these, for already in the 1680s coffee houses provided centres for news, intrigue and gossip. Tobacco had begun its long-term damage to Scottish health, for it was a luxury that many could afford occasionally. In the 1680s the potato, which had not yet begun the adaptation to a different climate and day length which eventually made it a staple food, had appeared. It was an interesting plant in the new Edinburgh Botanic Garden and occasionally grown elsewhere as a delicacy. For the most part the consumer goods of the 1680s were similar to those of the 1620s.

Consumption, even of a limited amount of goods, had to be paid for, and in a world of protection this was becoming difficult. The citizenry could not be expected to do without pots and pans, needles and books, which came from England and the Netherlands, nor could industry do without Scandinavian timber, Swedish iron or Bay salt. The section of imports that a political economist might have considered suitable for sacrifice was the whole range of luxuries brought in for the aristocracy. The landowning class had a large part to do with the more flourishing of the country's exports, but if the balance of payments was to be looked at in terms of a differentiated society it was hard to justify the imports of wines, spices, silks and so on, except on the grounds that the social and political predominance of the people who bought them could not be frustrated. Even with the weakening of the aristocracy this was still a valid claim.

In 1681 the Privy Council put up a scheme to reduce dependence on foreign manufactures by a system which gave to the entrepreneur at home a specially privileged position. The idea of solving social and economic problems together, by forcing vagrants to become a serf labour force in new manufactories, which had prevailed in the 1670s, but had never led to action, had been abandoned. Now the new plan, which may have arisen from the stimulus given to the Council by the presence of James, duke of York, was to forbid the import and use of certain foreign luxuries, and offer to those who undertook to manufacture them freedom to set up works anywhere, the right to bring in foreign workers to train local labour, freedom from various public burdens including the quartering of soldiers, removal of duty on raw materials and a prohibition on the export of the half-processed materials which could be of use, such as yarn or half-finished textiles. This policy was extended to cover various companies making soap, glass, paper, wool cards and, with lesser advantages, to sugar houses. Later on the privileges went also to works for cordage, silk, hardware, gunpowder and pottery. All commodities were possessed of a genuine local market. Under this regime the sugar houses seem to have been the most successful manufactories, for both positive and negative reasons – the local sweet tooth and the difficulties involved in transporting refined sugar any distance. Most of the other industries failed, though the paper mills survived by making paper for the use of the legal profession, which meant a market free from the variations of the business cycle. As far as offering substitutes for the imports of the upper and middling classes, these new developments were at best only a beginning. The best known of the 'new manufactories', the New Mills factory outside Haddington, not an entirely new venture, was run by a group of businessmen with well-developed commercial techniques and a readiness to adjust their policy in the light of market information, but it never managed to get beyond the 'infant' industrial stage of needing protection. Even insulation from the rough world of competition with English exports did not allow it to be very successful: it was failing by the early eighteenth century. In any case it relied on fine wool produced abroad, and the obvious source of such wool, England, had laid an embargo on its export, so this delicate child of protectionism depended on the smuggling trade.

It is significant that the special attempt of the government to promote industries came in 1681, for the 1680s as a whole was the period when the mercantilist restrictions on trade began to be felt. They became even more severe in the 1690s, for the war with France which followed the political revolution of 1688–9 placed enormous burdens on the economies and fiscal systems of all participants. The acute need for money with which to fight led to the raising of taxation levels, and this, at least for England, involved also getting rid of that survival of medieval taxation, customs duties on exports. The whole effect was to turn a world heading towards protection for reasons of intellectual preference into one urgently needing to use high duties for revenue. And at the same time French activity at sea endangered Scottish cargoes. The economy of Scotland was passing from a position of narrowly making ends meet into conspicuous failure to do so.

As outlets closed the Scots looked round for new mechanisms that would open trade routes. One theme in their thinking related to the expanding East India trade. The English East India Company was bringing to England commodities which readily found a sale elsewhere in Europe: these included spices, fine cottons and tea, none of which could be produced in Europe. This trade was the most rapidly growing for England, though still not large. It needed a considerable amount of capital, for the turn-round was slow and the profits variable. We can now recognize that neither for the Netherlands nor for England had this trade been a major plank in seventeenth-century prosperity, but this fact was less apparent in a world where the only widely known figures were those of the occasional sensational profit. Both companies worked by maintaining and using fixed trading posts in the east. There came to the mind of an enterprising Scot, William Paterson, the idea that a similar company might bring wealth to Scotland. It is not clear whether in his original idea he intended to set up a rival to the English East India Company on its own ground. There were plenty of disgruntled merchants in London kept out of the EIC's monopoly.

Though France and the Netherlands had a grip on part of the eastern trade, there appeared room for newcomers. So was launched in 1693 a scheme for a new company to trade with India and Africa, and two years later the company was afloat.

It is possible to see this episode as the manipulation of Scottish merchant ambition by a group in London rivalling the EIC on either commercial or political grounds. But as subsequent developments show, the Scots were good at breeding men of enterprise and initiative, and we should not see Paterson as simply the puppet of London capital. In any case he soon had to function without it, for a political storm was created by the idea of an Anglo-Scottish rival to the great Company in a Parliament where the Company was well represented. When the political mine was detonated the English participants were threatened with impeachment, as well as being directly prohibited from proceeding with the scheme. Pressure was put on European money centres to prevent foreign subscription. The Scots had either to abandon the scheme or go it alone, and unwisely, believing that a trading colony, certainly the only type of colony which might make money rapidly, would solve their economic problems, they went on. After all, the countries conspicuously richer than themselves all had colonial enterprises: might there not be a cause and effect from colonies to wealth?

The disastrous history of the 'Company of Scotland trading to Africa and the Indies' has often been told: how the Scots decided to raise funds on their own, and did so, but failed to show much grasp of reality, economic, political, climatic or strategic in their location of a trading base in Panama, or in the goods sent out with which to initiate business. Afflicted by disease, the active hostility of the Spanish government which claimed the territory and the passive hostility of England and the king, the main settlement, founded in 1698, had failed by 1700. The side line of trade with Africa made a moderate profit, but not enough to compensate for the loss of over £150,000 sterling and the destruction of irrational hopes.

The disaster was the result of an immature attempt to exploit the technical resources of the European world. It was accompanied by another event which showed that Scotland had still not attained immunity from failure in her basic activity, agriculture. In 1695 the harvest was short, and the country, already under strain from the war, was slipping towards famine. In 1696 the harvest was a disaster in the south, and it failed again everywhere in 1698. Even the relatively healthy crop of 1699 was not enough to prevent another season of severe local shortages. In some parts of the country 1700 also was a year of high price. Most areas thus received two or four years of dearth. The commonly used biblical phrase 'the seven ill years' was used in a threatening sermon before the disaster struck, but otherwise is neither contemporary nor accurate. But things were bad enough without such enlargement.

It was an old-fashioned harvest crisis, extended by inroads made on the store of seed corn by the starving peasantry, and accompanied by disease which made it Scotland's last demographic crisis. The bitterness of the occasion may have been accentuated by its unexpectedness. The lowering of agricultural prices in the 1660s and the long interval since the last general harvest failure might have encouraged the view that Scotland had outgrown such hazards. In a sense this view would have been right. The crisis came from an unprecedented spell of bad weather. But the country would continue to be a potential victim of harvest fluctuations until it had developed a marketing system and the internal welfare administration necessary to get food supplies to the people who needed them, and the industrial strength which would make possible the purchasing of enough food from abroad. Scotland did manage to bring in grain from Ireland in 1696, reversing rapidly a programme of self-sufficiency in which export was encouraged and import forbidden. This did not stop the Privy Council clamping back the restrictions in 1697, only to have to take them off in 1698. These oscillations of policy show weakness in communication as well as relatively primitive economic thinking. The harvest failures disrupted the growing similarity of prices in the country, showing that a unified market was not yet fully established. Many parishes attempted to carry their poorer population through the crisis, some by persuading landowners to support their own tenantry, some by compelling the tenantry to donate allocations of food. In one case, Bolton, the parish paid out of its reserves the harvest wages of the cottars, the class most at risk. But in general the situation was summed up by the parish clerk of Sprouston who stated afterwards that the parish still had a large number of poor 'in great necessity and poverty' which it had tried by driblets of money to support and that 'the acts anent the poors' maintenance' had 'not been put in operation'.

We do not know the size of the population in the late seventeenth century, or of the loss in the famine. Till recently the best estimate for the loss put it between 5 and 15 per cent of the population.

Recent work on Aberdeenshire now puts it as high as 25 per cent for that important area. It is clear from parish registers that it was not simply the age groups always at risk, the very young and the very old, who died, but also men and women who were needed to sustain the family economy. Famines usually leave peasant societies burdened by debt, and the loss of an adult's physical resources could mean destitution for the survivors. The fact that there were food riots in Glasgow reminds us that a famine not only lets little food get through to the urban sector but dries up its purchasing power.

The demographic effects of such a famine could well be more long lasting than those of the other main cause of population loss in the seventeenth century, emigration, for settlement abroad, to act as foreign mercenaries and as petty traders. On all these matters our figures are hazy. We know of particular groups who went on particular campaigns, for instance the Scottish troop of over 300 destroyed in Gudbrandsdal in 1612. Many Scots served as mercenaries in France, the Netherlands and the northern wars. Only a proportion of the 10,000 sent to Ireland under General Munro would have survived several years of seventeenth-century standards of military hygiene and the defeat of 1646. Ireland also received the early Ulster settlers, many of whom fled back to Scotland during the war period, and also a surge of immigrants in the 1690s. For this last migration a figure of some 5,000 a year has been suggested, and for emigration before mid century 20,000 a year. The departure of settlers would have a long-term demographic effect for they usually went as families. Service overseas was a standard way by which an undeveloped country with a relatively high pressure on rent or land exploited the socially more rigid structure of other countries. It usually meant the departure of adolescent and young adult males only, and these were often younger sons, unlikely to inherit the means by which they could hope to set up a family at home. Those who went more honorifically to become state servants might come home and marry or might settle abroad. Many of the soldiery died or were killed. Others deserted or were abandoned as sick. In one sense the loss of such men to their home country was absolute. In longer terms its impact was slight since social and economic conditions would not have given most of them the opportunity to marry. They were not 'breeding stock' whereas those who died in the famine often were. It is entirely possible that emigration took more than 100,000 Scots in the seventeenth century, but for only a fraction of this did it mean a lessened capacity of the country to sustain population growth. The departure of some of these for military service after 1660 may have been a necessary price to pay for the relative establishment of law and order in the Lowlands. A society in which lords had a large number of armed men hanging around, ready to accompany them to ostensibly peaceful encounters, or to make an affray when called upon, had given place to one where disputes were being settled by law. Men bred to arms would resent the prospect of other ways of gaining support, and it could be to the country's general advantage that they should look to foreign powers as a means of sustaining a fighting way of life.

6

Towards a New Settlement

For the first time for over three centuries the direct royal line ran out in Charles II and it was his brother James who succeeded him in February 1685, only to flee abroad at the end of 1688 and be replaced by the revolutionary decision to accept William and Mary, his nephew and daughter, as joint monarchs. This revolution was made in England for English reasons. It had been known since the mid 1670s that James was a convert to Roman Catholicism. His first wife, the vastly overweight Anne Hyde, daughter of the earl of Clarendon, had died on 1671 and he had later married Maria Beatrice of Modena. Both marriages had produced children, most of whom had died young: the late seventeenth century was a time of generally high mortality and also of pernicious ideas on infant feeding and medical treatment of the sick to which the rich, because they could afford to pay doctors, were particularly subject. By the time of his succession James's only surviving children were Mary and Anne, both born to his first wife in the 1660s.

It was unusual for the Scottish crown to pass to someone who had had long, adult experience of politics and whose views were known. James had experienced a major attack on his right to inherit in the years 1679–81 when the Whig party in England had attempted to get him excluded from the throne on the grounds of his religion. This had been resisted and eventually outwitted by Charles II who saw it as an attack on the whole concept of monarchy. If Parliament could unmake an heir then it could make a king, and monarchy could come to depend totally on its goodwill. The 'Exclusion' movement had had no support in Scotland. The Scottish parliament had already once put through a revolution accepting James VI as king while his predecessor was alive and still capable of claiming the throne, so the principle of Exclusion was not alien. But since the Interregnum the Scottish political class had been convinced of the unwisdom of direct opposition to the crown. To prevent extra trouble Charles II had sent James to Scotland for much of the period of unrest, where his presence gave Edinburgh a semblance of a court, and the intellectual and institutional advantages that could obtain from it. He had acted as commissioner to Parliament in 1681, since Lauderdale's rule had ended with the rebellion of Bothwell Brig, and in this parliament he had received explicit acceptance of his right of inheritance in the form of a Succession Act, and reaffirmation of royal control of Church matters with the ambiguous and confused Test Act. The oath that this Act required of all office holders shook out of the Church those who held a high view of its position, and out of Scotland as refugees two men of note, one who later became Scotland's most famous jurist, Sir James Dalrymple of Stair, and the other the most interesting political theorist of the day, the violent and articulate Andrew Fletcher of Saltoun. It also led to the trial, sentencing and flight of the earl of Argyll. The contemporary historian Burnet considered that James, when he came to Scotland, found Argyll too great a subject and had to decide either to break him or to ally with him. But it was also held by many that James and his brother wished to put pressure on Argyll not to destroy him but to force from him a surrender of some or all of his feudal powers. The numerous franchises of the earl and his superiorities made for unrest in the south-west Highlands. James, when king, intervened positively to give independence from the jurisdiction of the earl for part of their lands to the Camerons of Lochiel, and he had already knighted the old chief, Sir Ewen Cameron. It seems that James had embarked on a policy of building up his own following in the Highlands at the time of the trial of the earl, and may have encouraged his prosecution because the law of Scotland gave the crown a powerful weapon in silencing opponents. The flight of Argyll added to a growing and significant body of men, both English and Scottish, adhering to the court of William of Orange in the Netherlands and actively intriguing in British politics. William's wife Mary could expect to be heir presumptive when James succeeded to his joint throne, so the Protestant interest in both England and Scotland focussed on this court. Argyll, till this point in no way a conspicuous supporter either of presbyterianism or of civil liberty, came to stand for Whig opinion in Scotland.

The events of 1681 and after give some support to the idea that James was initiating a Highland policy in response to the consider- able presence that Highland armies had had in seventeenth-century politics. The policy was not thought out to any degree, but implied an attack on the heritable jurisdictions. By this date Highland chiefs were not unknow to Lowland society. It was already common for the sons of chiefs to be educated in the Lowlands, for their fathers were spontaneously seeing advantage in fulfilling this clause of the Statutes of Iona. Chiefs, as responsible for the behaviour of their clansmen, had frequently to go either to the Scottish Privy Council or to the king himself to fulfil this duty and explain episodes of trouble. Here Locheil's career is significant. It had been on such an expedition to Edinburgh that he had been knighted by James, and on another to London he was introduced to the court as 'the king of thieves', a remark that showed that James's stay in Scotland had made him familiar with the reputation of the Camerons. There is less evidence that James had thought out a positive policy for the Highlands beyond a desire to reduce the particular source of trouble, the franchises, but in his personal support of Locheil he had chosen one of the shrewder and more influential chiefs whose clan's posture of aggressive insecurity could make him a useful ally.

James was to need such allies, but at first all appeared well in his reign. It started with abortive invasions, of England by his illegitimate nephew Monmouth, of Scotland by Argyll. Monmouth had collected a sizeable army before he was defeated, but in Scotland defensive preparations had been made, in particular the confiscation of Argyll's jurisdictions in favour of rivals, and the putting of the western shores in readiness for attack. Various Highland chiefs had been ordered to stand by with companies of armed men, and the marquess of Atholl was placed at Inveraray with 500 followers. It is an interesting sidelight on the nature of Highland chieftainship that the removal of the formal instruments of authority from the earl of Argyll made it impossible for him to gain support. He was captured easily, executed on his earlier sentence, and the Campbells suffered little but the extra taxation to pay for the garrisoning by Atholl.

The effects of the two unsuccessful risings were, by removing Monmouth and hence his claim to Whig support for the crown, to focus Whig aspirations on William of Orange, and to create excessive parliamentary generosity towards James. His Scottish Parliament granted the excise in perpetuity. Monmouth's widow, the countess of Buccleuch, had her husband's portrait displayed on a vast canvas in the guise of St John the Baptist, but such idolatry could not give him a posthumous following in Scotland.

From this strong position in popular loyalty and finance James

VII's path was swiftly downwards in both kingdoms. He shared a pattern of miscalculation with his father, Charles I; the belief that if he had, or thought he had, a legal power he could act on it without the need to bargain and conciliate possible opposition. Even in an autocracy the monarch has to persuade and gain support, and neither kingdom was an autocracy. In England James saw that eventually he would have to repeal the Test Act which kept Catholics out of office, and that this would have to be done in Parliament, so he devoted his energies to the detailed restructuring of the power bases of local society to obtain a suitable Parliament. Meanwhile he used the dispensing power, of dubious legality, in Declarations of Indulgence, that is royal statements suspending the penal laws, in 1687 and 1688. In Scotland, where Parliament was known as less independent, he brought proposals before it in the spring of 1686. The bargain he tried to obtain was to be that the king would endeavour to secure 'a Free trade with England' and the Parliament would be mindful of the loyalty of the Roman Catholics and extend security and the right to their worship to them. Surprisingly the Parliament made an evasive reply, so in Scotland as in England James was forced back on his 'dispensing' power. Its legality had not been publicly called in doubt in Scotland as it had been in England under Charles II. James in Scotland certainly, and probably to a considerable degree in England, could have achieved the release of the Roman Catholic population from legal restrictions by simply dismantling any process of prosecution. Regular failure of conviction would, as it had done in the witchcraft trials of the 1670s, remove from those in local office any will to go through the tiresome and costly business of bringing cases to trial, without there being an issue of principle. In February 1686 James had issued his first Scottish announcement, allowing private worship to Roman Catholics and Quakers. He was still carrying on the attempt to force peace in the south-west by suppressing conventiclers. Even this cautious step was enough to persuade some of the nobility, including the normally hesitant duke of Hamilton, to refuse to sign the dutiful reply of the Privy Council. James pushed the Lord Advocate, Mackenzie, out of the government, and brought in a new type of civil servant politician in Sir John Dalrymple, Master of Stair. Most of the nobles on the Council were not prepared to show there the resistance they would show in Parliament, and the recent history of the earl of Argyll indicated that this was wise. In the summer of 1687 James went on to allow a general toleration of worship. The presbyterian ministers outed in 1662, or at least the survivors of this group, and those who had resigned since, were able to come into the open and organize a presbyterian Church, which was soon too strong to be repressed again.

James's policy was a severe blow to the established episcopal Church. In various episodes under his brother it had been forced to take orders from the state, on the issue of Indulgences to presbyterian ministers, on the dismissal of archbishop Burnet of Glasgow for protesting at the policy, and by the production of the Test Act of 1681 in Parliament with no prior consultation with the Church. Now it found itself shackled with a tradition of subservience to the crown while the non-established Churches had a free hand. Though it was unlikely that the bulk of the aristocracy would leave the established Church, James's two most immediate advisers, the Drummond brothers, holding the offices of Secretary of State and Chancellor, became Catholics.

Discontent in Scotland remained passive, though it can be discerned by resignations, by the abandonment in some cases of attempts to repress conventicles, and by the decision on the part of the leading lawyer of the day, Lauder of Fountainhall, to stop keeping a journal. In contrast to this passive lack of co-operation, and in striking contrast to the events precipitating the Great Rebellion, the Revolution of 1688-9 was solely made in England. The English political nation became alarmed at royal policy when this set out to break the link between the established aristocracy and political power. It was alarmed for the future by the birth of a son to James in June 1688, and further by the public promise of toleration in the second Declaration of Indulgence for England. True, this promised that a Parliament would be called, but in view of the changes of local power that the king had been securing this would not necessarily act as the aristocracy hoped. Even before it had become clear that the baby prince would survive contemporary child-rearing practices, the leading politicians of the day had written to William of Orange describing the discontent in the nation and inviting him to invade. By Christmas William and Mary were ensconced in Whitehall, James, his wife and son fugitives in France, and hardly a blow had been struck except where the invading officers had got involved in brawls. The aristocratic clique which had so manipulated things had established themselves in wealth and power and were to remain on top for the next two centuries.

It was not to be so easy a change in Scotland. There was no

powerful group of opposition lords ready to take over and even when the Parliament met issues and leadership were not clear. Because in Scotland monarchy had been mediated through a much weaker administration than in England, there was the less motive to repudiate its validity. On the other hand James had left the island, and any attempt to bring him back would mean conflict with the leaders in England. Hostility to James's Roman Catholic policy had had a divided base in Scotland, for none of the diverse elements, the presbyterians in their conventicles, the established Church, and the small bodies of outright dissenters, could claim to speak for as large a part of the nation as could the English Church. Rising respect for law and the rights of inheritance added to Scottish unease at disinheriting a king and his heir. The meeting of the Scottish Parliament took place a month after the English Convention Parliament had, without formally consulting the Scots, offered the crown of England to William. The delay was partly because all leading Scottish figures had rushed to London after the flight of James: experience of 1660 had taught that it would not pay to be away from court when drastic changes were being made.

It was a natural result of accepting a ready-made revolution that the Scots took some time to work out their detailed settlement. Yet once achieved it involved a much more drastic break with the past than did the English. The Scottish Revolution statements are the Claim of Right and the Articles of Grievances, and both go far beyond the cautious law-defining of the English Bill of Rights. The Claim of Right declared illegal several well-established practices, such as the quartering of troops on civilians or the system of extracting securities known as Law-Burroughs, and also declared that 'Prelacy', i.e. the existence of bishops in the Kirk, was 'a great and insupportable grievance' which 'ought to be abolished'. As an indicator of where power was to lie for the next 70 years it also labelled the proceedings against the late earl of Argyll unjust. In the ancient game of treason as played by the Scottish nobility the stakes had always been high for those unlucky enough to be caught on the losing side, and it was not normal for there to be posthumous rehabilitation. With similar ruthlessness the Articles of Grievances denounced the parliamentary committee, the Lords of the Articles. This attack, and that on bishops, are not surprising, for the Articles were compiled by a committee of eight nobles, eight shire representatives and eight burgesses, in other words a committee of the Articles as it would be without the controlling element of the

bishops. These statements set the stage for the two main new features of the revolutionary settlement, the independence of the
Scottish Parliament and the change in 1690 from an episcopal
Church government to presbyterianism. William and his consort
Mary had to agree to the dismantling of episcopacy because the
bishops held to allegiance to James: they had over the Restoration
period been deprived by government actions of any other base for
their episcopal theory than royalism. Parliament forced presbytery
on William, and this involved the restoration of the surviving outed
ministers from 1662 to their parishes, whether held by someone else
or not, and the removal of patronage from lay control to heritors and
kirksession combined. For a short while it looked as if the Church
would revert to the full ethos of Whig Remonstrance. Parishes had
been, in many cases, made available for occupation by systematic
'rabbling' of episcopal occupants. Crowds of unidentified men had
come, usually at night, and forced ministers to leave. There is
no reason to regard these disturbances as evidence of local
unpopularity, for everything points to an organized campaign of
thuggery to prejudge ecclesiastical issues.

Once prelacy had been declared a grievance, only those who had
been kept out of the episcopal Church could be regarded as free from
its taint. There were some 60 such ministers, who now declared
themselves the true presbyterian Church, formed the General
Assembly and proceeded to force suitable like-minded pastors on
the other 800 or so parishes. This process could not be carried
through quickly: in parts of the north-east it took several years. The
60 were under some harassment from William, who having asked
the Assembly to behave with moderation towards all those who
would accept the new political regime, could not help but notice
that, while protesting moderation, it was doing all it could to push
such men out on trumped up charges. The main difficulty in the
way of this policy was the fact that in parts of the north a whole
presbytery would be tainted with conformity so, until a vacancy
occurred naturally, there was no minister who could be recognized
as a bogus presbytery and used as a lever for the expulsion of others.

Much of this lay in the future, and the Scottish Parliament, when
it divided into 'Williamites' and 'Jacobites' over the basic question
of who was to be recognized as king did so without the realization
that the settlement would lead to systematic oppression of the
episcopalian element. Those who were Jacobite at this date included
those with personal involvement in James's rule, for instance

Graham of Claverhouse, now viscount Dundee, the Catholic clans in the Highlands, which category included most of the Macdonalds, those who opposed vigorously the power of the house of Argyll, about to be rehabilitated, and various individuals Catholic either by upbringing or sycophantic conversion. The episcopalian interest was half-hearted in loyalty. It had been thrown into disarray by the policy of James of insisting on total allegiance which implied in practice approval of his policy of promoting Catholicism. James's letter to the Parliament took this line declaring that the Parliament was in fact illegal, and, when read to Parliament, forced the more decided of the Jacobite interest to leave its meetings. Parliament was thus handed over to the Williamites, and this explains the strong language of the statements made. The crown, the Claim of Right declared, was forfeit, and was offered to William and Mary by a delegation of those established within Whig counsels who expected to do well under the new regime, the tenth earl of Argyll, not yet legally restored to the title, Sir James Montgomerie and Sir John Dalrymple, son to the great legist. It was not clearly stated to William but could be assumed that with the crown went acceptance of the Claim and the Grievances as a package deal.

Matters could not end with the coronation of William and Mary in May 1689 because much of the Jacobite interest remained unreconciled and unsubdued. James had already opened a campaign in Ireland to regain Britain. Some of the chiefs in the southern Highlands felt bound to support him for past favours or simple loyalty, others because their clans were unstable and based on no clear landholding status. Some, such as the Macgregors, the Macdonalds of Keppoch, the MacIans or Macdonalds of Glencoe and the Robertsons of Struan, had for long had a foothold in simple banditry. Dundee, forced for safety to leave the Edinburgh Parliament, retreated to the Highlands and collected a following there. At the end of July he fought his last battle, leading his Highlanders in the victory of Killiecrankie over Hugh Mackay of Scourie and government troops. It is ironic that this encounter should have seen oppose each other professional generals from Lowland and Highland, each in charge of a small army from the other's cultural group.

The Williamite government in Edinburgh, hearing of this defeat, showed that political issues were not seen in purely Scottish terms. It was prepared to abandon Scotland to the Jacobite forces, and return with an English army. This proved unnecessary, for after Dundee's death at the battle the Highland army largely dispersed. Only a small part remained to attempt to break through into the Lowlands, and was held by the covenanter regiment at Dunkeld.

Killiecrankie was, by any standards, a small, and in the event, inconclusive encounter. Its significance is as a repeat of the mid-century events when Montrose had brought Highlanders to play a major part in national politics. Before 1645 changes of clan power in the Highlands had not had much impact elsewhere. The growth of the territory controlled by the Mackenzies, and the intrusion into the main clan in Sutherland of a number of the Gordon family had not had wide repercussions, and for much of the early seventeenth century the trend of expansion of Campbell power had been held back by bad relations between the seventh earl of Argyll and the crown. The fracture of Clan Ian Mor, the southern Macdonald branch, into warring branches had led to great animosities and brutality, but had had relatively little impact outside its territory. In Alasdair MacColla (the son of Colkitto) in conjunction with Montrose, it had enabled the latter for a brief period to claim to have conquered Scotland, but Alasdair's aims had still lain in clan politics. Though he enjoyed defeating Lowlanders and Protestants his main ambition was to refound the strength of Clan Ian Mor and damage its immediate enemy, Campbell power. It was natural, perhaps inevitable, that after the battle of Kilsyth he should have left Montrose and gone back to the southern Highlands to fight for what he saw as his inheritance, and so it was in Kintyre eventually that his army had been wiped out. The defeat at Dunaverty ended for ever the idea of a resurrected Macdonald lordship of the Isles, though it still remained possible that a similar, almost independent lordship, would be created under the house of Argyll.

Later events in the Great Rebellion period show that the Highlands had come to accept more fully the concept of national identity. Clan chieftains and their men took part in the Engagement and Worcester campaigns. Iain Lom's poetry shows simple nationalist hostility to Cromwell's invasion, and Glencairn's rising drew on royalist and anti-English sentiment in many Highland figures. The adherence of Lord Lorne, Argyll's son and heir, to this campaign, while his father remained largely neutral showed that hostility to Campbell power could not be the full basis for support for Glencairn. It is likely that Glencairn would have received more support if he had been able to draw unambiguously on such hostility, but it is also the case that a genuine content of royalism was in existence by the 1650s in the Highlands. It was always easier for Highland society to think in terms of allegiance to a person than to either a policy or an institution. Personal adherence had been manifested in 1651, during Charles II's visit to Scotland, when the hereditary piper to MacLeod of MacLeod, Patrick Mor MacCrimmon, commemorated a brief meeting in his famous pibroch, 'I gave a kiss to the king's hand'. Argyll power again expanded in the Restoration period: the new earl had been left somehow to pay off the debts of the Huntly estate from the time that his father had controlled it, and he did so by prosecuting the debtors, particularly the McLeans of Duart, in his own court. He was given support in this by Lauderdale, whose policy was that of the unjust steward. The relationship between Campbells and the crown was broken by the exile of this earl of Argyll in 1681, and temporarily destroyed by his rebellion in 1685. This event brought the anti-Campbell clans to support James VII with a persistance in their loyalty which owed little to any qualities he had as an individual, though in the case of Locheil it was the result of active favouritism. National consciousness and regional injustice founded a more persistent 'loyalty' than that shown by the adherents of Montrose. The chiefs who had fought at Killiecrankie came to consider themselves bound to support James unless he released them from this obligation.

The adherence of clan leaders to national issues was a response to the fact that Montrose and Cromwell, separately, had shown that the Highlands could be successfully invaded. The main routes though the mountain blocks were known: the problems of supply had been mestered, and Inverlochy (Fort William to us) had been recognized as a vital base. The Restoration government therefore had not had a 'Highland problem' in the same terms as it had existed for earlier governments. Clan chiefs could be brought to heel when the central government wished. The chiefs themselves had developed a second persona. They wished to be landed aristocrats in much the same way as were Lowland nobles, though with extra powers over clansmen. Imperialism by one clan over the lands of another came to be by judicial rather than military process. The Highlands as a whole were sufficiently at peace in this period for the cattle droving trade to develop. The *Register of the Privy Council* gives an impression of constant concern over issues of Highland law and order, pursuing wrongdoers, taking sureties, even getting information about misdeeds by torture. There were groups of broken men engaged in plunder and cattle stealing, or extracting the protection money known as 'blackmail'. But this concern must be seen in perspective: it had not existed in the 1620s or 1630s, except when Highlanders raided into Lowland areas, because the Privy Council of those days had been aware that it had not power in the Highlands except by commissioning one clan to attack another. In the Restoration period Highland pacification and the spread into the area of authority of the central government were following, some 60 years later, the same track as had control of the Borders. In the fourteenth and fifteenth century the heads of the great Border surnames had acted as petty kings, even to the making of international treaties such as that made by the Douglases and the Lord of the Isles with Edward IV in 1462. They had been forced in the late sixteenth century to accept control by the crown, but until the 1630s their area had still been the setting for various types of banditry by groups fragmented from the great surname units. But since the Borders had become, in James VI's phrase, 'the Middle Shires', the monarchy had been able, admittedly by some degree of special exertion, to control these groups. It had had to do so because they were capable of disturbing the relationship between Scotland and England. Restrained and pacified, the border area turned to economic development and, eventually, to depopulation in the eighteenth century. Pacification of the Highlands was, at least under the later Stewarts, a less urgent priority. The disturbers of the peace there made no direct attack on the legitimacy of the Restoration government. The energies of that government had been deployed on the section of Scotland that did make such an attack, the south-west. So the task of completing the assimilation and subduing of the Highlands had been postponed until the mid eighteenth century, when it was to take place in a very different political, social and economic climate.

After Dunkeld, therefore, the government was concerned only with immediate and practical issues in the Highlands, and the outstanding one was whether the resistant Jacobite clans were to be pacified or defeated. With the end of the war in Ireland in the summer of 1690 this remained the outstanding security issue. In 1691 the chiefs and principal vassals were given until the end of the year to swear allegiance to the new regime. James VII's letter releasing them from his cause did not arrive in the Highland area until just on Christmas. Even if anxious to conform the more distant clan chiefs had not the time to comply. The troublesome small sept of the MacIans of Glencoe, well known as cattle stealers, one of those which had not conformed in time, was picked on for a display of terror.

The story of the misuse of power and abuse of hospitality which lies behind the small-scale massacre of Glencoe in February 1692 is well known. What marks it off in the bloodstained annals of clan warfare is the effect it produced. Partly for reasons of party politics it was used to drive out of power William's Secretary of State, Sir John Dalrymple, master of Stair, in 1695, with the parliamentary declaration that it had been murder, 'slaughter under trust' and therefore particularly heinous. This was a step in the assimilation of Highland and Lowland society. At the time of Montrose's campaign neither cultural group would have applied such an expression to treacherous dealings with the other.

Acceptance of the new monarchy involved Scotland not only in civil war and slaughter but also in participation in a large-scale European war from 1689 to 1696 and again from 1702 to 1713 in the so-called war of the Spanish Succession, the first of the long eighteenth-century wars for control of trade and colonies. Heavy demands were made for troops and money. Parliament experimented with new taxes, poll taxes in 1693, '95 and '98, the hearth tax of 1690 and the cess at a high level. Poll and hearth taxes, even when graduated, have a marked regressive character. It is difficult to say what level of taxation the economy could bear in normal years, but study of local records shows the demoralizing effects of the particular situation of the 1690s: war, dislocation of trade, harvest failure and the damage done to the developing system of poor relief by the 'outing' of episcopal ministers. Some of these ministers and their families were on the roads as vagrants, begging their way. So were discharged or deserting soldiers and sailors, and tenants evicted from failure to pay their rents. Poor law records for this period show the stresses of society even before famine struck. The main financial burden of the wars was borne, of course, by the richer country, England, and not unreasonably since the issues which had led to the wars, the Protestant succession, the alliances against France, the prevention of a major power in the Low Countries, imperialism in trade matters, were all much more markedly English than Scottish interests.

The story of Parliament in the reign of William III is paradoxical. It is the habit of historians, who look at things predominantly from the point of view of the desire of the executive to secure a smoothly working administration, to deplore the behaviour of the great magnates, Atholl, Argyll, the third and fourth dukes of Hamilton and the duke of Queensberry. These men are accused of concentrating on selfish aims for power and, since the interests of each clashed with those of the others, there was bound to be a majority of the great men working against the government, whichever of these was in office. But to be surprised at this, as it appears that William was, is to show a lack of understanding of the nature of public interest for a magnate. The first duty of a duke of Hamilton was to the interests of the house of Hamilton, and so of its supporters. In the case of this house the head had also a residual national obligation because if the succession were to go back to a link made before James VI the house stood nearest to the throne. The second strand of obligation is the reason why, in every crisis, the duke of Hamilton, whichever one he was, tried to sit on the fence. Argyll had inherited the posture of presbyterianism, and this gave what was basically a family stand a national dimension. The existence of their jurisdictions made these magnates petty kings within their own domain, and, like kings, they coveted territory and power beyond their domains. Politics in revolution Scotland is more understandable as a local manifestation of that early modern feature, international anarchy, than as a period in the growth of the self-conscious nation state. Traditionally the institutions of the state, which were poorly developed, had not been strong enough to create an aura of patriotism, except during foreign invasions, and the central government had whatever value it did have to such great men as an area for bargaining, a means of obtaining power over men and lands in return for occasions of military or political support. For a time in the later years of James VI the creation of a conscientious and united service aristocracy had given the crown a power base in the country, which Charles I by ignoring and by taking his advice from men of no standing, had destroyed. Charles I had attempted and Charles II had partly succeeded in using the episcopate as instruments of government. Charles II's main success had came from the willingness of a shell-shocked aristocracy to let the king's favourite, Lauderdale, run things. Since then the aristocracy had recovered much of its nerve and some of its power, and become much less governable.

War and taxation and the need for legislation meant that a Parliament had to meet every two or three years, and these meetings gave splendid opportunities for magnate disgruntlement. Temporary alliances would be made to thwart the ministry. The crown had not enough, in benefits, offices or privileges to build up inside the parliamentary body a strong court party. Those who think in terms of monarchic policy naturally see these opposition policies as negative or unpatriotic. But if it is remembered that the policy of the monarch was based on a combination of William's European policy, which had brought him to Britain in the first place, and English commercial interests, these adjectives become less appropriate. In the 1698 Parliament, for instance, the war was at an end for the time being and the central government had more room to manoeuvre; the country party, as the opposition had come to call itself, wished to have debated the bad state of the country, in another year of famine, a ban on the import of English cloth and French goods, a *habeas corpus* measure and the Darien Scheme. The court party prevented a vote on all these issues. It is difficult to see the court party in this instance as the representative of Scottish patriotism.

It was the Darien scheme in particular which showed the system of an independent Parliament in Scotland to be unworkable. The original proposers of the scheme in Scotland were probably not aware that the threat to the English East India Company would lead the English Parliament to resolve its own divisions and prohibit English participation. That was awkward for William's dual position. In any case, since English views on foreign policy were dominated by trade and colonial issues, and William's by the long-term balance of power in Europe, once it became clear that the Scots were going to upset Spain by planting a colony in Panama, the king had no option but to denounce and oppose them. Spain was a vital factor in William's European alliance. That the Darien venture was a failure arose from its inherent fatuosity, not the king's opposition. Its long-term significance was that it showed the king he could not continue to drive two unlinked horses. It also gave the Scots an unjustified sense of grievance against the English, which made their Parliament even more unmanageable. It is not surprising that the idea of a legislative union of the two countries, which had been raised and brushed aside in 1689 should be brought forward by William in 1700 and 1701, and considered seriously enough for commissioners from both countries to meet in ineffective discussion through the winter of 1702-3.

So from one point of view the Scottish political structure, as settled by the Revolution, was a failure It produced political chaos, religious bitterness and oppression and social stress. From another point of view it was remarkably successful as an interim stage. In the short period of a Parliament capable of making its own legislative programme various Acts which remained on the statute book for a long time and were of real significance came through. The Act of Patronage settled, for a generation, what was to remain a major issue in the Church and settled it against the interests of landed society and in the interests of the dominant presbyterian clique. The landed interest secured a valuable change in two Acts, one 'Anent lands Lying in Runrig', the other on 'Division of Commonties', which together gave it a freer hand in the control and development of open waste areas and easier reorganization of estates. When 'Improvement' became the fashion in the later eighteenth century landowners found the clarity of this legislation a means of avoiding the expense of private enclosure acts. In the Act for Settling Schools of 1696 an important step was made in the future pattern of local government. It was not this Act which was the source of the system of parish schools: the formative statutes for this had been those of 1616 and 1633. But the Act defined the financial obligations for the support of these schools. Landowners were to be rated for them, but could pass half the burden to their tenantry. A similar rating division was later adopted if a parish had to raise money for poor relief by assessment. The administration of poor relief in assessed parishes thus came back from the estate to the parish, an important step in making for effective support.

The main legislation of this period has as common feature the defining and emphasizing of the position of the possessor of land, that is of property rather than feudal superiority. Landowners, whether tenants is chief or not, were given rights and duties which tended to emphasize the unity of the landowning class and cut it off from its tenantry. The position of the lairds, enhanced by the inflation of earlier days, the reorganization carried through by Charles I and the advantages won during the Great Rebellion, thus received legislative recognition. Upward progress of the landowning class was accompanied by the reduced independence of lesser folk. Coal miners and salt-workers had, by legal definition, been pushed into serfdom, a state which only enlightened self-interest of the owners of the mines had prevented from being extended to lead miners. The relatively independent birlaw court had been submerged in the more authoritative baron court, and now the concept of property in land was becoming absolute.

Local government was, however, shown by the famine years of the 1690s to be as yet unable to cope with a major disaster. The Privy Council put out proclamations and Parliament passed Acts, one giving statutory power to the proclamations, the other containing different definitions, but even those parishes which attempted in this confusion to fulfil their duties experienced famine-based epidemics and demographic crisis. The central government was not yet strong enough for it to penalize parishes where powerful landowners refused to support their tenantry. All 'the same eighteenth-century local government was to be based at the parish level on the legislation of the 1690s.

Part of the contrast between the chaotic nature of political life after the Revolution and the creativity of the liberated Parliament may be due to the quality of the men William chose to serve him. When he came from the Netherlands the king was in the habit of listening to advice from refugees such as William Carstares who certainly knew the complexion of opposition politics under Charles II, and he also put faith in the Dutchman Bentinck, who received the English title of Portland. Neither refugees nor Portland did very well in assessing Scottish politics as they had developed in the 1690s. William tried to govern through a mixture of refugees and their kinsmen, Lord Melville, James Johnston, Sir John Dalrymple, master of Stair, and the medium level of landowning nobles who had sustained previous administrations, the marquess of Tweeddale for instance. These lesser families were, in many cases, to show themselves as determined in their promotion of family interest as were the magnates. At times it was almost as if, as in the later sixteenth century, the king's own servants were to be the source of brawls and distrubances. The Privy Council not only found itself unable to exercise influence over the General Assembly: it also was often forced to recognize that important decisions on Scottish affairs were being made in London and with weight given to the advice of English ministers. From 1700 on, under William and his successor Anne, James, VII's younger daughter, the Council ceased to have any independence in government. Its function was to do the will of the London court as smoothly as possible, which meant that under William mainly the king, but under Anne the English ministry decided things. So much is clear from its surviving record.

At the time that Scottish policy became dominated by the English cabinet the government of England was only slowly on the way to stability itself. In the 1690s the English political scene was as sectional and unstable as the Scottish. It was only under Anne that the party system began to coalesce into large opposing groups, the manipulation of 'places' and other benefits became a regular system of maintaining the core of a government, the attempt to remove all place-holders from Parliament was turned into a more limited scheme requiring their re-election, and opposition parties abandoned the system of 'tacking' by which measures unwelcome to the administration were attached to vital finance bills. The English Parliament, after a fairly rough time, saw the dominant parties prepared to live with each other by defined rules. The Scottish Parliament, new to the pleasures of extremism, was taking a little longer to get there.

Settling down in this way would mean accepting the basic features of the constitution, and in an important aspect this was a harder lesson to learn in Scotland than in England. The Scots were coming to focus their political life on Parliament: though an important aspect of it was still conducted in the General Assembly there was no longer any suggestion of effective legislation by the body which historically had most closely overlapped Parliament, the Convention of Estates. But the Scottish Parliament never attained to the position of the true centre of national identity held by the English. This maybe a reason why parliamentary kingship, which was all that the last two Stewarts could be credited with, was a less acceptable solution to political problems than in England. In this period Jacobitism, that is the political expression of a desire to revert to the older Stewart line, becomes more evident than it had been in the immediate Revolution period. It was sustained by a very real sense of episcopalian grievance. It took some time for the 60 who made the General Assembly to get rid of over two thirds of the clergy. In some parishes they were never able to force out ministers who had acquiesced in episcopacy and were protected by powerful patrons. But the policy of ejection was continued for many years and produced a deep alienation from the presbyterian Church and the Whig political system which promoted it, especially in the north-east. Landowners, who resented being deprived of patronage and the kin of the outed clergy held a sympathy for it in other areas. In England genuine Jacobitism existed in some old-fashioned and some predominantly Catholic areas, and most political leaders kept contact with the court in exile as an insurance policy, but that was all. In Scotland the sentiment appealed not only to those who valued hereditary rights in land but to all who disapproved of presbyterian intransigeance, high wartime taxation or the whole trend of a changing society. For many years Jacobitism appeared to supply an acceptable alternative.

The Jacobite issue became active again in 1700 with the death of the only child of the princess Anne who had seemed likely to grow to adult years. In response to this and in a flurry of irritation with William the English Parliament settled the crown, with some limitations, eventually on the surviving Protestant line of descent from James VI, that of Sophia, wife to the Elector of Hanover. It did not bother, any more than it had in 1688, to discuss the matter with the Scots. Meanwhile, though, there was still Anne as heir presumptive, and the princess, though a poor physical specimen, was only in her late thirties. There was plenty of time for the Scottish Parliament to develop its own ideas about the crown of Scotland.

This was the background to the abortive Union negotiations of 1702-3, held after Anne's succession, and to the later ones of 1705-6. By 1705 the Scottish Parliament had done much to show that the existing relationship between the two countries of Britain was unworkable. Politicians had been given a rich opportunity towards this when Anne's English advisers encouraged her to evade the requirements of the Act of Security of 1696, to adjourn the meeting of the Scottish Parliament until the War of Spanish Succession was well under way, and then to reconvene illegally the old Parliament. The opposition delayed business and created such heat that a genuinely legal new Parliament called in 1703 was also intractable. The recognition that Scottish affairs were effectively being decided in London led to drastic legislation by this Parliament, the Act anent Peace and War of 1703 which insisted on the right of the Scottish Parliament to decide such issues for Scotland, and the Act of Security, delayed in acceptance by the crown but eventually forced on it, reaffirming the right of the Scottish Parliament to make a different choice of monarch from the English after Anne's death if Scotland had not by then been granted freedom of trade with England and her colonies. The Scottish Parliament had reminded the English unpleasantly of its rights over Scottish trade by allowing the export of wool, on which the English cloth interest wanted an embargo, and the import of wines from France. With the impossibility of preventing smuggling across the Border between the two countries both Acts were seen by the English as blows at English mercantilist policy.

The Scottish demand for freedom of trade with England and her possessions was not new. There had been frequent representations by the Scottish Privy Council to Charles II about particular features of English tariffs. That the Scots did not hold by free trade as a general policy is shown by their willingness to put restrictions on Irish commodities: it was the special privilege of the rich English market they wanted. James VII's Indulgence policy had held this out as an offer to them though there is no reason to think that it was his to give. By then the Scots were conscious of suffering from the isolating effect of the Union of the crowns. Tied to a foreign policy increasingly dictated by English imperialism, they had been forced to engage in wars with their overseas markets. By the 1680s these markets were closing, partly because of these wars, though also partly because of deliberate protectionism. Only the English market, always the most important to Scots when available, was not affected by war, but it too was at risk from protectionism. The new high levels of duty made necessary by the recent and expensive wars were contracting Scotland's trade. The result was that in a time already notable for its economic and social stress, there was a growing balance of payments crisis. This was shown in the export of money, and that export dried up internal business. The famine of the 1690s, involving expensive grain imports, and the losses of Darien, followed by a bank crisis in 1704 all accentuated the cash problem.

Of course in part the economic crisis was artificial. The balance of payments could have been righted by a patriotic policy of self-denial. Some of the imports were necessary items for her own production; iron, timber, salt and cordage all come in this category. Also necessary was the whole spectrum of sophisticated manufactures which gave the Scots tools and household comforts. A further category of imports was simply luxuries for the upper classes – sugar, wines, dried fruits, silks, spices, pictures, hangings and arms. Theoretically in a period of national emergency these could have been dispensed with: this would be the policy of a modern government faced with such a problem. But in practice at this time no administration could have forced the powerful citizens who used these goods to do without luxury. Even if such rulings had passed through the aristocratic Parliament, the country did not have a civil service capable of enforcing the policy at the ports. The Scottish coast line was an invitation to smuggling, and the venality of the customs service an invitation to fraud.

The economic crisis was showing itself in the trade depression of 1704, and a spate of pamphlets was produced over the future of Scotland and the issue of Union. There was a body of sophisticated merchant opinion well aware of economic problems. It is not clear how much of this, except in very general terms, got through to the consciousness of the landed aristocracy. But landed society as a whole was deeply affected by anything that threatened the sale of estate produce. This included the leading Scottish exports of linen and cattle, and others also had significance; wool, coal, salt fish and grain. Linen and cattle found their market entirely in England. It was a blow to this vital trade when the English Parliament set out to bring the Scots to heel in 1705 with the Alien Act, the threat to cut off these trades and to treat all Scots as foreigners if the Scots did not open Union negotiations. The effect of this would have been damaging to more than landowners, for there were many groups of Scottish merchants settled in England. Union negotiations would, of course, involve settling the Scottish succession in the same way as the English.

Union negotiations had not only taken place just before, at the start of Anne's reign, but at various times during the seventeenth century, usually under pressure from the crown but with no great enthusiasm from the two countries. Those of 1669 had failed apparently through Scottish intransigeance, but perhaps (the evidence does not support a closer identification) also with royal complicity. In 1689 things had never got off the ground, but the discussions of 1702–3 had settled basic terms, so that each country knew what the other would regard as essential. An incorporation of Parliaments would be the English demand, freedom of trade the Scottish. Further features had also been worked out before the uncertainties of the Scottish parliamentary situation and the heat generated by the apperent illegality had stalled discussion.

Since freedom of trade had been dangled in front of the Scots by James VII and had been clearly defined in these negotiations as essential, it is somewhat surprising to find modern historians prepared seriously to doubt whether the politicians of Scotland entered into negotiations for this purpose, rather than for their own immediate political advantage. The correspondence of the politicians is used as evidence for the latter theory, and since in all ages a week is a long time in politics one should not be surprised that this correspondence tends to support the belief that all that mattered to these men was what could personally be secured in the next few days. On the same sort of material it would be open for scholars to decide that in the mid eighteenth century Britain had no economic policy, even though the country was pursuing an imperialist and exclusionist policy over trade and empire.

Any treaty of Union would have to be acceptable to the men represented in Parliament, that is the gentry and the town merchants, and these were groups intensively, if not unanimously, interested in trade. To any landowner trade was the elastic sector of his estate's economy and therefore the quickest away to wealth. The merchant class, though desirous of expansion in trade, was nervous of anything that might alter existing patterns. Small merchants and craftsmen in the royal burghs were at risk from English rivalry in trade and manufactures. The English market was less significant to burgesses than to landowners because most of the trade with England did not originate in the burghs. But within the merchant group there were men with close relatives or business associates settled in England and therefore threatened by the Alien Act. There were also men who hoped to gain a share in trade with America or to join the East India Company. A sizeable section, therefore, of the voting power in Parliament had economic interests which would be promoted by Union. But these people were also open to the influence of the Church, and the Church opposed Union on the grounds that it would put the established presbyterian order at risk. English bishops sat in the House of Lords, so episcopacy was built into the political system. The English Church was regarded as dangerously erastian because it allowed influence or control by the central institutions of crown and Parliament. The covenanting remnant came to join the established Church in Scotland, while claiming that in the past this remnant had been the only true Church, and Union with England would involve the acceptance of a continued uncovenanted Church in England. It would in fact embarrass both countries by forcing the recognition that Churches would be allowed to differ. The past history of each country gave grounds for suspicion that closer contact would lead to attempts to subvert one or other of the Churches. Scots could recall the anglicizing policy of Charles I and the English had the express words of the Solemn League and Covenant to heed. The Church, as such, had now no formal representation in the Scottish Parliament but it was the body most easily able to raise a mob through inflammatory preaching, so its views had to be listened to.

Trade and religion were thus motives mutually in opposition. In practice Union would have to be devised by the politicians, the small group who provided holders of office. For these, trade was more important than religion, but at any moment the permanent aggrandizement of the family of an individual would take precedence over other motives, for that was what sent men into politics. The course by which the country headed for Union was bound to be erratic. One crucial step was the breakaway from the opposition 'country party' of what came to be called either the 'new' party or the 'Squadrone Volante', a group of frustrated politicians anxious for office, and led by the marquess of Tweeddale. Opposition parties are always liable to disintegration since they lack the material advantages of power and profits which can hold together a court party in spite of internal animosities. The English political structure had only recently seen a similar drastic breach and reassembly. The existence of this 'new' party altered the map of Scottish politics. For one thing it simplified the state of the Country party, making it nearer to a party of principle and less a miscellaneous voting partnership. The figure of Fletcher of Saltoun became conspicuous in it, and we can see his aims in the amendments he had tried to make to the Act of Security. These would have created a weak executive and a powerful Parliament in which the influence of the aristocracy was balanced by greater power to the gentry, the 'baronage' of Scotland. The constitution would have been reminiscent of that of 1641, but was of doubtful practicality. Greater representation of the gentry would not have appealed to an aristocratic Parliament, nor the loss of royal influence to the Court party. Opposition to the Court party also included the hard core of Jacobites.

The breakaway Squadrone made things more unstable but opened up possibilities. It did not stop the anti-English feeling, which was conspicuous in the year 1704–5: indeed since at the crucial time it provided the commissioner, Tweeddale, it acquiesced in such feeling so far as to put through the judicial murder of three members of the crew of the *Worcester* (an English ship accused without evidence of piracy against the Darien traders) as well as the Act of Security. The reaction to Scottish intransigeance in England was not only the Alien Act, but also the restoration of the old Court party under Queensberry, and it was in his ministry that the last negotiations for Union were initiated.

Union, as worked out in the spring of 1706 took forward what had been settled in 1703, the Scots agreeing on the Hanoverian succes-

sion and that Union should be incorporating, the English on opening trade. It also carried out what had been raised before but not
settled, compensation for the demise of the Darien scheme. A good
deal of negotiation took place over the levels of taxation, understandably since England had recently become a nation with a high
burden of tax. From these discussions came the Equivalent, a
payment of nearly £400,000 to compensate the Scots for their future
share in funding the English debt, and for paying off their own
crown debts as well as subsidizing the Darien investors. A period of
reduced tax level for Scotland was agreed, and a further Equivalent,
money set aside to promote industry. In a period where the hand of
government was accepted as light there was no insistence on
uniformity of law. The Scottish heritable jurisdictions were
deliberately left alone. In many lesser matters of government,
weights and measures, coinage and the practices of the Exchequer,
the English system was to prevail. More significant of English
domination was not so much the small size of the Scottish parliamentary representation, 16 peers and 45 members of Parliament,
but the fact that this was to be the engrafting of Scottish membership into the existing English Parliament. English parliamentary
traditions and procedure were much more advanced than Scottish,
and the role of Parliament in English life so much more significant,
that this step may have seemed essential to the English commissioners. But since Scottish national identity was a long-established
concept, it was a major surrender for the Scots.

By the autumn of 1706 the treaty was worked out, and enough
inducements promised to give a reasonable prospect of Parliamentary success for the measure. A sophisticated machinery for
securing the adherence of enough voting power to see parliamentary business was to be set up later in the eighteenth century,
starting crudely in 1714 with a Commission of Police which rapidly
became a collection of lucrative sinecures. Enough of such a
machinery already existed to smooth the conduct of affairs, yet in
fact the distribution of honours and money on this occasion was
small. Some peerages were given, and some payments of arrears of
salary, amounting in all to £20,000, were secretly made. The sums
were small even in the terms in which the parliamentary classes
worked, in the revenues of their estates, the benefits to be made
from office or the fines which in the past had been incurred through
political mistakes. Their smallness suggests that they really were
arrears and not bribes. The main offer which the English dominated

government could make to Scottish politicians was of course a share in power, and about this there were reservations not yet apparent. In the upper strata of government and the army Scots would be eligible during the eighteenth century for the second place only, but this was never openly stated.

It was still necessary to get the volatile Scottish Parliament to agree to the treaty. A vital step in this process was to be an Act assuring the Scottish Church establishment. Even with the prospect of this, discontent from the presbyterian faction was one of the elements which gave at least the appearance of uncertainty to the whole final parliamentary session in Scotland. Parliament also meant an opportunity for politicians to display in their rhetoric the values which they thought ought to prevail. Not all of these pieces of oratory should be taken at face value. The discussion opened with a speech by Seton of Pitmedden, of Squadrone affiliation, whose theme was expressed in one sentence which set the seal on Scotland's economic prospects: 'This nation, being poor, and without force to protect its commerce, cannot reap great advantage by it, till it partake of the trade and protection of some powerful neighbour nation.' It was answered by some splendid language from Lord Belhaven: 'None can destroy Scotland, save Scotland's self.' 'If we unite' he stated, 'we want neither men nor sufficiency of all manner of things.' It was a patriotic declamation which would ready better if Lord Belhaven's idea of patriotism had not allowed him to let his tenantry starve in the famine of 1690 when he and the other heritors of the parish of Spott refused to fulfil their obligations in relief.

The issue was not as simple as either speaker implied in 1706. The majority of the Scots were prepared to surrender nominal independence but the terms were more than the apparent ones of an offer of trade. So long as there was a claimant to both the thrones of England and Scotland, there was no way in which the Scots could have their own separate monarch without the prospect of eventual war with England over the claims which such a monarch must necessarily have to the English throne. Peace within Britain was a tacit but not a negligible part of the bargain. It might be necessary for Scottish self-esteem for there to be riots in Glasgow, near riot in Edinburgh, petitions, addresses and hostile sermons, for the thoroughly unpopular measure of Union to pass, but there was realism in its acceptance.

7

Working Out Union

Eighteenth-century Britain, in which Scotland was now an integral part, was a country where government kept a low profile. The function of ministers was foreign policy, not home affairs. The latter were left to local landowners in one or other capacity and to burgh councils. Taxation was at a high level, but there were strong forces acting against the raising of it effectively. Once the issues of succession and Church establishment were settled early in the eighteenth century there was little demand for major change, and Parliaments met usually without a programme of legislation. The changed position of Scotland therefore did not much impinge on her ordinary citizens, many of whom did not come within the scope of central institutions even in matters of law and order. This basic fact makes it difficult for the much governed people of today, in a world still dominated by the nineteenth-century intrusive concept of legislation for social ends, to appreciate the impact of Union in its own century. For most people in most matters life was unchanged, the culture they lived in still local or national according to their status, the issues within which choice had to be made still local, the regulating powers of Church, state and neighbourhood, which attempted to control them, still wielded by the same men as before. Central government became even weaker than before, for in an unwise decision for party advantage the Privy Council was abolished in 1708. That was the only important change.

Union did, however, alter things for those with a foothold in any aspect of local power, and it rapidly altered things for the worse as the calculated generosity and good temper of 1706–7 wore off in England. The Scots who had suspicions that their country's views would be swamped in a largely English Parliament were proved right, and so were those English who feared that Scots in Parliament would give, servilely, new strength to the administration. The

Scottish fears were first justified over the extension in 1709 to Scotland of the English law and penalties for treason, the English by the creation of sinecure offices in Scotland. The Kirk came to see the protection given by the Act of Security as inadequate. Merchants in England found the Scots engaged in making quick profits on imports before the new high level of custom duty was established, and subsequently building up their capital by systematic customs fraud. Merchants in Scotland found that free trade, granted, did not immediately open markets, and that in particular it took a long time to get in on the attractive Indian trade. There was scope for disillusionment. A particular Scottish grievance suggests carelessness or venality on the part of their Commissioners for Union, when it was shown that the drafting of the Act carefully left room for appeal from the Court of Session to the House of Lords. That one of the early cases which established this, Greenshield's case, was, in practice, concerned with the right of an episcopalian minister to use the Anglican prayer books, was an affront to many decades of liturgical prejudice. The Union Commissioners were drawn from the group of men who attended court and it is unlikely that they were unaware of the appellant jurisdiction of the House of Lords or that the wording of the treaty left a neat space for its insertion.

A further pressure, which might be seen to have a more narrow impact but which was, all the same, felt to be a national slight, came out over the refusal of the House of Lords to allow the duke of Hamilton to sit there for a new English peerage. The Lords were nervous of increasing the administration's voting power. The mechanism of electing the Scottish peers was crude, involving for most peers the decision to vote entirely either for the list of the government or that of the opposition, and so tended to mean the implanting in the Lords of 16 hand-picked government supporters. But the exclusion vote bent the terms of the treaty of Union.

A more serious bending was the restoration of Church patronage in 1712, which directly overruled the Church's Act of Security. This was a blow against the presbyterian system as settled after the Revolution. It was also a reaffirmation of the rights of landed property. The abolition of patronage in 1691 had done much to push the landowning class into the episcopalian confession: its restoration did not bring it fully back to the fold, and so in many parishes patronage lay in the hands of men who were not members of the Church. There could easily develop a local feud between elders and heritors, and in cases where the issue of patronage led to the active intervention of the presbytery over an appointment the feud could be lasting.

The discontent produced by Parliamentary decisions was voiced in an attempt to get the Union dissolved in 1713. This was unsuccessful since the discontented Scots were a small minority in Parliament. It culminated in the support or acquiescence of many Scots in the Jacobite rising of 1715. There had been a threat of invasion by the Jacobite claimant, James VII's son, the 'Old Pretender', then a young man, in 1708, and the issue was made likely to recur by Anne's death in 1714, particularly since the Hanoverian hair was not the lively old intellectual, Sophia, but her very Germanic son, George. However, the English Tory party, which had been dabbling in Jacobite intrigue just before this event, was disrupted by an internal dispute when the queen's health suddenly failed, and the succession of George I took place smoothly. It was a snub and dismissal given by George I to a Scottish politician, John Erskine, sixth earl of Mar, who had done much to manage the passage of the Act of Union through the Scottish Parliament, which triggered off the rising. Mar was able to gather into an army not only the anti-Campbell clans of the south-west Highlands, but also a considerable contingent from the northern Lowlands, as well as the men he forced out from his own estate. The presence of an individual in a Jacobite army did not necessarily mean possession of enthusiasm for the cause of the Old Pretender, for a man might be there by force, as an insurance policy for his family's future position, for discontented episcopal sentiment or for pending bankruptcy. It is also possible to see in this rising a protest over the steady loss of power by northern Scotland to the south, which had been going on for two centuries: from the early sixteenth century all major political decisions had been swung by the south.

Those kept out of power by the Revolution settlement and who went in to the rising were able to raise a large army which, if properly handled, ought to have defeated its government forces under the duke of Argyll and broken through to the central valley. All descriptions of the forces show a strong preponderence on the Jacobite side. Credible estimates of the numbers suggest an army of 12,000 under Mar, with 4,000 present at the final battle, and 4,000 under Argyll, also shrinking for the encounter. Conscript Highlanders tended to melt away homewards whenever their chiefs were not present. Most landed families had representatives on the rebel side, and there was widespread ambivalence, sometimes passive support, probably increased by Mar's promise to secure the repeal of Union. The main core of support lay in the Lowlands benorth Tay and in the central and south-western Highlands.

Unfortunately for the Jacobite claim neither popular support nor a military preponderance of at least three to one could make the earl of Mar into a general or the Old Pretender into a charismatic leader. The comment on the Pretender's management of affairs by Fletcher of Saltoun sums up this latter handicap: he stated that 'it convinces everybody who formerly did not believe it that he is of the Family'. After occupying the upland areas of Perthshire for some weeks of exceptional hard weather and fighting an inconclusive but bloody battle at Sheriffmuir, the Jacobite army began to disintegrate, and the Pretender took ship for France. The legal establishment of Scotland then did its effective best to ensure that practically no penalties could be brought to bear on those involved.

The rising shows that there was a considerable reservoir of discontent in Scotland, particularly in the episcopalian north-east, but London policy did nothing to meet this. The episcopal Church had been so obviously involved that the tacit toleration which had been extended to it was ended, and efforts were made to close down episcopal 'meeting houses'. This did little to win over sentiment in the north-east, and the established Church in that area experienced many episodes of violence and feuding in presbytery meetings which relates more probably to religious resentment than to native barbarity. Eventually episcopalian sentiment in the Lowlands was to become confined to groups in the upper classes, and at its strongest to take the form of refusal to take the oaths of allegiance rather than any positive activity. This policy prevented its holders serving as Justices of the Peace or freeholders to elect Members of Parliament (in some cases till nearly the end of the century), and so did not trouble government much.

National resentment against each other continued in both countries after the 1715. English merchants in the early 1720s were complaining, and on good grounds, of customs fraud. For several years the quantity of tobacco exported from Glasgow and on which a 'drawback' of duties paid was claimed, was greater by over a million pounds in weight than the amount legally imported. By this deceit Scottish merchants were building up their capital from the pockets of those who paid more, if not complete, attention to the laws, a process which was to be crucial in the ability of Glasgow houses to compete in the more highly capitalized trade of the mid century. The customs service was obliged to send up to Scotland more English officials, in the hope that they would not rapidly develop venial connection, and on the same theory, to move Scottish port officials every three years from one port to another. A strong element in Scottish thought at all social levels was that customs and excise regulations should be treated as advisory rather than mandatory.

A more acute resentment, this time on the Scottish side, arose with the more resolute attempt, under Walpole's rule, to extract a revenue from Scotland. The policy was the raising of the malt tax which Scotland had paid at a specially low level since 1714. In 1725 it was to come up to half the English rate. The tax was a heavy and regressive part of the total British tax burden. At the prospect of the change rioting broke out in Glasgow, if not with the connivance of the burgh council, at least with its passivity. The outbreak, the Shawfield riots, was not only a serious breakdown in law and order but also showed the risk of a national movement. The maltsters in many other burghs were on the edge of refusal to pay taxes or to make malt until the policy was reversed, and this would have created in many towns the same mixture of mob violence and council acquiescence. There are indications too that the judges sympathized with the protest, and judges at this date carried considerable administrative authority.

For once an eighteenth-century government had force ready when it wanted it, There had been need to send troops to Scotland in 1719 to deal with a complicated international Jacobite scheme, which ended rather ineffectually in the landing or some Spanish soldiers in Kintail. The event had at least reminded Whitehall that there were large areas of the Highlands normally unpoliced. In 1724, perhaps as an aftermath of the Atterbury Jacobite plot in England, members of the government had been in correspondence with various people in Scotland's upper tier about how to impove law and order on the one hand, and how on the other to pmomote economic growth in the Highlands. Part of the policy then worked out was to encourage both developments by sending General George Wade to disarm the Highland clans, build and police roads, and generally to present a military presence in the area. Wade had campaigned in Spain in the Succession War and was consequently used to rough terrain. He had arrived in Scotland with several companies of dragoons and a battery of artillery, which he was dispatching to the north, when the news of the riots arrived. The troops received new orders, to march on Glasgow and keep it in check. Meanwhile the earl of Islay, heir presumptive to Argyll and a vital link in goverment control of Scotland, who held the office of Lord Justice General, arrived in Edinburgh to browbeat the bench of judges. The risk of a national demonstration faded. There is, though, probably a connection between the patent discontent of the burghs at this time and the establishment soon after, on a recommendation from the Convention of Royal Burghs, of the 'Board of Trustees', an unpaid committee of upper class men to administer £6,000 from the Scottish excise for the promotion of industry and fisheries. The second Equivalent, promised 20 years before in the Union treaty, was thus now to be paid.

The Board of Trustees can be seen as a sign of the accommodation of Scotland to the fact of Union, and a recognition that if economic benefits were to come from it these would not arrive as if by magic but by hard work and wise investment of the narrow range of resources in the country. It was to be an uphill struggle, for what the Board would feel free to promote would be industries which did not compete with the woollens of England which sustained her exports. This was to mean, in particular, expanding the Scottish production of low-quality linen. Indirectly this helped to develop the infrastructure of transport and communications which were eventually to widen the area of the market economy. There was no pot of gold to be found.

Union provided, though, once the '15 was out of the way, the political stability which was to make economic growth possible, and also the forces that overcame the fragmentation of Scottish politics. It carried on the process of reducing the great territorial magnates who had controlled their followers at times by coercion to influential political figure with followings based on the prospect of local advantage transferred by patronage. The system of voting for the representative peers bound these magnates into large factions. The tendency of political parties to divide into supporters and opponents of the house of Argyll kept the Squadrone in existence as the minority Whig group, containing much of the greater Scottish nobility, only at intervals able to gets its hands on the source of political influence but never so weak as to be ignored. The climate of politics had permanently changed from that of the later Stewarts. Rivalries had now to be worked out entirely within the law, and as one of the most significant professional legal families, that of the

Dundases of Arniston, supported the Squadrone, the law was used pretty evenly between the two dominant parties. A significant change was the shift of effective local power from the great feudatories to the landed gentry. The attention of great men was focused on London, where ministries were made and remade. Local dominance could not command their attention, and so slipped from their grasp.

Such changes were not only at the expence of feudal superiority: they confirmed landed authority over the tenantry. The system of low-profile government, at national level, was founded on a local system of concentrated authority, under different hats, by the landed class. Heritors effectively ran parish affairs as patrons, often, when not episcopalian in allegiance, as elders in kirk sessions. Almost always the 'ruling elder' representing the parish at high levels of the Church was landed. As payers of stipends, supporters, of the material fabric of church, manse and school, as the main source of funds for the schoolmaster's salary as well as for poor relief, the landowners had wide opportunities for intervention in Church and social matters. Civil government at local level, such as there was of it, was carried on through the landowners by their baron courts, by the meetings of the Justices of the Peace and by the most long-term significant local body, the Commissioners of Supply, who had the powers of raising whatever local revenue was needed.

The weakening of magnate power was making possible the creation of a structure of county government. The Scottish county was never to establish the sense of upper-class community found in the corresponding English unit, but it made important progress in its identity in the eighteeth century, though still handicapped by the overlap between its jurisdictions, under sheriff and Justices and the franchises, and by a lack of clear distinction between the powers and duties of its three units, the sheriffs, the Justices and the Commissioners of Supply. The latter two groups contained many of the same people, which reduced the effects of confusion. There has not yet been enough study of the policy of these local bodies and their impact for there to be any certainty about the quality of local government. The Quarter Sessions of the Justices in the early eighteenth century show them controlling, or attempting to control, the movement of grain in years of dearth, regulating the ownership of dogs, controlling wages in a downwards direction, of course, and, in some matters, prices, allocating contracts for work on road repair and administering the 'statute labour' on the road by the tenantry, placing vagrants in gaol or ordering them out of the county, coercing the parishes over the support of their poor, and ordering the children of cottars to hire themselves as farm servants. In which, if any, of these fields, their orders were obeyed, is not as yet clear, but there is no doubt that in their own eyes they were playing an important part in government.

It was the accepted ethos of the day that the mass of society should be closely controlled in their daily lives. That sexual and social irregularities should be stamped out seemed generally appropriate, and within the religious context essential if the local congregation was to be able to regard itself as part of the Christian Church. It was an affront to God as well as to society if members of congregations fought out their quarrels with blows or words, slandered each other, failed in charity to the poor, carried out their normal business, unless it was Church business, on Sunday or, even worse, sat tippling in an ale house then or indulged in sex outside matrimony at any time. Some failings, though deprecated, did not lead to outright denunciation. Drunkenness was tolerated on weekdays, wife beating accepted as normal marital control, and though parents were enjoined to send their children to school, they were not reproved if they did not, or if they withdrew them once reading but not writing had been attained. The kirk sessions recognized that many families needed the labour of their children.

Vagrancy was an area where Church and State might disagree in their views of control. It was illegal to beg, but local standards of poor relief were usually so low that it was taken for granted that those in need would do so. In fact enhanced allowances would be paid to those unable to beg. Begging from parish to parish was another matter. In time of dearth or disorder this would be on a scale beyond control, and there were also reservoirs of a begging population who would turn up to receive alms at weddings and christenings of the upper class, and also would flock to communions to receive alms. Whatever Proclamations or Acts of Parliament might say, the Church would not deny alms at communions and the upper class regarded largess as a duty. The Church was capable of censuring individuals who obeyed the law without due kindness: in 1737 the kirk session of Penninghame censured a man for sending on a beggar after housing him for two nights with the unfortunate result that he died on the road: it was 'Unchristian and blameable conduct', whatever the law might say.

Church and State at the local level were deeply concerned about the problem of the vagrant poor, who were a source of disorder, and also a shifting burden which could overwhelm local capacity. In the relatively tranquil period of the 1720s there were schemes being put forward, initially by the Church at presbytery level, but taken over by the Justices, for control of vagrancy, with the necessary corollary of insistence on adequate arrangements for relief in the parishes. Starving men and women would take to the road if they were denied support at home. The Justices of various counties started to put steady pressure on their parishes to control the giving of alms to vagrants and to raise funds for adequate relief by assessment. Most parishes still continued to find whatever sums they regarded as necessary voluntarily, but assessment, particularly in the southern counties, began to spread. When a parish assessed itself, whether from an inescapable shortfall in voluntary supplies or under the pressure of the Justices for better provision, it did not now pass the obligation to landowners simply to fulfil or neglect, but kept the management of relief in a joint committee formed from landowners and kirk session. The parish was becoming part of a system of local government, though still a unit of considerable independence. In the only occasion in the first half of the eighteenth century when there was serious risk of general famine, the year 1740, there is evidence from some areas which suggests that in the rural Lowlands the Justices and the parishes managed together to stave off disaster by making available supplies of subsidized food. The Midlothian parish of Currie, for instance, passed a unanimous resolution to provide for all indigent poor, and carried it out. The towns did not get by so successfully, for the impact of severe weather was exacerbated by the problems of war, and in particular the cessation of coastal transport for fear of the press gang. Edinburgh city suffered a sharp epidemic of measles with a considerable number of deaths, which suggest malnutrition. Deaths rose sharply also in the few towns within the Highland area, and there is no reason to believe that the sense of public responsibility which lay behind the efforts and assent to expenditure of the landowners and kirk sessions were mirrored in the landward parts of the Highlands. Clan disagreements and rivalries still prevented the parish being an effective unit of government, and many Highland counties lacked Justices altogether, from an unwillingness of suitable people to take the oath of allegiance, and further unwillingness to be put in a position where they might be expected to exercise authority beyond their clan while knowing that this was impossible.

It cannot be said that the system of relief in the Lowlands, even when responding to pressure from landowners was either efficient or generous, but at low cost it provided a life support in temporary emergencies and also enabled the old to keep body and soul together without total loss of dignity or institutionalization, and with only a small amount of moral bullying. It was the product of a genuine concern for good order on the part of landowners, and possibly an element of national pride. Certainly the men who worked in this period under a sense of patriotism for the economic improvement of Scotland were deeply embarrassed by the level of destitution that at times prevailed.

Other efforts of local government can be seen to blend public duty and individual advantage. This was particularly so in the matter of road improvement. Some roads, particularly the military roads for basic communications built in Galloway and the Highlands, were financed by the central government. In the Lowlands roads were maintained by the Justices, supported by a rate on landowners and six days compulsory labour, with carts and horses, by the tenantry. The fact that grain prices appear to have become linked and unified in the 1730s shows that transport in the Lowlands had become adequate for normal needs, though as late as the 1760s it was possible for the market system to fail to get grain regularly to the main cities. In this matter the efforts of local government linked to the economic pressures leading to the development of an economic infrastructure, the expansion of the resources of banking with the creation of the Bank of Scotland and the Royal Bank, improved contact with the outside world which kept two Edinburgh newspapers going and the steady expansion of postal services.

Part of this collection of minor improvements in information and movement of goods and money was the result of pressure by the trading and industrial community. Part was a conscious effort to provide the country with a system of government suitable to a modern country. The main sector of society concerned was the landowning gentry. Their superiors, the aristocracy, expected to gain direct advantages from government, rather than to spend on it. The hope was for a place in government or in military or diplomatic office. The size of the great houses which the aristocrats could afford to build, the policies which they could lay out, the marriages they could secure on the English market, all show how successful they could be. A glance at Floors Castle, at the grounds of Castle

Kennedy or at the portraits in Drumlanrig all support this point. They show that the great families valued and adorned their Scottish bases, at great cost, but they also remind that the funds for such adornment came from office secured through presence in London. The vacuum of power created by their absence there for most of the year was filled by the gentry.

By combining the resources of Church and State a Scottish laird was in a surprisingly powerful position of local power, and the bodies on which he was represented were conscious of their significance and dignity. The Commissioners of Supply for Midlothian, for instance, met in the outer house of the Court of Session: The Justices for the Lothian counties worked hand in hand with the judges of this Court in their schemes for the promotion of poor relief and the suppression of vagrancy. In the baron court there were no such pretensions, yet, even though deprived of much of its criminal power during the Cromwellian interlude, it could be of real value to a landowner in reinforcing his own interests, particularly in protecting his sporting rights and timber. Even where landowners were under the nominal control of some other body, for instance likely to be ordered by the presbytery to repair a church, build a new manse or provide a parish school, a judicial laggardliness could postpone payment for a long time and bring pressure to bear on an individual minister.

The parish schoolmaster received a salary less than adequate for subsistence from the landowners, between 100 and 200 merks, and 100 merks was a little over £5 11s. He expected also to receive fees from the children taught, or in cases of severe poverty from the parish on their behalf, and usually also had a salary as parish clerk. In the first half of the century, before basic prices began to rise, these would give him an income higher, though not by much, than that of most of the tenantry. He might also receive extra donations from landowners, or further fees from tutoring their children. Both minister and schoolmaster could be severely inconvenienced in their work, as well as hampered in their personal life, by hostility from a domineering landowner. Both would normally share the contemporary belief that education and spiritual ministrations did not exist to encourage social subversion but rather to support the social system, and in particular the existence of landed power. It was difficult for a parish to support its poor, whether it was assessed or not, without the real co-operation of its landowners.

The judges and advocates were building up Scots law on the intellectual framework set up by Stair, and had a marked tendency to build it up in ways which suited landed property. A judicial decision of 1744 declared 'It is the privilege of property that the proprietor can be put under no restraint'. The lawyers promoted property against long-standing rights of feudal superiors which were felt to be archaic, such as their control over the alienation of land by vassals, or the choice of a wife. Such rights may have been appropriate when feudalism genuinely meant that the superior would call on military support but in the world which the lawyers thought of as modern were inappropriate. Power for the aristocracy came thus to be replaced by persuasion, and the instrument of persuasion was 'influence' or the careful use of patronage. The parliamentary franchise, for instance, was based on superiority, and a peer could not directly use the superiority of his own estate in voting power. But by the careful carving up of such superiority into parcels of the minimum voting size (valued at 400 pounds Scots a year, or forty shillings by the Old Extent) he could create a party among lesser landowners which would give him a considerable share in the choice of Member of Parliament. This again was the use of persuasion rather than coercion. Even within the great franchises there had been a tacit surrender of some aristocratic powers, and since 1708 the right of repledging, that is of having a case transferred to a regality court from the crown's court, had been curtailed.

The lawyers were also emphasizing property against lesser folk. One area of this was the law of hypothec, the privilege of distraining for rent and thereby controlling land-use even beyond the terms of a tenancy. Judicial decisions over poor law money in the mid century did much to encourage the belief of landowners that all money and property on an estate was at their disposal, but since in practice most landowners did not wish to be at the trouble of carrying out detailed poor law administration, these decisions were more important in the creation of intellectual atmosphere than in the actual use of power. Whatever might be held to be the explicit law of hypothec, no landowner in fact was going to ride into a farmyard and select the sheaves of corn he considered most suitable for his rent, nor, whatever his powers were in poor law matters, was he going to check whether 6*d*. a week was more than enough for an old woman who could no longer beg. But so long as rents were paid mainly in kind and service these powers gave the landowner a right to influence the personal conduct of his tenants.

In economic terms the trend of the eighteenth century was for the enhancement of the larger estates at the expense of the smaller, not through any cataclysmic changes, or even severe economic pressure, but probably by the combined influence of increased opportunity for the indulgence of expensive tastes which led the incompetent into debt, and by the joining of estates together by the marrying of heiresses. Certainly even in those parts of Scotland where there had become established a large number of small landowners – the class that Walter Scott was to christen 'bonnet lairds' – Ayrshire and other parts of the south-west, Stirlingshire, Clackmannanshire and Kinross-shire, these men were under pressure. In most parts of Scotland the percentage of land held by great estates was increasing, though in these 'bonnet laird' counties estates of under £100 a year in value still included over 10 per cent of the land in 1770.

The group above this level, landowners of moderate wealth, was closely connected with the burgeoning of thought and artistic achievement for which eighteenth-century Scotland has long been famous. Men in this movement had often been trained in law, and added to their landed income fees as practising advocates or a judicial salary. Law obliged them to spend much of the year in a city, usually in Edinburgh, where they squeezed their households into the better flats of the old town. They were often joined in the city by others of their class who came there for the winter to conduct lawsuits, educate their children and enjoy the assemblies, plays and concerts that these cities, like other regional capitals at this time, were making available. The combination of a core of trained professional men, lawyers, doctors and university professors, with men of similar means but more leisure, all obliged through the restricted nature of their housing to seek their social life in taverns made possible the sudden proliferation of clubs and debating societies on which the Scottish Enlightenment was to be founded.

Even in the seventeenth century the interest of some men had moved from concentration on family promotion, politics and religion to matters of form, elegance and intellect. There were the discreetly handsome and formal houses of Sir William Bruce, heavy in underpinning but of architectural distinction, often sensitively related to their garden grounds. Bruce's work was somewhat interrupted by stretches of imprisonment after the Revolution, caused by his close association with James VII, but he still managed to produce late masterpieces, including the early work on Hopetoun House, and the taste for symmetry and elegance continued. Old and sprawling big houses were refashioned, smaller ones built from scratch, and the landowning class included in Sir John Clerk the younger of Penicuik at least one skilled architect. Sir John's view of what should be 'a family House' is worth attention, for it indicates a shift in the concept of the social function of such a building:

A family House especially for a Man of Quality ought to be large and have in it one good Apartment at least consisting of a dining Room, drawing Room, Bedchamber, dressing Room and closet . . . above all a good family House should be divided in three parts viz. the Body or main House with a large pavilion on each side. . . .

The main or chief Body of the House ought to be at Least double the Bigness of each pavilion, and may serve chiefly for lodging the Master of the family and the better kind of Guests who come to visit him. One of the pavilions ought entirely to be appropriated for women and children and the other ought to contain the kitchen, with apartments for Men servants and such like conveniences. . . . The principle floor in the main block is for the accommodation of the Family with a privat dining room.

Apart from arousing curiosity as to where Lady Clerk was to be located, this description shows that a landowner using such an architectural model would be giving up the old dual function of the big house, which had been both a gathering point for local support and the kin group, as well as a possible reception place for men of higher status. The new house retains the socially upward looking concern of the old, but changes its local impact to being a place of private entertainment by a married couple or the husband alone of social equals. The new outlook of the upper class was to be displayed permanently in stone.

The clubs and social gatherings of the cities provided the groundwork for some sort of a cultural revival and was the scene of Allan Ramsay the older's publications of his own poems and also of traditional Scottish songs. The Scottish language, which might be used in these, came to be seen as an embarrassment to those who wished to make their way in the south, even though there was a renewal of interest in it as a literary medium. More important in emphasizing the significance of the potential Scottish contribution to culture were developments within the academic world. Edinburgh University pioneered the changes which were to make for raising the intellectual content of university education; the abandonment of Latin as a medium for teaching and publication in favour of the vernacular, the change from regenting to specialist teachers, and the creation of a medical school in which scientific subjects were taught. The other Scottish universities followed suit, Glasgow with rapidity, Aberdeen slowly.

Most of the great period of the Enlightenment lies outwith the scope of this book, but certain names of long-term significance had made their mark before 1745. Francis Hutcheson, as professor of Moral Philosophy at Glasgow, is the key link in the development from the philosophy of Shaftesbury to the Scottish school of common sense, and had a considerable influence on the Enlightenment thinkers; Colin Maclaurin, whose true mathematical precocity brought him a Chair at 19, figured as the most distinguished British mathematician of his day, though overshadowed abroad by the Bernoullis and Euler. He was a gemoetrician, suspicious of the new techniques of infinitesimals, a prejudice which placed him on a relatively slow-moving area of the front of discovery. Yet in his *Treatise of Fluxions*, the first systematic work on Newtonian lines, he showed how much of what came to be the special field of calculus could be handled purely by geometry. The greatest name, though, in this period just before the Enlightenment, is that of David Hume, whose *Treatise of Human Nature* fell, as he said, 'dead-born from the press' in 1738, but who, in 1741, managed more successfully to bring his intellect within range of public understanding by publishing part of his *Essays, Moral and Political*. It was to take some time before the powerful solvent of his sceptical reasoning was to be appreciated.

The self-contained world of upper-class society was thus nurturing men who were to share in the making of a considerable impact on educated culture all over the known world. Not much of this impinged on the bulk of people. It is difficult to assess the popular culture of the age for this has in most material aspects been replaced by the mechanized products of a later day. That technical standards of craft work were not high seems clear from the surviving objects such as gravestones, which though more competent at representing objects than they had been still show an engaging awkwardness combined with a strong traditional line in motif. There are other carvings, on doorways, gateposts, fountains and sundials which often show a cramped vigour, but we do not know, for many of these, whether they were made by local or imported labour. The level of decoration on objects of use such as communion tokens, pewter tankards and armaments was not high, and these were certainly native-made. On a few surviving items of daily use such as bottles crude workmanship does not obscure the irregular charm of the basic material. Gravestones and door lintels sometimes display the instruments of a man's craft, suggesting that skill was an important possession both to the deceased and to the carver, and indicating that it ensured membership of a social group. Urban craft incorporations still held men together for social activities as well as mutual support.

The ability to participate actively in intellectual matters depended largely on literacy. Recent work has delivered some blows to the traditional view that Scottish parish schooling produced a predominately literate population in the early-eighteenth-century Lowlands. There is a basic difficulty of evidence in the topic. What can be measured for varying groups is readiness to sign one's name on occasions calling for a signature, usually on dealings with the establishment of either Church or State. The percentage able to sign for court matters appears low, relatively higher in the merchant community than elsewhere. When in 1737 the kirk session and deacons of Dalkeith petitioned the patron of the town during a quarrel with the town clerk, all could sign. In the 1740s a similar appeal by the burgesses of Wick to their patron had two names attested only by a cross and several signatures which indicated that their perpetrators were not in the habit of wielding a pen. Estimates have been made that some 20 per cent of men could sign their name, and markedly fewer women, but these have to be set against descriptions by visitors of congregations following the reading of the Bible in church in their own copies. Reading skills could be acquired by most in two years of schooling, but writing skills would take more time and involve higher fees. The kirk sessions tried to set a good example by keeping pauper orphans at school until they could read well, but not much longer: it was normal for poorer families to wish for income rather than the little-used skill of writing, and withdraw children at eight or nine years old to have the advantage of their labour. Girls were more likely than boys to have their education curtailed for industrial work. Really poor families did not send their children to school at all. In general it does not look as if, outside landed and professional groups, or merchant society, there was yet the pressure on people to learn to read that is provided by the modern wealth of printed material, but there was strong pressure from the Church that the skill be acquired. In inventories of goods made after death, surprising bundles of books turn up occasionally in humble settings, suggesting that the skill, once learnt, remained of value of some owners, and that to those of determination a taste for reading could be indulged.

The main aspect of verbal culture offered to the masses was, of course, theology in the sermon, and the quality of those surviving in print, which may not of course be typical of all those offered, shows an assumption of doctrinal sophistication in the audience which was probably not misplaced. These writings also suggest considerable staying power in both deliverer and audience. Ministers were expected to preach their way through the Bible, verse by verse as text, taking an hour at a time, and the quotations and allusions made in preaching had a tendency to concentrate on well-worn sayings. The effect of preaching was to give the congregation both a general understanding of the Bible, which included the less famous books, a close familiarity with biblical imagery, and a firm grasp of neo-Calvinist dogma.

Evangelism within Calvinism still retained a popular following in Scotland, and this was to be expanded in the religious controversies of the early eighteenth century. The venomous orthodoxy of the 1690s, which had secured the execution of the youth Thomas Aitkenhead for scepticism and blasphemy, had modified, but it was still assumed that orthodox religion should be expressed in stereotyped phrases: language which broke the accepted mould suggested dangerous new thinking. Two issues brought this point up in the 1720s, one the question whether the Glasgow professor of Divinity had lapsed into arminianism, the other whether an old book originating in England, *The Marrow of Modern Divinity*, reprinted in 1718, did not open too wide a door to grace through pointing out that God's pardon was not offered in terms of election or reprobation, and was to be assumed as available for all: grace, which would come only from God's irresistible will, could be taken as free to anyone. The issue of the first case was probably one that continued to trouble men in the nineteenth century, the existence of 'natural' religion, but this cannot be established for certain since both the professor, John Simson, and his opponents put up a cloud of obfuscation. On the latter topic the problem was how 'free' could 'free grace' be in an organized Calvinist Church: it was a particularly weak point in Calvinism that its view of the selectivity of the offer of grace was in direct conflict with many passages in Scripture. The General Assembly prevented the expulsion of Simson in a way which foreshadowed the later Moderate domination, but decided that the *Marrow* was heretical – a difficult point to support since, being written as dialogue, the book could be taken not to support any single point to view. Much the same accusations could have been made in both cases, that selected passages of a text could be strung together to produce unacceptable doctrine, and that expressions and emphasis were not those conventionally accepted.

The combined decisions, which were disliked by many, made the occasion of the first significant schism within presbyterianism, for they naturally suggested that the Assembly was prepared to tolerate high-placed heresy, but would suppress a work valued for its impact on ordinary men and women. But behind this and later breakaway movements, as a greater real cause, was the relationship of Church and State. Various groups within the Kirk had not abandoned the aim expressed in the Solemn League and Covenant, the ideal of the later covenanters of control over the State exercised by a self-appointed group of godly. To these the restoration of patronage in 1712 was a gross affront, the reversal of an important decision made in the period of the Great Rebellion, and again after the Revolution, by a parliament largely English and therefore episcopal in its Church government. The first break, in 1733, was in response to the decision of the General Assembly that in cases of appointment where the patron's right had lapsed, the presbytery should ask, not the congregation at large to choose, but only the heritors and elders. Ebenezer Erskine, probably the finest preacher in the Church, chose to attack this decision in an important sermon, was rebuked and suspended with other supporters, and refused to make even nominal apology. The group of ministers instead formed itself into 'the Associate Presbytery' and claimed, in essence, to be the true Church of Scotland. Among the lengthy and angry pamphlets produced by the split, most interesting is that in which Erskine attacks the Act of Union as sinful, since it involved accepting the idea of security for the Church of England. He was harking back to 1643.

The Assembly had not expected the breach: till now factions within the Kirk had been held there except for a small and scattered remnant of Cameronians. On the other hand no other group had, under the guise of presbyterianism, launched such an attack as Exrskine's on the somewhat haphazard use of the Assembly's authority within presbytery. The existence of a dissenting Church was an invitation to those who felt that the established Church was too ready to accept a narrow concept of who might be taken as saved, as well as those who disapproved of its accommodation to the world. Some of the schismatic ministers were approvers of the *Marrow*. The theology of Erskine was within traditional Calvinism, since he held that salvation was only for a few, but his stress on the irresistible nature of divine grace encouraged passivity and hope and could be seen as stressing free grace. The seceders soon came to see themselves as the only body of the elect, which meant in practice distancing themselves from the idea of such grace in favour of the more traditional idea of the congregation embodying the elect. Still, the existence of schism between men who all held by the same confession encouraged those who sought religious reassurance to see that there was no inescapable connection between congregations of established or dissenting Church and the elect. The road to salvation might not lie through one group only. Popular evangelicalism was able to see in this a way round the Calvinist belief that salvation was already settled and for only a small minority of worshippers. Evangelicalism, both within the bounds of neo-Calvinism and without them, was to remain an important element in popular culture, sustained by voluntary societies for prayer and reading.

The most important puzzle in popular culture is one that was not voiced overtly, for various reasons. It is, how far the populace in general accepted the social and economic structure of their day. Certainly differences in power and wealth between great men and the mass of the population appear to have been taken for granted. If resistance to the activities of a landowner occurred, it is not evidence of repudiation of the world of individual property and the rights derived from it, but of some particular extension of property rights or some particularly burdensome assertion. Thus, for instance, many landowners had difficulty in protecting plantations of trees from despoiling to keep cottage fires alight. This seems particularly acute, in the papers of Archibald Grant of Monymusk, in an area which he had cleared of tenantry so as to make the plantations. The work ethic had been acquired by many of the tenantry at school, but in practice some young men and women were unwilling to hire themselves out for farm service, and the rate of turnover of servants in big houses could be very fast: in Mellerstain, a well-drilled household, the average servant stay was three weeks. There were undoubtedly practices which enabled workmen to claim for hours that had not been worked, for instance masons would expect to be paid for working a seven-day week, when in fact their working week was six days only. These instances seem simply local instances of loss of control by individuals in charge.

Church discipline seems also, if sometimes grudgingly, to have been accepted. The low level of illegitimacy for most of Lowland Scotland, and the continuation of the system of public penance for sexual offences, argue for consensus. Occasionally, under provocation, men might assert themselves in defiance, but the assertion was usually withdrawn later. In 1702 one Robert Garner, when found with Janet Watson by an old woman 'in scandalous posture at the entry to the grammar school' in Dalkeith and threatened with delation to the kirk session, 'spoke very slightingly and irreverently' of the session, but later accepted public rebuke. It was not rare for a man to deny paternity of a child conceived in fornication, but it was rare for him to persist in such denial in the face of persistent enquiry. Rarely did a woman protest, but there is a case of female insubordination recorded by the kirk session of Penninghame. In 1710 Christian McKie said about her parish rulers, 'ye of the session take the poor's money to keep your purses with on Saturday and Sunday and give it to the skybes of gentles'. There was, of course, some fuss over this, and she and her husband, he presumably guilty of failing to control her, were made to apologize. Over 20 years after the event when the parish treasurer died it was found that Christian had been right. In one of the rare instances of embezzlement of poor funds, the treasurer had been systematically and secretly lending it out to his friends, some of whom were proving poor investments. His son made refunds: no apologies were offered to Christian. The story is exceptional for as yet women did not publicly denounce the organs of the society within which they lived. It is also unusual, in that money was often held in the hands of fairly humble people as kirk session treasurer, almost always without being misused. The ability of most Scottish parishes to manage their funds and administer relief is evidence of a high sense of social duty and also of popular support for the governing system of the Church.

But in one area there was real resistance to the claims of property. This was the famous episode of the 'Galloway levellers' in 1724, the men who went out at night in well-organized bands with specially shaped poles to push over the stone walls of cattle enclosures. The cattle trade to England was expanding after the Union, and this had encouraged some landowners in the south of Galloway to evict tenantry to create large stock farms. There were disturbances which showed that some of the cattle were illegal Irish imports, and there appears to have been a connection between some of the protesters and the continuing bodies of organized covenanter communities. Suppression of the troubles was fairly lenient, but the basic property right was left with the owners. The episode is the only important Lowland protest from those 'cleared' or 'reorganized' in the interests of more profitable landowning in the eighteenth century. The lack of further such movements may indicate that wisdom was learnt by the event, and that subsequent reorganization was approached in a less wholesale way by landowners. It may, on the other hand, mean that the Scottish people acquiesced in the absence of tenant right.

The impact of market forces on the Scottish agrarian system appears to have changed only slowly. By mid century at least in the Border area farming was market-oriented, the market in this case being English. Farms were not yet specialized even there: a sheep farm would also have to support its manpower on home grown grain, yet its money income would come from the sale of sheep and be sensitive to English price changes. The details we have of such farms shows them as yet only partly monetized. Labour would receive its wage in a complicated structure of payments in kind, and many of the work obligations were left in general terms. These features and the changing pattern of work over the year prevented a farmer from knowing what any one farm operation really cost, and thereby prevented any impulse to reduce the work force. Also the varied pattern of work reward made the position of the labour force similar to that of tenants, for they had still a strong concern in the actual yield of land and flocks. Elsewhere, even where payments of rents or wages were nominally monetized, they might in practice be made in kind. The depersonalizing aspect of economic development was to be held at bay for another generation even in the pastoral uplands, the most economically developed in the country, and in the arable areas of the Lowlands, so long as grain prices remained low, there was little pressure for basic economic change. The forces of improvement' in the first half of the eighteenth century were mainly deployed in industrial developments, though some change in the countryside were taking place. There were a few more hedges and walls, forming enclosures, and there was even a nursery in the Borders near Kelso supplying growing shoots for hedges; the potato was to be found occasionally as a field crop (it figured as such in Islay in the 1740s for instance) and there was the occasional meeting of The Honourable the Society of Improvers: the early model villages, such as Cuminestown and Ormiston, in which landowners attempted to use surplus rural labour to promote industries, had been set up. But in the world of improvement there was as yet a high ratio of talk to activity.

One interesting area of the failure of improvement was the attempt by the second duke of Argyll in the 1730s to raise rents and provoke better farming in Tiree. Tiree, though an island renowned for its grain potential, had, even before the late seventeenth century, seen declining yields from overcropping. The Argyll estate hoped that putting farms up for competitive bidding would lead to higher rents, and the higher rents to better farming, which would have benefited both landowner and tenantry. The farms were to be 'set' with no particular attention to the claims of clanship.

As it turned out it was too early, and the economic climate too unfavourable, for this policy to succeed. Concepts of money values were shaky, and of clanship strong, so that the bidding for farms became contests between the Campbells brought in by the superior and the men they had pushed out. By the mid 1740s rent arrears were accumulating and the duke had seriously damaged the unity of his own clan. His brother and successor reversed the policy.

Elsewhere in the Highlands the pressure for higher rents, particularly for increases in the money part of rent, was pursued more cautiously, and was feasible because of the rise that Union had brought to cattle prices and the expansion of the market in England. Cattle were the commodity most easily got to market without the aid of roads. They could be swum across from the inner islands – there was no concern at that date for the feelings of the beasts in this matter – and could walk through the upland tracks till well over the Border. It is estimated that about half the price of the beasts thus sold went in rent, and the rest was used to bring in extra supplies of oatmeal. The Highland peasant farmed intensively what arable land he had and left his cattle out on the hill for most of the year. He might have little straw to feed them on in winter if lack of a nearby mill forced him to *graddan* his grain, that is roast it by burning the straw and husk. Expansion in the number of cattle held could not be, as it was in the Lowlands, an encouragement to reduce overcropping and so did little for the diet of the peasantry except in the form of milk, for little use could be made of the dung for manure. It was almost a separate enclave of farming. The peasants bred cattle for the rent and grew grain for food. There are signs that the holdings for grain were becoming smaller even before 1750. Population pressure, even though population growth was slower as yet than in the Lowlands, was leading to subdivision rather than stimulating agricultural development.

The coastal dwellers in the western Highlands made little use of large-scale fishing, in spite of the presence of quantities of fish that startled observers. There was, perhaps, a cultural aversion to the sea, but in any case they were undercapitalized for exploiting it. In the Northern Isles fishing had developed, largely under the control of a class of landowners who had come in since the deposition of earl Patrick and who demanded rent in fish or fish products. The customs accounts of Shetland show that in the eighteenth century the export of the islands was almost entirely fish, and in both island groups, dried fish provided a reserve diet when crops failed.

The expansion of the cattle trade, by increasing the payment of rent in money, met the need of the chiefs for higher spending power, but added to the forces cutting these men off culturally from their clans. Highland chiefs were making use of Lowland education and sometimes of state offices, which might include the command of a Highland company for peace-keeping purposes. They were purchasing luxuries that could not be produced in the Highlands, and they might move about in the Lowlands, when they had enough cash, as ordinary gentry. The relative tranquillity of the area meant that there was seldom risk of their arrest for past misdemeanours of their own or their clansmen's if they went to town. They retained their status as chiefs, and would assume the right to force out their clan on a campaign and lead it, though most of them had little knowledge of military matters. The clansmen's retention of their Highland culture was also under pressure from both within the clan and from outside. There is evidence at least from the peripheral areas of the Highlands, such as Easter Ross and Atholl, of great unwillingness to participate in the military event of the '45 on either side, and even in the 1715 the level of desertion in the Highland army suggests an abandonment by many of the old military ethos. Two contrasting views of Highlanders were often voiced in the eighteenth century. One was that this was a martial people valuing military achievement and despising other activities, the other that here was a peasantry scraping an arduous living in inclement conditions. The latter seems the more convincing.

Opinion of those in governing circles was that Gaelic culture needed to be superseded by teaching the polulation the virtues of

Hanoverian rule, English speech and Calvinist doctrine. The recipe, it was hoped, would produce a docile and industrious population, which might become prosperous. One step in this direction was the creation of the Scottish Society for the Propagation of Christian Knowledge in 1709, with the intention of raising voluntary funds to support schools in the Highlands. These schools were not to override the obligation of Highland heritors to support a parish school but to supplement it, with perhaps further aid from the heritors, by temporary schools in large parishes. Schoolmasters, with less than a living wage from salaries, were sent to the Highlands and expected to win the support of parents for the education of the children. All such education was to take place in English. While this, of course, placed an almost unsurmountable pedagogic hurdle in the way of the teachers themselves, who had had little training anyway, it is a not surprising demonstration of cultural imperialism, for there was in existence at this time practically no printed literature in Gaelic other than the book of Psalms. The bilingual chiefs show, in the irregularities of their spelling when using Gaelic, that it was to them simply an instrument of oral culture. The orthography created to cope with the inflexion system of the language, which in itself has proved a considerable block to literacy, was largely unknown in the area it was designed to serve. The lack of a Gaelic Bible meant unfamiliarity in the Gaelic-speaking area of the normal imagery in which Lowland culture was expressed, and this imparts to surviving Gaelic literature an old-fashioned and separate quality. Highland culture was intensely aural. There was little scope for the visual arts and the standard of any work done in them was low. Music and poetry together produced the dominant medium of song.

The Church of Scotland could not take the ruthless approach of the SSPCK to the use of Gaelic. It hoped to see the language decline, but meantime it had to ensure that ministers given parishes in the Highlands were competent to preach in the vernacular. Arrangements were made to find sums to support potential candidates from the Highlands at university and to have their preaching examined by bilingual ministers, but there was a continual shortage of candidates. The ministers in the Highlands were, though, even if out of sympathy with many aspects of culture there, and particularly with the clan system and Jacobitism, conscientious men carrying out a difficult task with little to help them.

A mainstay of Highland society in many areas in the early

eighteenth century was under attack by the 1730s; the tacksman. The tacksman held land by virtue of kinship to the chief, an unstable position since kin is a wasting asset: the tie becomes weaker with each generation as men of common ancestry separate. His duties were to organize the farming, playing a personal role somewhat similar to that of a Birlaw court, and to be ready to gather the clan for fighting or for the recapture of stolen cattle. The apparent peace of the Highlands in the 1730s was reducing the value of such men, and some chiefs were beginning to feel that payment for their duties was a burden on the peasantry and a loss of revenue to the chief. Argyll's attempt at reorganization in Tiree dispossessed a particularly powerful group of Campbell tacksmen who acted as subordinate chieftains, to put instead a simple landlord – tenant relationship exercised through factors, and to give more rent to the duke without overburdening the peasantry. Only part of the scheme was achieved, and it ignored the ways in which a resident upper class could act as rural leaders, supporting and coercing the tenantry in ways only available to an independent élite. Some at least of the economic confusion which resulted seems to stem from the fact that the peasantry were not yet in the way of making and carrying through the decisions needed by successful farming. Some areas of the Highlands did not have tacksmen. The Atholl estate had as its gentry class propertied vassals who did not share the chief's surname. But in most areas the tacksmen were the central link in clan sentiment and loyalty, and the trend against them, which continued through the eighteenth century, did much to fragment and disorganize Highland society.

8

New and Old Themes of the 1740s

The 1740s was a decade in which, in some aspects of society, changes began which were to be long standing. In other aspects there were residual impulses from the past. The idea that the society of either the past or of the future was intrinsically better should be abandoned. What matters is that they were very different from each other, and it is worthwhile thinking of the significant events as either backward- or forward-looking.

The Act of Union had allowed the Scottish peerage to compete for places in the House of Lords but had ostensibly kept it from expression in the Commons. The eldest sons of Scottish peers were expressly disqualified from representing a Scottish constituency by a clause introduced late on in the Union debate, which looks like an attempt to restrict the power of great houses. The constituencies were the counties, with the voting power in the hands of tenants in chief, and the royal burghs grouped into bundles. In the past control over the elected part of Parliament had not concerned the Scottish magnates, even after Parliament escaped from the stranglehold of the Lords of the Articles, for there were many ways in which pressure could be put on individuals. It was as a final demonstration of this fact that the duke of Atholl had called on his vassals to attend him when he went to Edinburgh to oppose the Act of Union. The smaller burghs were easily controlled by local landowners or feudal superiors, but the county electorates were larger and not directly bribable. 'Influence' had to take over from domination. Great men took to controlling county elections by creating ficticious qualifications out of their feudal superiority, and conveying these to those of the landed gentry who could be considered as supporters. Legislation to control such breaches of the spirit of the law cumulatively put a strain on the conscience of the would-be voter, and on the organizing power of the magnate. Nominal transfer had to take place more than two months before the Michaelmas Head Court of the county made up the electoral roll, and over a year before an election. The need for advance planning of votes kept out English intrusion. An oath might be offered to each 'freeholder' that he did 'truly possess' the superiority on which he claimed to vote: malpractice in the interests of one party or another by the sheriff and sheriff clerk came to be penalized. But the need of great men for the mechanism of influence and the desire of country gentlemen to get to Parliament found new ways round or direct breaches in the law. It is in the 1740s that this system of fictitious votes seems to extend to all counties, and also at this time that the Court of Session began to intervene and receive complaints about malpractice. The Court could clean up particularly outrageous misdeeds, for instance those in which the praeses (chairman) of the county meeting had simply refused to allow qualifications no shadier than any others to be added to the roll, when he allowed those of an opponent, but it could not outface perjury. The risk of having to fight cases in the Court, certainly by the cost of such matters, did put some pressure on men to behave, but not a great deal. The development of these election frauds was not desirable. It was an instance of the corruptions brought by prosperity which had inspired some of the puritanical rhetoric of opponents to Union. In another light it can be seen as a continuation of the process by which direct magnate power gave way to influence and patronage. To maintain control over a county the great lord now had to secure benefits for his followers from his association with the court, and one of these benefits was a place in Parliament. In return he expected support and loyalty in political matters. From the lower social levels he still expected servility.

The filaments of patronage went through all levels of society like the mycelium of dry rot through old woodwork. When the third duke of Argyll, never one for pomp, stayed the night in Edinburgh or Glasgow on his way to Inveraray he would be 'waited upon' by the Lord Provost, bailies, resident nobility and all people of distinction. The town council of Glasgow commissioned a full-length portrait of him to show its respect. In return the duke spent many hours a week carrying Scottish affairs in the interests of his supporters, through the relevant offices in London. A miserable schoolmaster, failing to pay his respects to the second duke of Atholl as soon as he arrived in the parish would be treated in a way which produced a cringing letter of apology. The earl of Marchmont would be appealed to by the wife of one Joseph Hume, condemned to death for killing a man in a brawl, and expected to intervene because of the common surname. Patronage as a system sprang partly from the idea that the owner of land was entitled to have a following, even if now this did not mean a military one, and the patron fulfilled his obligations to those below him to maintain his legitimate interest.

At the top of this structure of influence and interest were the crucial political links between Scotland and London. The eighteenth-century system of government did not require a chain of command from the central executive power to any locality, but it did need information and influence, particularly on appointments to judicial or administrative office. There had to be a Scottish minister in London, some member of the Cabinet who would ensure that Scottish appointments were such as to support the total government network, but who might also use his cabinet position to influence policy in the interests of Scotland. There was also the duty of leading the Scottish Members of Parliament through the divisions of the House of Commons, and even speaking as their representative. This task came to be that of the Lord Advocate. Finally some one or more person in Scotland had to manage electoral business, and this person need not be one occupying any particular post. For a time the Scottish Secretary of State had performed the London aspect of Scottish business, but this post had often been held by a member of the Squadrone party which was only part of Scotland's electoral strength, and in 1725 the Secretaryship was allowed to lapse. The Prime Minister, Walpole, had decided to ally with the rival Argyll interest and not with the Squadrone. The office was recreated on Walpole's fall in 1742, apparently for the sole purpose of giving a post to the fourth marquess of Tweeddale, son in law to the Prime Minister Carteret, and the conspicuous failure of Tweeddale to cope with the emergency of the '45 was enough to lead to the suspension of the office in 1746 for over a century. The Argyll party was strong without the aid of such a post. The second duke of Argyll had not been an easy man to get on with, and he had finally broken with Walpole over the government's decision to punish the city of Edinburgh for the Porteous Riot of 1736.

In cause the Porteous Riot stemmed, as did the Shawfield Riots, from the confirmed Scottish view that indirect taxation should be avoidable. It arose from the use of force by the captain of the city's guard, Porteous, in securing the execution of a smuggler, in the course of which people in the crowd were killed. Porteous was condemned for murder, and when respited, lynched by a well-organized exercise which involved all levels of Edinburgh society. The event had a content of national feeling, though this was not as dangerously evident as in the Glasgow riots, but from the government's point of view it was simply a denial of the rule of law. After the event Argyll swung his electoral influence against Walpole, and this partly explains the fall of the Prime Minister after the 1741 election when he found himself without his customary Scottish support. But Islay, Argyll's brother and heir, took on what he could of the management of Scottish affairs, and after 1743 when he succeeded his brother as third duke, reunited and enlarged the Argyll influence. Apart from the unstable period of Squadrone supremacy, with Tweeddale in office, he was to hold Scotland at the service of the government till his death in 1761. He used Lord Milton, Lord Justice Clerk, as his Edinburgh agent, re-established the unity of clan Campbell, and thereby the control of the county of Argyll, and became eventually the confidant and adviser of all leading Cabinet figures. For some 15 years he personally provided the link that kept Scotland in touch with the political system, satisfied the needs of the Scottish political class and resisted unwise or unpopular legislative proposals. Scotland was content, in and after this regime, to be North Britain.

This process of harmonization of Scotland into Britain might well have been interrupted by the last flash of active Jacobitism, the '45. By the late 1730s the concern that London had shown over the securing the quiet of the Highlands in the previous decade had abated. Wade's roads were still there, and the Highland companies, formed from the Whig clans, for the sake of somewhat one-sided law and order, but in 1739 these companies were banded into a regiment and later sent, grumbling and mutinous, abroad. No force replaced them in the Highlands, and even before this, various of the smaller and more aggressive clans had been extracting blackmail from Lowland and Highland neighbouring areas. Clan Campbell was demoralized by the second duke's adherence to the position of landlord rather than chief. There prevailed a destabilizing conviction in legal and political circles that, with the abolition of the Privy Council, had gone any power for subjects to take up arms in the defence of government. Into this vacuum of power came the dramatic appeal of Prince Charles Edward to the Jacobite sentiment of a few of the chiefs. By chance, by force and by the failure of various nominal adherents of the government to decide promptly on which side their loyalty lay, the Jacobite army was built up and able to get through the passes into the Lowlands effectively unopposed.

One of the odd features about the rising of 1745 is that it received relatively little aid from that part of Scotland most evidently and sincerely Jacobite, the north-east Lowlands. This discontented area had suffered the imposition of presbyterianism with a good deal of riot and disorder, and the episcopal Church now proscribed had lost most of its general support. A real distaste for the Whig and Hanoverian structure of politics kept many landowning families out of the established Church and out of government office, but their Jacobitism was largely passive. Some of the Highland chiefs who took or sent their men to the Pretender's cause had a genuine desire to see the events of 1688–9 reversed, notably most of the various branches of Macdonald, though even then not all of these were prepared to expose their clansmen to war. The McGregors had little reason to keep them from opposing an established government, and among the Camerons, Mackinstoshes, Robertsons and some branches of Gordons there was real support for the older Stewart line. It is difficult not to see motives as mixed among some others who joined in. The earl of Cromarty was on the verge of bankruptcy, staving off disaster by the fact that no one could sue him in his own court: Lovat was a man to whom intrigue was as necessary as air: Macpherson of Cluny probably ready to accept advantage from anyone who offered. If the Hanoverian forces could have put an efficient army promptly in the central Highlands to hold the passes it is probable that most of the clans would have been glad to go home. As it is they were able to march to Edinburgh almost unopposed, and to defeat an army outside the city in a few minutes, eventually to march into the English midlands.

The basic story of the '45 is almost too well known, but there are points in it worth stressing. The rising got little active support in the Lowlands except from a few quixotic gentlemen and several Edinburgh goldsmiths, but it revealed a high level of tolerance. Upper-class society, long deprived of a court, enjoyed having a prince about: the Royal Bank of Scotland moved its base into Edinburgh castle when the city opened its gates to the rebels, but continued to do business with both sides. The administration of Scotland had retreated to Berwick, as it had been ready to do in 1689. Little in the way of looting of homes appears to have happened but the rebels collected various stores of grain and oatmeal rents from landowners and also interrupted the flow of taxation funds to the south. The Prince declared that the Act of Union would be repealed, but this could not mean an effective separation of the two countries, and in royalist thinking no power on earth could wipe away the Union of Crowns for the essence of the Jacobite claim was indefeasible hereditary right. The march into England was launched to give a chance to the numerous Jacobites, thought to be ready in England, to join: indeed at the time the man who claimed to be the leader of the English Jacobite party was part of the coalition government. When recruits conspicuously did not show up and the duke of Cumberland, recalled from the war on the continent, showed signs of outflanking the army, the long retreat from Derby began, to end on Culloden moor in April 1746. The rebel army had never been large and in this final battle probably numbered only 3,000. The defeat, though aided by bad tactics, was inescapable, for in Cumberland the Highlanders had met a man prepared to train his men to stand against their initial charge. Though for an event which had thoroughly frightened the government the executions for treason were not many, the rising was put down in the Highland area with a considerable display of brutality, probably the legacy of the split in cultures between Lowland and Highland which had become so marked in the seventeenth century. In any case the policing of a disturbed and remote area by soldiery was likely to create hardship and starvation in communities living on a very narrow margin at best, and this not only in Jacobite areas, for the government's forces were not discriminating.

The long-term effects were to demoralize and burden with debt some communities, and to destroy both in law and in loyalty, the system of clanship. This was a change which had been on the cards for a long time. Ever since Cromwellian troops had defeated Glencairn it had been clear that a determined attack on Highland military independence backed by English force would win, but from the 1650s until the 1740s no government had offered the trouble and expense to carry it out. In the 1720s there had been suggestions made by Edinburgh lawyers that bringing Lowland levels of peace-keeping to the Highlands and thereby freeing the clansmen from domination by the chiefs would be part of a policy of 'compleating the Union'. From the mid seventeenth century the government had been able to prevent Highland disorder spilling over into any of the Lowlands but the immediate fringe, and this in itself had increased the likelihood of the region becoming open to market pressure. The expansion of the cattle trade and the modest export from the

Highlands of other pastoral products and some linen were all signs of market penetration. Now the government brought various disciplining Acts through Parliament. The banning of Highland dress because of its association with war, enforced disarming, the compulsory buying up of the heritable jurisdictions and the exiling of many of the chiefly leaders and even the sending of lesser men to the colonies as indentured labour, were all blows against the clan system.

The ending of clanship was not as traumatic as many historians have claimed. That part of upper-class authority which was an anachronism was cut away, but Highland society remained still hierarchical. Chiefs had been increasing their rent rolls at the expense of their personal standing in the clan for some time. The enforced absence of many in exile for a generation completed the process of making them little more than landowners. The bitterness of the Gaelic poetry of this period against the whole disastrous enterprise of the rising is a sign that, whatever clanship might continue to mean in social and emotive terms to local communities, it would no longer mean blind obedience.

The '45 not only depended for its launching on a social and political anachronism: its aims were backward looking too. It relied on the sort of society suppressed in the Lowlands by the events of the 1640s and '50s, when Lowland magnates had sent their followings equipped for fighting to support their personal or political interests. The ultimate aim of Jacobitism, for good or ill, was to turn the clock back behind 1688, to abandon the Protestant succession and link Britain in alliance with France. Yet the French wars since 1688, of which the third one was then still undetermined, were not mere flashes in the pan. They arose out of a profound rivalry in trade and colonial power from the two great powers. Jacobitism had no remedy for this competition.

Since 1707 Scotland had nominally been a participator in the benefits of British imperialism. She had not yet obtained much of a position in the East India Company, for that took time, but the colonies of settlement were providing markets and products of value by the 1740s. It was in this decade that the colonial market developed sharply and became the foundation of future wealth. Even in the 1720s some Glagow merchant houses had been selling the Virginian tobacco, to which French taste was tied, to France, while many Glasgow firms were building up their capital. The Scottish store system in the Chesapeake area made the trade an expensive one, involving long credit, so merchants had to develop links with the main sources of credit, the banks in Scotland. The precocious development of banking techniques was already under way, with the 'cash credit' system and the optional clause, and even the branch structure, later so significant, had been experimented with under the powerful stimulus of competition between private banks, the Royal and the Bank of Scotland. Characteristically it was through a commercial tip from a banking firm that the Scots merchants picked up the prize tobacco contract, that for the French monopoly in 1740. War between the two countries was no obstacle to this trade. The value of this large contract was that though the French chose to buy the cheapest tobacco they could force onto their countrymen (the Gaulloise cigarette develops from a long period of low standards), they paid cash for their purchases and this cash could lubricate the whole credit-based system of Scottish trade and industry.

Another important element in the Scottish economy experienced a sharp upward step in the 1740s, the linen industry. It was already benefiting by having £2,650 from the £6,000 annually distributed by the Board of Trustees to promote industry. The money was used to impose quality control by the inspection and stamping of all linen cloth brought to market, but it was also dribbled out in smell grants to help developments such as lint mills for the dismembering of the flax into fibres, and a few plash mills for washing flax. A special area which needed not only money but also technical skill, was that of bleaching, and here again the Board not only gave financial help but, by encouraging instruction, some control of quality. Some money went on awards for the growing of flax, probably a waste of the Board's resources, for flax growing, beyond the immediate needs of a farmer's household, was not popular in Scotland. The plants did not do well in the cloudy summer climate and the wide range of possible yield made it an unattractive venture for the more commercially minded farmer likely to respond to the Board's initiatives. The figures of the official sale of Scottish linen had mounted in the 1730s but were still not high, and we know nothing of the level of linen work done by private contract. In 1742 the Convention of Royal Burghs persuaded Parliament to put a bounty on the export of coarse, cheap, undyed linen cloth to the colonies. Before the Scottish presence in this downmarket area had been made difficult by a drawback offered to cheap German linen. The bounty, enlarged in 1746, more than redressed competition with the German cloth. The sales of Scottish linen to the colonies, mainly for clothing the slave population, began to expand. The historian of this industry reckons that nearly 20 per cent of Scottish product was finding its way into this outlet by the end of the 1740s. A growing industry can benefit disproportionately by a moderate but secure overseas market, and the Scottish production of linen began a rapid climb.

These economic developments were eventually to have considerable social consequences. In the 1740s these were not yet conspicuous, but even so there were some indicators of the future. Tobacco did not directly generate much employment, though the expanding tobacco firms needed some hands to handle and pack bales, and most of the small towns in Scotland would have a tobacconist, a man who made and sold twists of tobacco, or grated it into snuff. The outward cargoes which stocked the tidewater stores were at first largely imports from England of the Netherlands, but some basic country products, leather, cheese, grain would be included. As the fine branch of linen manufacture developed round Paisley its products also went to America, for use by the planters themselves, and in general America provided an expanding outlet. Linen made full-time work for many weavers and some spinners, though the appalling drudgery of spinning enough to keep body and soul together made it the last chosen of employments. Even so, the industry prevented destitution. More widespread was the impact of part-time spinning. Every household had a spinning wheel, no housewife or servant was expected to have idle hands on a weekday, and some part of the work done was for the open market, some for contract. Spinning came to provide an extra cash income for the great bulk of Scottish households, and was a significant element in the rising standard of living.

New employment and higher incomes were an element promoting social mobility. The increase in incomes made it possible for more parents to send children to school, if there was one within reach. The parish and burgh schools could send some children to university, and poor boys of ability might be sent for this 'higher' education by bursaries provided by groups of parishes from their poor funds, and these funds themselves depended on the income level of the ordinary peasant. Patronage, by offering tutorships in upper-class households, might bridge the gap between the Arts degree and the further study of divinity, and patronage again get a lucky individual a parish ministry. Most, however, of those who went from rural schools to the university must have returned again to a parish school in the lowly, underpaid, role of schoolmaster.

The burgh school candidate had better prospects. He came to university in his early teens, and had local contacts. He might find his way into a merchant or banking house, and as trade expanded this became easier. The leading figures in the Glasgow tobacco trade had come from outside the merchant community, though not from lowly status. Industrial expansion needed intermediaries and technicians: the linen industry in particular had posts for those who would study Dutch or Irish bleaching techniques, or help to manage a bleachfield. At the bottom end of this, teaching in a spinning school gave a more varied work load and higher pay than simple spinning.

The interesting question, on which as yet no systematic work has been done, is how open was society at the top, the landowing level. Entry into a merchant house or a manse could not be a route by which to get to the landowning sector. The profession with which landowning was linked was that of advocate, and entry into this group from any but a landowning base was rare. By parliamentary usefulness the richer landowners might get sons into the East India Company or government service in the colonies: in the third quarter of the eighteenth century Scots were to figure notably in both areas. Merchants or bankers might decide to put accumulated wealth into buying an estate. There are seventeenth-century examples of this practice, and the two Midlothian families Dick of Prestonfield and Clerk of Penicuik became landowners in this way, but there is less evidence from the early eighteenth century. For the most part the landowning world, which was where power lay, was one to which birth was the entry.

The trade developments, themselves the result of commercial initiatives and political advantages, link up with an increase in the range and sophistication of the goods that the country could put on the market. In 1730 or 31 (the writer of the memoir is uncertain) there had been an attempt to boost the fine-linen industry by holding an assembly in which everyone was to wear Scottish textiles. The literary and intellectual clubs of early-eighteenth-century Edinburgh were branching out, and would soon start patriotically also to promote the home production of domestic comforts. Blankets and tinplate were particularly aimed at. Behind these schemes stood the injured patriotic pride of a small group of men we name the 'Improvers' who hoped to see Scottish agriculture and industry develop and hold their own with those of other countries, eventually to provide a better income for the producers. Mackintosh of Borlum had stated in 1729 that the fact that Border landowners had to send to Berwick for good meat 'raised his blood' and Cockburn of Ormiston angrily described Scottish beer as 'stupefying'. The personal success of these early champions of better things was not marked. Borlum ended his days imprisoned in Edinburgh castle for refusal to be adequately penitent about his Jacobite past, and Cockburn in bankruptcy through unwise industrial ventures. But their writings are a sign of the willingness of some men to question existing practices.

Such questioning was economic rather than social in its targets. The difference in life style and influence that went with landed estate was not questioned, even by the relatively self-made men of the expanding professions. Alexander Munro, the main initiator of the Edinburgh medical school, in a long letter of sententious advice to his daughter, advised her to marry a 'man of independence', that is a landowner, and the rights of property were safeguarded from the critical intelligence of Enlightenment thought. There was, however, one right which did lead to vocal protest, that of patronage in the Church. Besides causing schism, it also made for complaints from those who did not wish to make a break within the Church but objected to the choice, by a patron, of some particular minister. Some of this was based on an unreasonable demand that each sermon be used as a means of conveying the essence of Calvinist theology in stereotyped and easily recognizable language, but more probably on the fact that the minister had to carry on much of his work with the eldership of a parish and doubts about belief or personal commitment could make this difficult. Disputes over appointments could lead to a Call, that is to the collecting of the votes of heads of families, or of male heads only, or by the decision of the Assembly in 1732, of the heritors and elders. The mixture of personal matters and principle which could arise in a parish kept issues alive. There was also knowledge of the evangelical movement which had started in England, of field preaching and organized prayer societies. All these features were involved in the 'Great Wark' of 1742, the Cambuslang revival.

This revival took place in a parish with a long-standing record of bad relations between landowners and populace, and a recent history of internal feuding within the kirk session. The principle heritor, the duke of Hamilton, had been defeated by parish resis-

tance over the choice of minister. Some of the landowners were episcopalian, and therefore grudged subscription to poor relief as
organized by the session. None of this explains the fact that in
February 1742, after a weekday lecture held in response to news of
the English evangelical movement, various people experienced a
personal religious revolution. After that, preaching and prayer took
place daily, often out of doors because of the great throng of people,
and dramatic conversions took place. Whitefield, the English
evangelical, already planning a Scottish visit, came and preached,
but to confirm, not cause the movement. There were dramatic
meetings also in other parishes near by.

For many years after, an annual reminder meeting of the revival
was held. The 'preaching braes', an open hillside, made the setting.
A special outdoor pulpit and communion tables would be set up,
vast crowds came in, and large subscriptions to the poor of the
parish were collected. The owner of the land on which these events
occurred, whose fences and pastures suffered as a result, and who
was in any case episcopalian, attempted to put a stop to these com-
memorations by legal action, claiming that the financing of these
occasions was an improper use of parish funds. He won his case,
though it was later discounted as a precedent in parish law. He and
the judges could hardly have done more than this to mark the gulf
between the upper class and its priorities on one side and popular
evangelicalism on the other.

The movement was a forerunner of a major later development,
the fusing of popular evangelical sentiment with the old claims for
an independent Church, and kept patronage as an issue in the
popular mind after the General Assembly had settled down to work
it as part of the law of the land. The experience of free grace among
humble folk was a cultural boon that more than compensated for the
hardness of their lives, but it was to carry into the nineteenth
century the seeds of self-righteous legalism on both sides of the
patroonage issue. The Cambuslang Wark must be seen as an event
which tied the rancours of the seventeenth century to those of the
nineteenth, though the terms of the patronage issue were to change
between the two periods.

There are also early signs of a worker ethos expressing itself in
religious matters. In 1740 when it was proposed within the Church
that the minister of Monimail be transferred to the large and
flourishing parish of Inveresk, a body of weavers in Inveresk, said to
number 80, protested. The transfer would, they claimed, be based

on love of money, not on spiritual edification, and they did not want a minister open to such influence. At this date most organized working-class activity would have been illegal and therefore secret since it would usually be 'in restraint of trade', so this manifestation of some level of organization among workers is an interesting signal for the future.

Another theme of the 1740s, with vast long-term results, was the upturn in the rate of population growth. Population appears to have recovered only slowly from the impact of the famine of the 1690s, probably not replacing its lost numbers until 1740: then it expanded. We do not know, as yet, whether this growth came from a rise in births produced by earlier marriage, as in England, or by better survival, but such slight indicators as we have suggest a family structure moulded by pressures very similar to those in England, in which case it is to the economic expansion of the 1740s that we should attribute the new level of growth.

The link between population growth and economic growth is hypothetical, of course, and may appear far-fetched, for it is only in the late 1740s that most of the industries of Scotland appear to expand. The exception to this, though, is very important, linen: its upward trend already shows in official statistics of linen 'brought to sale'. The expansion here may well have been greater than the statistics show for much linen was produced in response to specific orders. The spinning and weaving which enabled country lairds to carry the enormous stocks of shirts and nightshirts necessary in a society with rising standards of cleanliness and limited washing facilities often never led to market sale. Another area for which there is evidence of expansion is commercial activity, and such commerce would be unlikely to be based entirely on the goods of other countries, and may have used commodities for which the output figures are not known. Certainly without extra business it would be difficult to explain the considerable increase, even before 1740, of the necessary aids to business in a modern society, the economic infrastructure as it is often called, of news, postal services, banking opportunities and transport.

Another sign of a better-equipped economy is the fact that so few starved in the harvest failure of 1740. Money could be raised, and was, at short notice to bring in extra grain, and the joint system of Church administration and landowner support made food available where it was needed. An interesting sign, though, of the changing concern of the upper classes lies in the complaint of Sir John Clerk younger of Penicuik of how little credit the Midlothian landowners received for the £2,000 they donated to relief. In the seventeenth century the status anxieties of the upper class had been directed at their social equals, with passionate concern over the seniority of ennoblement; now in the eighteenth century landowning society's worry was that the lesser ranks might not appreciate the benefits it could confer, and would try to conduct their lives without using the patronage of the upper class.

This concern for deference and admiration was partly because property had become more important than lordship, and property was a commodity which could easily change hands. The great estates were fairly secure, for the economic climate of the century was to favour and build them up, and they were further buttressed by entail. But the holders of these lands, except in the case of the third duke of Argyll, sat fairly loose to Scottish issues. It was in the lesser nobility and gentry, whose focus was still on Scotland, that the nervousness over deference existed. Given the narrowness of the base of the political nation, the proportion of the population that exercised the vote or influenced the vote of others, which was much smaller than in England, this nervousness seems exaggerated. Landowning power was unlikely to be shaken off any major area of activity.

Property, with its attendant privileges, was pervasive. It influenced, though it did not fully control, the Church, even before the Moderate party set out on a deliberate policy of co-operation with the powers that be. Resident lairds, if they had not deserted presbyterianism, could easily become elders and ruling elders, and if they had disqualified themselves for direct office they could get their agents installed instead. On the urban scene the narrow pattern in which power moved and the domination of many burghs by local great men led to some outright bribery in elections and much more 'influence' and pressure. There might not be much in the way of government posts and benefits to be conferred in Scotland but what there was was carefully applied, so that political strength could appear to hinge on the appointment of a cess collector for Aberdeenshire or the sexual favours conferred by the wife of a Dundee customs official.

The same system of government concern extended into the Church, but here the control by the manager, the third duke of Argyll, was constrained by the actual limitation of crown patronage, as well as by the needs to pander to the popular distaste for too overt influence. The structure of Church courts was a more independent aspect of the Church than were appointments. The presbyterian system placed some landowners in all the upper courts, but these men did not necessarily act simply in the lay interest. That there was rivalry between Church courts and landed society is shown in the way in which in the 1720s the Justices of the Peace of West and Mid Lothian took up the initiative towards improving the poor law from the presbyteries of the area, and made up their own scheme which they pressed on the parishes. It was shown more overtly in the landowner move for total control of parish funds in the network of legal cases at the end of the 1740s. Kirk sessions, in their programmes of moral discipline, had to realize that they could do little to keep landed society under control, or even the domestic servants of that society. Otherwise moral discipline, as experienced by the mass of the population, was still running as an independent steam roller in the 1740s and forcing the population to toe the line.

Patronage and influence had replaced landed power in the Lowlands: in the Highlands the changes of the 1740s had produced a temporary vacuum. Old jurisdictions had been ended, and new ones were not yet effective. The picture we have, ascribed to the 1750s, is one where chiefly domination persists, yet already chiefs had for some time been thinking in commercial terms, and also seeking government office. The concern for posts had been acute even before the 1745. The change after was not so much in the relationship of clan chiefs to government as in their attitude to the clan lands, or as it was considered, their estates. Chiefs had regarded themselves as landowners since the later seventeenth century: now they became simply such owners, for the social and political claims that the clan had made on them were removed. The new pattern of society was not the result of the creation of a new relationship but of the removal of a balancing element. There had been a shift of emphasis within existing limits.

The same is true of the English dimension. Despite the fact that the nations had been separate in institutions until 1707 there had been considerable cultural interaction in the seventeenth century. The two societies had long had much in common, and can be seen as showing differences mainly in the stages reached at any one time in a similar development. Family structure and concepts of local government were sufficiently alike for the two to merge easily. Landownership had become similar: the patterns of trading enterprise were alike, and so were the social systems within the towns.

The languages, Scots and English, had been so alike even before 1603 that men could move from one to the other without the aid of dictionaries or interpreters. Local variation was maintained by the habit of even landed society of speaking dialect much of the time, reserving courtly English for politics, scholarship and religion. There was no particular difficulty for Scots in accepting a British patriotism and adding it to an existing Scottish one. For many, this was thought of not as becoming 'British' but 'English', for, for so long as England remained richer, offered more opportunities for careers and the acquisition of wealth, was more liberated from ecclesiastical pressures and in closer control of the joint political system, it was natural for enterprising Scots to seek cultural assimilation. Yet, as early as the 1740s, when the cultural changes began in Scotland which were to bring her to the great days of the Enlightenment, and which were not shared with England, it was clear that Scotland was still more, a great deal more, than 'the knuckle end of England', as Sydney Smith was later to call it.

A Note on Further Reading

General

Two of the volumes in the *Edinburgh History of Scotland* series cover the period of this book, Gordon Donaldson, *Scotland: James V to James VII* (Edinburgh, 1965) and William Ferguson, *Scotland: 1689 to the Present* (Edinburgh, 1968). Both are scholarly works, equipped with excellent bibliographies, but conceived within traditional ideas of historiography, and therefore relatively weak on the economic and social aspects. Also the focus of each author lies away from the period where the books meet, and so the joint coverage of Restoration and Revolution is thin. The essential documentation of political events up to 1707 is to be found in the third volume of W. Croft Dickinson and Gordon Donaldson, *A Source Book of Scottish History* (2nd edition, 1961), from which students requiring greater depth will of necessity find their way to the *Acts of the Parliaments of Scotland* volumes IV-XII (1816–1875) and the three successive series of *The Register of the Privy Council of Scotland* (from volume VI of the first series, Edinburgh, 1884, to volume XVI of the third, 1970). There is no general economic history taking the reader right through the period, but there are valuable partial studies in S.G.E. Lythe, *The Economy of Scotland 1560–1625 in its European Setting* (Edinburgh, 1960) and H. Hamilton, *Economic History of Scotland in the Eighteenth Century* (Oxford, 1963). The gap between these two can partly be filled by I. Whyte, *Agriculture and Society in Seventeenth Century Scotland* (Edinburgh, 1979), T.C. Smout, *Scottish Trade on the Eve of Union* (Edinburgh, 1963) and R.A. Dodgshon, *Land and Society in Early Scotland* (Oxford, 1981). For social history the essential and pioneer work is T.C. Smout, *A History of the Scottish People* (2nd edition, London, 1970). No general work on ecclesiastical history for the whole period can be recommended as combining a reasonably detailed grasp of the facts and only a moderate element of sectarian rancour, but a recent bibliographical article by David Stevenson, 'Scottish Church History, 1600–1660: a Selected, Critical Bibliography' in *Records of the Scottish Church History Society* 21 (1982), will guide the reader through the minefields for half the seventeenth century. There are numerous works on the architecture of Scotland: the various products of the Commission on Ancient Monuments are the place for detailed study and John Dunbar, *The Architecture of Scotland* (London, 1966) is a well-illustrated survey. Colin McWilliam, *Scottish Townscape* (London, 1975) provides a humbler urban picture to set against the rural emphasis of the other works.

Those needing to approach history from the angle of prosopography get great help on the peerage from the nine volumes of *The Scots Peerage* (Edinburgh, 1904–14) and the shorter but often meaty entries in Vicary Gibbs and others, *The Complete Peerage* (13 vols. London, 1910–40). There are so-called histories of various families and clans, often biographical surveys of the clan chiefs and principal landowners, and much of Scottish landed society can be traced in *The Complete Baronetage* (6 vols., Exeter, 1904–9), if due care is paid to faulty paging in the index, and successive issues since 1836 of Burke's *Landed Gentry* (London) can add detail to what is available in M. Stuart and J.B. Paul, *Scottish Family History* (Edinburgh, 1929) and J.P.S. Ferguson, *Scottish Family Histories held in Scottish Libraries* (Edinburgh, 1960). Two professional groups are well provided in basic information: G. Brunton and D. Haig, *Senators of the College of Justice* (Edinburgh, 1836) and G.W.T. Omond, *The Lord Advocates of Scotland* (2 vols., Edinburgh, 1883) cover the more distinguished of the Faculty of Advocates and the eight volumes of H. Scott (ed.), *Fasti Ecclesiae Scoticanae* (Edinburgh, 1915–50) give basic information on the lives of ministers of the Kirk. Other individuals, if the reader is lucky and the entry reasonably scholarly, may be picked up from *The Dictionary of National Biography* (London, 1908–9) or from Robert Chambers, *Biographical Dictionary of Eminent Scotsmen* (3 vols., London, 2nd edition 1875).

The publications of the early-nineteenth-century historical clubs, Abbotsford, Maitland and Bannatyne, and the Spalding and New Spalding Clubs for the north-east, the Scottish History Society, Scottish Record Society, Scottish Burgh Record Society and Wodrow Society are heavily slanted towards seventeenth-century material, and there are also publications relevant for the period of this book by the Stair Society, the Scottish Text Society and the Scottish Gaelic Text Society. The problems posed by unusual Scottish words can usually be solved with the aid of the full *Oxford English Dictionary* (12 vols., Oxford, 1933) which was largely edited by Scots, and on the rare occasions when this fails there is the *Scottish National Dictionary* (10 vols., Edinburgh, 1933–76). On local history the aids are not good. There are two pairs of volumes A. Mitchell and C.G. Gash, *A Contribution to the Bibliography of Scottish Topography* (Scottish History Society, Edinburgh, 1917) and P.D. Hancock, *Works Relating to Scotland* (Edinburgh, 1959 and 1960), neither of them very thorough. The *Handlist of Scottish and Welsh Record Publications*, edited by P. Gouldesborough, A.P. Kup and I. Lewis for the British Records Association (London, 1954) is of considerable value. For the central archives which in Scotland carry a large amount of local and private material, there is J.M. Thomson, *The Public Records of Scotland* (Glasgow, 1922). Collections of early maps are to be found in various libraries including the National Library of Scotland, university libraries, West Register house and various public libraries, and the negative of General Roy's mid-eighteenth-century map of all Scotland is in Edinburgh University Library.

Chapter 1: Government by the King's Pen

The most useful primary material is the *Register of the Privy Council*, series I, volumes VI-XIV, illuminated by the introductions of David Masson. Changing social structure can be seen in T.C. Smout, *A History of the Scottish People, 1560-1830* (London, 1970) and J. Wormald, 'Bloodfeud, kindred and government in early modern Scotland', *Past and Present* 87 (1980). The final chapter of this author's volume in this series, *Court, Kirk, and Community: Scotland 1470-1625* (London, 1981) points out the problems of monarchy after 1603. The role of the king and his policy is shown in Gordon Donaldson's volume in the Edinburgh history, *Scotland: James V to James VII* (Edinburgh, 1965) and more fully in Maurice Lee, *Government by Pen* (Champaign, 1981) and Alan G.R. Smith, ed., *The Reign of James VI and I* (London, 1973), while he himself has expressed it in *Basilicon Doron*, edited by J. Craigie for the Scottish Text Society (Edinburgh, 1944). The Church as an organization is well set out in W.R. Foster, *The Church before the Covenants* (Edinburgh, 1975) and in the works of G.D. Henderson mentioned in the general bibliography, and particular aspects of Church history require two articles in D. Shaw, ed., *Reformation and Revolution* (Edinburgh, 1967), W.R. Foster, 'A Constant Platt Achieved; Provision for the Ministry, 1600-38' and I.B. Cowan, 'The Five Articles of Perth'. Use should also be made of D. Stevenson, 'Coventicles in the Kirk, 1619-37: the Emergence of a Radical Party' in *Records of the Scottish Church History Society* 18 (1972-4) and, of course, the same author's bibliographical article mentioned in the main bibliography, 'Scottish Church History, 1600-1660: a Selected, Critical Bibliography' in the same journal, 21 (1982) and of William D. Maxwell, *A History of Worship in the Church of Scotland* (Oxford, 1955). For special aspects of Church and society there are two works on witchcraft, Christina Larner, *Enemies of God* (London, 1981) and C. Larner, C.H. Lee and H. McLachlan, *A Source Book of Scottish Witchcraft* (Glasgow, 1977), which together give an explanation and a measure of this social misfunction. John Hardy, 'The attitude of the Church and State in Scotland to sex and marriage, 1560-1707', Edinburgh University M. Phil. thesis (unpublished, 1978) has important points to make. Some further aspects of social structure have been taken from H. Paton, ed., *Parish Registers of Dunfermline* (Scottish Record Society, Edinburgh, 1911) and J. Stuart, ed., *Lists of Pollable Persons within the Shire of Aberdeen, 1696* (Spalding Club, Aberdeen, 1844). For the economy, the book by S.G.E. Lythe is essential: and there is a useful revision article in *Scottish Historical Review* 50 (1971), T.M. Devine and S.G.E. Lythe, 'The

Economy of Scotland under James VI'. M. Perceval Maxwell, *The Scottish Migration to Ulster in the Regin of James I* (sic) (London, 1973) displays the significant population flow of this period.

Chapter 2: The Rule of Charles I

Insight into the structure of Scottish politics and society in the reign of Charles I can be gained from C.V. Wedgwood, *The King's Peace, 1637-41* (London, 1955), David Matthew, *Scotland under Charles I* (London, 1955) and Maurice Lee, 'Charles I and the End of Conciliar Government in Scotland', *Albion* 12 (1981), this last a vital article. For finance see D. Stevenson, 'The King's Scottish Revenues and the Covenanters, 1625-1651', *Historical Journal* 17 (1974). Charles's relations with London are shown in R. Ashton, *The City and the Court* (Cambridge, 1979). A minor, enjoyable aspect of Scottish life is shown in M.R. Apted, *The Painted Ceilings of Scotland* (Edinburgh, 1966). Some of the intellectual and theological currents can be found in A.H. Williamson, *Scottish National Consciousness in the Age of James VI* (Edinburgh, 1979), J.F. Scott, *A History of Mathematics* (London, 1958), chapter 9, Walter J. Ong, *Ramus: Method and the Decay of Dialogue* (Cambridge, Mass., 1958), H. Trevor Roper, *Tyninghame Library* (privately published, 1977), J. Durham and J. Kirk, *The University of Glasgow* (Edinburgh, 1977), G.D. Henderson, *Religious Life in Seventeenth-Century Scotland* (Cambridge, 1937), *Autobiography and Diary of James Melvill* (Wodrow Society, Edinburgh, 1842), Sir Thomas Craig's treatise *De Unione Regnorum Britannicae* translated for the Scottish History Society by C.S. Terry, (Edinburgh, 1909), R. Gillespie's anonymous tract, *Reasons for which the Service Booke, urged upon Scotland ought to bee refused* (1638), S. Rutherford, *The Last and Heavenly Speeches and Glorious Departure of John Viscount Kenmuir* (Edinburgh, 1649) and W. Forbes, *Considerationes modestae et pacificae Controversiarum de iustificatione purgatorio invocatione sanctorum et Christo mediatore et eucharistia* (London, 1658). I have found of use M.C. Kitshoff, 'Aspects of Arminianism in Scotland', University of St Andrews M. Litt. thesis (unpublished, 1968), and for background information the *Register of the Privy Council* 2nd series, volumes I-VII. Revolution theory is explained in Lawrence Stone, *The Causes of the English Revolution 1529-1642* (London, 1972), chapter 1. For the English development of these years, a dimension which cannot be ignored, see Conrad Russell, ed., *The Origins of the English Civil War* (London, 1973), and Trevor Aston, ed., *Crisis in Europe, 1560-1660* (London, 1965) has some relevant themes.

Chapter 3: The Great Rebellion and Interregnum

Essential reading for this period are two books by David Stevenson, *The Scottish Revolution 1637-1644* (Newton Abbott, 1973) and *Revolution and Counter Revolution in Scotland, 1644-1651* (London, 1977), and the same author's *Scottish Covenanters and Irish Confederates* (Belfast, 1981) explores some of the links between Irish and Scottish events. For a general under-standing of the Irish aspect, see T.W. Moody, F.X. Martin and F.J. Byrnes, eds., volume 3 of the *New History of Ireland, Early Modern Ireland, 1534-1696* (Oxford, 1976). W. Makey, *The Church of the Covenant* (Edinburgh, 1979) is a difficult but supremely important study of develop-ments within the Church, covering some of its relationship with the political revolution. On the financial side, Stevenson again in 'The Financing of the Cause of the Covenants', *Scottish Historical Review* 51 (1972): on the strategies of the English Civil War, C.V. Wedgwood, *The King's War* (London, 1958). For the price revolution, F.P. Braudel, 'Prices in Europe from 1450-1750' in *The Cambridge Economic History of Europe* 4 (Cambridge, 1967). Aspects of the world picture of the covenanters are explored in S.A. Burrell, 'The Apocalyptic Vision of the Early Covenanters', *Scottish Historical Review* 43 (1964) and on C.V. Wedgwood, 'The Covenanters in the First Civil War', *Scottish Historical Review* 39 (1966). The English Parliament's need for Scottish participation is shown in J. Hexter, *King Pym* (Cambridge, Mass., 1941). The best display of Scottish political and ecclesiastical thinking still lies in the three volumes of Robert Baillie's *Letters and Journals*, edited for the Bannatyne Club by David Laing (Edinburgh, 1842). Particular issues and events in the Highland area are explained by A. McKerral, *Kintyre in the Seventeenth Century* (Edinburgh, 1948), E.J. Cowan, *Montrose: for Covenant and King* (London, 1977), David Stevenson, *Alasdair MacColla and the Highland Problem in the Seventeenth Century* (Edinburgh, 1980) and A. MacInnes, 'Scottish Gaeldom, 1638-1651: the Vernacular Response to the Covenanting Dynamic', in John Dwyer, Roger A. Mason and Alexander Murdoch, eds., *New Perspectives on the Politics and Culture of Early Modern Scotland* (Edinburgh, 1982). For the political developments of the late 1640s an understanding of English affairs is necessary, and two useful works here are L.M. Lamont, *Godly Rule* (London, 1969) and D. Underdown, *Pride's Purge* (Oxford, 1971).

For the Cromwellian period the best detailed description is Lesley M. Smith, 'Scotland and Cromwell', Oxford University D. Phil. thesis, (unpublished, 1980). F. Dow, *Cromwellian Scotland* (Edinburgh, 1979) is useful on Glencairn's rebellion. Some first-hand impressions of the period can be gathered from three diaries, John Nicoll, *A Diary of Public Transac-tions* (Bannatyne Club, Edinburgh, 1830), *The Diary of Mr John Lamont of Newton, 1649-1671* (Maitland Club, Edinburgh, 1830) and *The Diary of Alexander Brodie of Brodie* (Spalding Club, Aberdeen, 1863), though the first two are guarded and the third more interested in his spiritual state that in material circumstances, and there is also, to redress the balance in a worldly direction, the Bannatyne Club's *Letters from Roundhead Officers* (Edinburgh, 1856). For the Highland scene there is the confused but absorbing Wardlaw Manuscript printed by the Scottish History Society, editor James Fraser, as *Chronicles of the Frasers* (Edinburgh, 1905).

Chapter 4: Restoration Government and Society

The best political outline for this period is W.L. Mathieson, *Politics and Religion* (2 vols., Glasgow, 1902), but W. Ferguson, *Scotland's Relations with England* (Edinburgh, 1977) has valuable insights. The basic documentation is to be found in W.C. Dickinson and G. Donaldson, *Source Book of Scottish History*, volume III (London, 1954) and the *Register of the Privy Council*, 3rd series, volumes I-X. Parliament, and its development, is analysed in C.S. Terry, *The Scottish Parliament: its Constitution and Procedure 1603-1707* (Glasgow, 1905). Of value for government is Sir George Mackenzie, *Memoir of the Affairs of Scotland from the Restoration of Charles II* (Edinburgh, 1821).

On Church matters there are W.R. Foster, *Bishop and Presbytery* (London, 1959), Julia Buckroyd, *Church and State in Scotland 1660-1681* (Edinburgh, 1980) and I.B. Cowan, *The Scottish Covenanters* (London, 1976). It is impossible not also to use R. Wodrow, *The History of the Sufferings of the Church of Scotland from the Restauration to the Revolution* (2 vols., Edinburgh, 1721) in any detailed study because it includes much original documentation not easily available elsewhere, but those who use it should pay attention to the evaluation of the historiography of Wodrow in Marinell Ash, *The Strange Death of Scottish History* (Edinburgh, 1980). From the same historical school also, unfortunately, and at a low level of editorial skill comes the only edition of the papers of the principal political figure of the day, in O. Airy, *The Lauderdale Papers* (3 vols., Camden Society, London, 1884-5). The work of the Church at parish level can be seen in two volumes of kirk session material privately published by H. Paton, *The Session Book of Kingarth* (1932) and *The Session Book of Dundonald* (1936), as well as Rosalind Mitchison, 'A parish and its poor: Yester in the second half of the seventeenth century' in *Transactions of the East Lothian Antiquarian and Field Naturalists' Society* 14 (1974). The problems of the Church in the Highlands are shown by W. Mackay, ed., *Inverness and Dingwall Presbytery Records* (Scottish History Society, Edinburgh, 1896), and the level of non-Christian belief in some areas is brought out more clearly in Martin Martin, *A Description of the Western Islands of Scotland* (London, 1703).

Aspects of upper-class culture are shown in Rosalind K. Marshall, *The Days of Duchess Anne* (London, 1973), and the significance of James, duke of York's court in Scotland in Hugh Ouston, 'York in Edinburgh: James VII and the Patronage of Learning in Scotland 1679-1688' in John Dwyer, Roger A. Mason and Alexander Murdoch, eds., *New Perspectives on the Politics and Culture of Early Modern Scotland* (Edinburgh, 1982) and also in *Memoir of Sir Ewen Cameron of Lochiel* (Abbotsford Club, Edinburgh, 1842). Witchcraft and its relationship to the claims of religion is investigated in Christina Larner, *Enemies of God* (London, 1981), and the criminalization of women is discussed there and in an article by the same author, '*Crimen Exceptum*? The Crime of Witchcraft in Europe', in V.A.C. Gattrell, Bruce Lenman and Geoffrey Parker, eds., *Crime and the Law* (London, 1980).

Legal developments in this period are shown in an article in the same volume, S.J. Davies 'The courts and the Scottish Legal System 1660-1747: the Case of Stirlingshire'. A.E. Whetstone, *Scottish County Government in the Eighteenth and Nineteenth Centuries* (Edinburgh, 1982) brings out the long-term significance of the Commissioners of Supply.

Rural life is shown in two baron court books published by the Scottish History Society, G. Gun, ed., *Records of the Baron Court of Stitchill 1635-1807* (Edinburgh, 1905) and D.G. Baron, *Records of the Baron Court of Urie 1604-1747* (Edinburgh, 1892): many more exist in estate papers. I. Whyte, *Agriculture and Society in Seventeenth Century Scotland* (Edinburgh, 1979), chapter 4, expounds the use of Parliament by the landowning interest, and R.A. Dodgshon, *Land and Society in Early Scotland* (Oxford, 1981) shows the social and economic sides of land use.

Chapter 5: The Economy in the Later Seventeenth Century

The rural sector of the economy is better explored than the urban, and besides those books mentioned in the general bibliography there are important articles: R.A. Dodgshon, 'Agricultural Change and its Social Consequences in the Southern Uplands of Scotland, 1600-1790', in T.M. Devine and David Dickson, eds., *Ireland and Scotland 1600-1850* (Edinburgh, 1983); T.C. Smout and A. Fenton, 'Scottish Farming before the Improvers', *Agricultural History Review* 13 (1965); D. Woodward, 'A comparative study of the Irish and Scottish livestock trades in the seventeenth century', in E.M. Cullen and T.C. Smout, eds., *Comparative Aspects of Scottish and Irish Economic and Social History* (Edinburgh, 1977). For estate management there is I. McFaulds 'Forfarshire landowners and their estates 1660-96', University of Glasgow Ph.D. thesis (unpublished, 1980) and A.H. Millar, ed., *The Glamis Book of Record* (Scottish History Society, Edinburgh, 1890). A valuable book which covers the actual work in the field and the crops is Alexander Fenton, *Scottish Country Life* (Edinburgh, 1976).

Specialized studies and materials with a bearing on Scottish demography and economy are A.B. Appleby, *Famine in Tudor and Stuart England* (Liverpool, 1978), M.W. Flinn, ed., *Scottish Population History from the Seventeenth Century to the 1930s* (Cambridge, 1977), part 3, G.Marshall, *Presbyteries and Profits* (Oxford, 1980), G.P. Insh, *The Company of Scotland* (London, 1932), J.D. Marshall, ed., *Miscellany of the Scottish Burgh Record Society*, 'Report of Thomas Tucker' (Edinburgh, 1882), E.J. Graham, 'The Scottish Marine during the Dutch Wars', *Scottish Historical Review* 61 (1982), W.R. Scott, *The Constitution of English, Scottish and Irish Joint-Stock Companies* (Cambridge, 1912) III, P.H. Brown, ed., *Early Travellers in Scotland* (Edinburgh, 1891).

Chapter 6: Towards a New Settlement

There is little in the general histories of Britain, since T.B. Macaulay's *History of England from the Accession of James II* (4 vols., London, 1849 and 1855) which pays serious attention to James VII's rule in Scotland or to the impact of the Revolution there. Some insights on his stay in Edinburgh can be found in Hugh Ouston, 'York in Edinburgh: James VII and the Patronage of Learning in Scotland 1679-1688', in John Dwyer, Roger A. Mason and Alexander Murdoch, eds., *New Perspectives on the Politics and Culture of Early Modern Scotland* (Edinburgh, 1982) and in *Memoir of Sir Ewen Cameron of Locheil* (Abbotsford Club, Edinburgh, 1842); Sir John Lauder of Fountainhall's *Historical Observes* and the two volumes of his *Historical Notices* (both Bannatyne Club, Edinburgh, 1840 and 1848) are good sources for the gossip in governing circles.

The legislation which made the Revolution is to be found in W.C. Dickinson and G. Donaldson, *A Source Book of Scottish History* 3 (London, 1954), pp. 200-8. For the massacre of Glencoe the most balanced work is Donald J. Macdonald, *Slaughter under Trust* (London, 1965). On the Darien expedition, John Prebble, *The Darien Disaster* (London, 1968) tells a well-known story vividly. The Highland problem is set out in David Stevenson's book on Alasdair MacColla, already mentioned, and the government's perception of it is to be found in the Maitland Club publication *Papers Illustrative of the Political Condition of the Highlands of Scotland 1689-96* (Edinburgh, 1845). Jacobitism has recently been explored in detail by Bruce Lenman, *The Jacobite Risings in Britain 1689-1746* (London, 1980). The policy of the presbyterian establishment is shown in A.L. Drummond and J. Bulloch, *The Scottish Church, 1688-1843* (Edinburgh, 1973), chapters 1 and 2.

The problems faced by the crown in forming a Scottish ministry after the Revolution are fully displayed by P.W.J. Riley, *King William and the Scottish Politicians* (Edinburgh, 1979). On Union the same author's *The Union of England and Scotland* (Manchester, 1978) is another detailed study of the political manoeuvres of a narrow group, with little attention to opinion in the wider constituency, and sets out the view that the motivation of the Scots was the immediate satisfaction of political and private needs. The same line is taken by W. Ferguson, *Scotland's Relations with England* (Edinburgh, 1977), though with greater knowledge of the issues in law and Church matters. The economic case is set out by T.C. Smout, *Scottish Trade on the Eve of Union* (London, 1963) and the same author's 'The Road to Union', in G. Holmes, *Britain after the Glorious Revolution 1689-1714* (London, 1969). The details of the Parliamentary debates are given in D. Defoe, *History of the Union between England and Scotland* (London, 1785), the Act itself is to be found in G. Pryde, *The Treaty of Union of Scotland and England 1707* (Edinburgh, 1950). J. Mackinnon, *The Union of England and Scotland* (London, 1896) remains a sound account of the whole story. The economic issues, as they seemed to a contemporary, are shown in J. Spreull, *Accompt Current betwixt England and Scotland* (Edinburgh, 1705).

Chapter 7: Working Out Union

The political system of Scotland after 1707 is examined by John Simpson, 'Who steered the Gravy Train, 1707–1766', in N.T. Phillipson and Rosalind Mitchison, eds., *Scotland in the Age of Improvement* (Edinburgh, 1970) and in Alexander Murdoch, *The People Above* (Edinburgh, 1980). A key figure in the administration is displayed in G. Menary, *Duncan Forbes of Culloden* (London, 1936). The government's problems in the Highlands are shown in another article in *Scotland in the Age of Improvement*, Rosalind Mitchison, 'The Government and the Highlands, 1707–1745'. The complexities of the county electoral system are shown in Sir James Fergusson, 'Making interest in Scottish county elections', *Scottish Historical Review* 26 (1947). On control of the Church there is a useful study by Henry R. Sefton, 'Lord Ilay and Patrick Cumming: a Study in Eighteenth-Century Ecclesiastical Management', *Records of the Scottish Church History Society* 19 (1977).

For a general survey of economic development there is Bruce Lenman, *An Economic History of Modern Scotland, 1660–1976* (London, 1977). There are also interesting detail and valuable references in S.G.E. Lythe and J. Butt, *An Economic History of Scotland* (Glasgow, 1975). Two successive volumes of comparative studies of Irish and Scottish development contain significant essays, the first, L.M. Cullen and T.C. Smout, *Comparative Aspects of Scottish and Irish Economic and Social History* (Edinburgh, 1977), has, for this period, its main impact on the economic side and the second, T.M. Devine and David Dickson, *Ireland and Scotland: 1600–1850* (Edinburgh, 1982), has valuable studies of social history. On particular economic activities there are: T.C. Barker, 'Smuggling in the eighteenth century: the evidence of the Scottish Tobacco trade', *Virginia Magazine of History and Biography* (1954), T.M. Devine, *The Tobacco Lords* (Edinburgh, 1975), A.J. Durie, *The Scottish Linen Industry in the Eighteenth Century* (Edinburgh, 1979), Baron F. Duckham, *A History of the Scottish Coal Industry*, vol. I: 1700–1815 (Newton Abbot, 1970), G. Gulvin, 'The Union and the Scottish woollen industry 1707–1760', *Scottish Historical Review* 50 (1971) and S.G. Checkland, *Scottish Banking, a history, 1695–1973* (London, 1975).

There are interesting essays on changing land use in M.L. Parry and T.R. Slater, eds., *The Making of the Scottish Countryside* (London, 1980) as well as an important article on landownership by Loretta Timperley, 'The pattern of landholding in eighteenth-century Scotland'. On Highland land policy there is E. Cregeen, 'The Tacksman and his Successors', *Scottish Studies* 12 (1969). A vivid picture of the Highlands exists in the book attributed to Edmund Burt, *Letters from a Gentleman in the North of Scotland* (2 vols., London, 1754). Shifts in law in favour of the landowning class are shown in two articles by Rosalind Mitchison, 'Patriotism and national identity in eighteenth-century Scotland', in T.W. Moody, ed., *Historical Studies* 11, *Nationalism and the Pursuit of National Independence* (Belfast, 1978), and 'The Making of the Old Scottish Poor Law', *Past and Present* 63 (1974). A landowner's problems in controlling his work force are shown in Rab Houston, 'Coal, class and culture: labour relations in a Scottish mining community', *Social History* 8 (1983). The most considerable display of resistance to landowning policy is discussed in J. Leopold, 'The levellers' revolt in Galloway in 1724', *Journal of the Scottish Labour History Society* 14 (1980).

David Horn, *A Short History of Edinburgh University* is a useful starting point for the appreciation of the Scottish educational system. For popular culture there are David Daiches, *Literature and Gentility in Scotland* (Edinburgh, 1982), David Craig, *Scottish Literature and the Scottish People* (London, 1961) and B. Willsher and D. Hunter, *Stones: Eighteenth Century Scottish Gravestones* (Edinburgh, 1980). There is a debate on literacy levels between R. Houston, 'The Literacy Myth? Illiteracy in Scotland, 1630–1760', *Past and Present* 96 (1982) and T.C. Smout in the next volume of the same journal, 'Born again in Cambuslang: New Evidence on Popular Religion and Literacy in Eighteenth-Century Scotland'. The material circumstances of upper-class life are shown in R. Scott-Moncrieff, ed., *The Household Book of Lady Grisell Baillie* (Scottish History Society, Edinburgh, 1911).

Chapter 8: New and Old Themes of the 1740s

The concerns of aristocrats are shown in the Historical Manuscripts Commission publication *Polwarth* 5, ed. H. Paton (London, 1961) and of the gentry in Sir James Fergusson, *Lowland Lairds* (London, 1949). The social setting of upper-class Edinburgh is described in D.D. McElroy, *Scotland's Age of Improvement* (Seattle, 1969), and some of the impulses that came to make the Enlightenment in N.T. Phillipson, 'Lawyers, landowners and the Civic Leadership of post-union Scotland', *Juridical Review* 21 (1976) and in E.C. Mossner, *The Life of David Hume* (Oxford, 1954).

For the '45 and after, James Fergusson, *Argyll in the 'Forty five* (London, 1951) gives a picture of the response to the rising of an area supporting the government, John Prebble *Culloden* (London, 1961) is clear on the military side and sensitive to events after and W.A. Speck *The Butcher* (Oxford, 1981) explains the campaign but has no curiosity towards its Scottish base. Andrew Lang, ed., *The Highlands of Scotland in 1750* (Edinburgh, 1898) is a reprint of an eighteenth-century account of the area before it had adjusted to the end of clanship.

A glimpse of Lowland society at the peasant level can be gained from A. Fawcett, *The Cambuslang Revival* (London, 1971).

Appendix: Chronological Table

1603	Accession of James VI to the English throne
1607	Failure of the king's plans for more complete Union in the English Parliament
1616	Act of the Privy Council for setting up parish schools
1617	Return visit of James VI to Scotland
1618	Issue of the Five Articles of Perth
1622–3	Famine period
1625	Accession of Charles I
	Act of Revocation
	Restructuring of the Privy Council
1633	Coronation visit of Charles I to Scotland
1634–5	Trial of Lord Balmerino
1637	Issue of Charles I's prayer book
	Setting up of 'the Tables'
1638	The Covenant
	The meeting of the General Assembly of Glasgow
	Abjuring of Bishops and Five Articles of Perth
1639	First 'Bishops' War'
1640	The English 'Short' Parliament
	The 'Cumbernauld Bond' signed
	The Second 'Bishops' War'
1641	The English 'Long' Parliament opened
	Charles I's second visit to Scotland
	The new Scottish constitution
	Start of the Irish rebellion
1642	Scottish army sent to Ulster
	Opening of the English Civil War
1643–4	The Westminster Assembly
1643	Signing of the Solemn League and Covenant
1644	Scottish entry into the English Civil War
1644–5	Campaign of Montrose
1646	Charles I surrenders to the Scottish army
	Last severe outbreak of plague in Scotland

1647	The Engagement
1648	The Second English Civil War
	Battle of Preston
	Whiggamore Raid
1649	Execution of Charles I
	Act of Classes
	First effective poor law legislation for Scotland
	Abolition of patronage in the Church
1650-1	Charles II in Scotland
1650	Battle of Dunbar. English occupation of most of Scotland
	The Western Remonstrance
	The Resolution
1651	Battle of Worcester. English conquest of Scotland completed. Commonwealth set up, and Scotland incorporated in England
1653-4	Glencairn's rising and Highland campaign
1654-8	Oliver Cromwell Lord Protector
1659	General Monck's march south
1660	Re-establishment of the English Long Parliament
	Restoration of Charles II
	Reissue of English Navigation Act
1661	Act Rescissory
1662	Re-establishment of episcopacy and patronage
1666	Pentland Rising
1669 &	
1672	Indulgences to presbyterian ministers
1672	Act reducing the privilege of Royal Burghs
1678	The Highland Host
1679	Battle of Bothwell Brig
1679-82	James duke of York on long visits to Scotland
1681	Test Act
	Privy Council's policy to encourage manufactures
1683	English Rye House Plot
1684-8	The Killing Time
1685	Succession of James VII
	Argyll rising
1687	James VII's proclamation for toleration
1688	The English Glorious Revolution and flight of King James
1689	Claim of Right
	The crown offered to William and Mary
	Battle of Killiecrankie
1690	Establishment of presbyterianism
1692	Massacre of Glencoe
1695	Founding of Bank of Scotland
1696-1700	Famine period

1696	Act for settling schools
1698	Start of Darien expedition
1702	Accession of Anne
1702–13	War of the Spanish succession
1707	Act of Union with England
1709	Founding of the SSPCK
1712	Patronage reintroduced
1714	Accession of George I
1715	Jacobite rebellion. Battle of Sheriffmuir
1719	Jacobite invasion of Kintail
1725	Shawfield Riots
1727	Establishment of the Board of Trustees
	Founding of Royal Bank of Scotland
1733	Original Secession
1736	Porteous Riot
1742	Cambuslang revival
	Start of bounty on the export of coarse linen
1745	Jacobite rebellion
1746	Defeat of the Jacobites at Culloden

Index